THE
LUGER STORY

THE
LUGER STORY

The Standard History of the World's Most Famous Handgun

JOHN WALTER

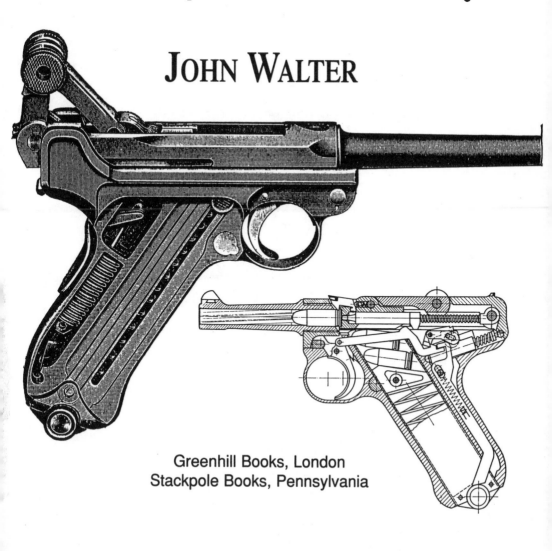

Greenhill Books, London
Stackpole Books, Pennsylvania

FOR ALISON AND ADAM

Greenhill Books

This edition of *The Luger Story*
published 2001 by Greenhill Books,
Lionel Leventhal Limited, Park House, 1 Russell Gardens,
London NW11 9NN
and
Stackpole Books, 5067 Ritter Road, Mechanicsburg, PA 17055, USA

British Library Cataloguing in Publication Data
Walter, John, 1951–
The Luger story: the standard history of the world's most famous handgun. –
(Greenhill military paperback)
1. Luger pistol – History
2. Luger pistol – Collectors and collecting
I. Title
683.4′32′09

ISBN 1–85367–436–2

Library of Congress Cataloging-in-Publication Data
Walter, John, 1951–
The Luger story : the standard history of the world's
most famous handgun / John Walter.
p. cm – (Greenhill military paperbacks)
originally published: 1995.
Includes bibliographical references and index.
ISBN 1–85367–436–2 (pbk.)
1. Luger pistol – History. I. Title. II. Series.
TS537.W353   2001
683.4′32–dc21
00-066096

Publishing History
The Luger Story was first published in 1995 by Greenhill Books. It now appears in paperback,
complete and unabridged, with a small number of revisions.

Typeset by DP Photosetting, Aylesbury, Bucks
Printed and bound in Great Britain

Contents

List of Illustrations

Drawings

Books by John Walter

2001	The Dictionary of Firearms (in preparation)
	Modern Military Rifles (in preparation)
2000	Allied Small Arms of World War One
	Modern Machine Guns
1999	The Guns that Won the West
	Kalashnikov
	Central Powers' Small Arms of World War One
1998	Rifles of the World II
1997	Secret Firearms
1995	The Luger Story
	German Military Letter Codes
	Guns of the Elite II (as 'George Markham')
1994	The Kaiser's Pirates
	Rifles of the World
1991	Guns of the Wild West (as 'George Markham')
1990	The Rifle Book
	Guns of the Empire (as 'George Markham')
1989	Guns of the Reich (as 'George Markham')
	Emden: The Last Cruise (editor)
1988	The Navy Luger (with Joachim Görtz)
	Handguns (with John Batchelor)
	Guns of the First World War (editor)
1987	The Pistol Book II
	The Airgun Book IV
	Guns of the Elite (as 'George Markham')
1986	The Luger Book
	Victorian Military Equipment (editor)
1984	The Airgun Book III
1983	The Pistol Book
1982	The Airgun Book II
1981	The Airgun Book
1980	German Military Handguns, 1879–1918
1979	The German Rifle
1977	Luger
1976	The German Bayonet
	Japanese Infantry Weapons of World War II (as 'George Markham')
	German Ersatz Bayonets (illustrator)
	An Interim Director of German Leatherware Makers
1974	The Bayonet (with Anthony Carter)
1973	The Sword & Bayonet Makers of Imperial Germany
1971	Russian Infantry Weapons of World War II (with A.J. Barker)
1969	A Primer of World Bayonets I (with Gordon Hughes)
	A Primer of World Bayonets II (with Gordon Hughes)

Foreword

The Luger is a fascinating tool. Excepting the Colt Peacemaker, no other handgun has excited as much interest nor supported such a vast industry.

Owing to sophisticated design, high-quality manufacture and ready availability, the Luger was greatly coveted as a souvenir of the trenches of 1914–18. But the reputation founded in this desirability had nothing to do with its efficiency as a weapon, its design, or its engineering. It had much more to do with its appearance and the myth of Teutonic excellence.

The Pistole 1908 is pleasant to shoot, recoil being surprisingly light though the rise of the toggle through the line of sight can be disconcerting. It also balances exceptionally well, with a natural 'pointability' that may be matched by the best revolvers but seldom in a semi-automatic with nineteenth-century origins.

As a symbol of the technology of war, however, the pistol has had its share of detractors. Hugh Pollard, writing in *Automatic Pistols*, noted that 'As a piece of design it is curiously efficient, but its small calibre, high velocity and rather delicate lockwork are points against it as a purely military arm. It is really very German in its psychology – it is wonderfully designed – theoretically capable of great things, but when taken practically it tends to break down through over-organisation, and its very virtues become defects.'

The key to the mystique of the Luger lies in its diversity. The Colt-Browning has been distributed as widely, but lacks the Luger's incredible variety of proof-, inspectors' and unit markings. Excepting perhaps the Mauser and Lee-Enfield rifles, no other firearm offers as broad a canvas for research.

The Luger Story inevitably retraces steps taken in *Luger* (1977) and *The Luger Book* (1986). Some readers disapproved of the carefully subdivided entry-by-entry nature of the latter, so a reversion has been made to a single-volume narrative aimed more at the Anglo-American reader than the Anglo-European. The term 'Luger' has been broadly favoured at the expense of 'Parabellum', footnotes have been removed entirely – they are so often a coward's way out of problems! – and the flow has been assisted, I hope, by the elimination of superfluous German words and phrases. In an era in which ever-increasing specialisation is becoming commonplace, therefore, *The Luger Story* seeks simply to present a reliable single-volume guide to the many facets of the pistol.

Invaluable additional research has been completed in the years since *The Luger Book* appeared, and it is thanks to the painstaking work of Joachim Görtz and Reinhard Kornmayer in Germany; Don Bryans, Jan Still and Charles Kenyon in the USA; Georges Machterlinckx in Belgium; and Bas Martens and Guus de Vries in the Netherlands that *The Luger Story* has progressed as far as it has.

Special appreciation is due to James Hellyer of Fish Hoek, Republic of South Africa, who has supplied me with detailed information about the markings on Lugers which have passed through his hands. His sketches have provided the basis for my drawings.

I am also pleased to acknowledge the assistance of Major a.D. Hans-Rudolf von Stein in Nettetal, Dr Rolf Gminder of Heckler & Koch GmbH in Oberndorf, Masami Tokoi in Düsseldorf, and Erma-Werke GmbH in Dachau, Germany; Henk Visser in Wassenaar, and Jan Lenselink of Koninklijk Nederlands Leger- en Wapenmuseum 'Generaal Hoefer' in Delft, the Netherlands; Per Jensen in Denmark; Anthony Carter, Gordon Hughes, Dr Geoffrey Sturgess, David Collier, Robin Wigington, David Penn of the Imperial War Museum, Colin Greenwood of *Guns Review*, Mark Jarrold, and Herbert Woodend of the Pattern Room Collection in Britain; John Pearson, John Martz, and Mark Armstrong of Mitchell Arms in the USA; Heikki Pohjolainen of the Finnish Arms Collectors' Association, and Markku Melko of the Sotamuseo in Finland. David Brown helped greatly by proof-reading the draft manuscript.

The illustrations have been credited in individual captions, though most were cheerfully supplied by Rolf Gminder.

Publication would not have been possible without the support of Lionel Leventhal of Greenhill Books, who was responsible, in our Arms & Armour Press days, for my earlier Luger books and was brave enough to take a chance with this third attempt.

Without the love, support and encouragement of Alison and Adam, however, *The Luger Story* would simply have remained a blank page in my typewriter.

The opportunity to prepare *The Luger Story* for a reprint has allowed a few small corrections to be made to the text, and a change to be made to the optimistic 'happy ever after' ending to the story on page 241. The Luger did not quite make its centenary after all. But who knows what will happen in the next few years. Will there be another revival? I have a feeling that the inexplicable lure of the pistol will ultimately prove greater than commercial *nous*...

John Walter, Hove, England, 2001

Glossary

German spellings have been retained for personal and town names – eg München for 'Munich', and Nürnberg for 'Nuremburg' – but not for provinces such as Bavaria and Prussia, unless they occur unavoidably in company names. The *Wörterbuch der Waffentechnik* by Glöck & Görtz (Journal-Verlag Schwend GmbH, Schwäbisch Hall, 1972) provides more comprehensive coverage.

Abteilung: battalion (artillery), detachment.
Abzug: trigger.
Abzugsbügel: trigger-guard.
Abzugsfeder: trigger spring.
Abzugshebel: trigger lever.
Abzugsstange: sear or trigger-bar.
Aktiengesellschaft: joint-stock company.
alter Art (a.A.): old pattern.
Allgemeine Kriegs-Department (AKD): general war department, Prussia.
amtlich: official.
Ansteckmagazin: detachable magazine.
aptiert: adapted.
Armee: army.
Artillerie: artillery.
Aufrüstung: rearmament.
Aufschlag: impact.
aufsteckbar: detachable.
Ausführung: pattern, model, type.
ausrüsten: to arm, equip, outfit.
Ausschuss: scrap, waste.
Ausstosser or *Auswerfer:* ejector.
Auszieher: extractor.
automatisch: automatic.

Bataillon: battalion.
Batterie: battery (of artillery).
bayerisch: Bavarian.

Bayern: Bavaria.
Bedienung: operation.
Befestigung: attachment, fastening, fortification.
Behälter: case.
Behörde: authorities.
Belgien: Belgium.
belgisch: Belgian.
Beschreibung: specification.
Beschuss: proof.
Bestimmung: ordinance.
Bewaffnung: armament.
Bewegung: action (*doppelte Bewegung*, double-action).
Blättchen: flakes.
Blech: sheet.
Blechbehälter: sheet-metal container.
Blei: lead.
Bleigeschoss: lead bullet.
Blitzkrieg: 'lightning war'.
Boden: base, bottom.
Böhmen: Bohemia.
Bolzen: bolt, stud.
Braunschweig: Brunswick.
breit: wide.
Breslau: Wroclaw, Poland.
brüniert: blued.
Brünn: Brno, Czechoslovakia.
Büchse: gun, rifle.

Bund: state, federation, federal.
Bundesheer: Federal army (Austria).
Bundesrepublik Deutschland: Federal
   Republic of Germany.

Dachkorn: barleycorn (inverted 'V' or
   pyramidal) sight.
Dämpfer: buffer.
Dauerfeuer: automatic fire.
Deckel: cover, lid.
Deutsche Demokratische Republik:
   German Democratic Republic, East
   Germany.
Deutschland: Germany.
Dichtung: seal.
Dienst: service.
Donau: Danube.
Drall: twist.
Drehverschluss: rotary action.
Druck: pressure.
Durchmesser: diameter.

Einbau: assembly.
einfach: simple.
Einführung: adoption.
Einheits: standard, universal.
Einsatz: insert.
einschüssig: single-shot.
Einstecklauf: sub-calibre barrel insert.
Einzelfeuer: single-shot.
Einzellader: single-loader.
einzeln: singly.
Eisenkern: iron core.
Elsass: Alsace.
Entladung: discharge.
erproben: to test.
Ersatz: substitute, replacement.
Ersatz-Abteilung: training unit.

Fabrik: manufactory.
Fallschirmjäger: paratrooper.
Faustfeuerwaffe: handgun.
Feder: spring.
Feld: field, land (rifling).

Feldartillerie: field artillery.
Feldzeugmeisterei: quartermaster's
   department.
fest: compact, rigid.
Feuer: fire.
Firmenzeichen: factory sign, logo.
Flieger: airman.
Frankreich: France.
französisch: French.
Fremdgerät: foreign equipment.
Führung: guide.
Fussartillerie: foot artillery.
Futteral: holster (Switzerland).

gasdicht: gas-tight, gas-sealed.
Gasdrucklader: gas-operated.
geändert: altered.
Gebirgsjäger: mountaineer, mountain
   troops.
gehärtet: hardened.
Gehäuse: housing, receiver, breech.
geheim: secret.
Geheime Staatspolizei (Gestapo): secret
   police.
geladen: loaded.
Gelenk: joint.
Genossenschaft: association, co-operative.
Gemeinschaft: union, commune.
Geräte: equipment.
geriffelt: ribbed, cannelured.
Geschoss: bullet.
Geschwindigkeit: velocity.
Gesellschaft: company.
gesichert: secured.
Geweer: rifle (the Netherlands).
Gewehr: rifle, shotgun.
Gewehr-Prüfungs-Kommission (GPK):
   rifle-testing commission.
Gewinde: thread.
gezogen: rifled.
glatt: smooth.
gleiten: to slip, glide.
GmbH (Gesellschaft mit beschränkter
   Haftung): limited liability company.

Griff: grip, handle.
gross, groß: large.

Hahn: hammer.
hahnlos: hammerless.
Hannover: Hanover.
Halter: catch.
Hand: hand, shoulder.
Handfeuerwaffe: small-arm.
hart: hard, solid.
Hebel: lever.
Heer: army.
Heereswaffenamt (HWaA): army
   weapons office.
Hersteller: manufacturer, producer.
Hilfskorn: auxiliary front sight.
Hinterlader: breechloader.
Holland: the Netherlands.
holländisch: Dutch.
Holz: wood.
Hülse: case, chamber (of a rifle).

Inspektion: inspection, perusal, section.
Inspektion für Waffen und Gerät (IWG):
   the predecessor of the Heereswaffenamt.

Jäger: hunter, rifleman.

kaiserlich: imperial.
Kaiserliche Marine: imperial navy.
Kaliber: calibre.
Kampf: combat, struggle, fight.
Kampfstoff: poison.
Kartusche: cartridge(-case).
Kasten: box.
Kavallerie: cavalry.
Kennzeichen: marking(s).
Kimme: sight notch.
Klammer: clasp, latch.
Klappschaft: folding stock.
klein: small.
Klemme: clamp.
Kompagnie (pre-1918), *Kompanie* (post-
   1918): company (of a regiment).

Köln: Cologne.
königlich: royal.
Königliche Gewehrfabrik: royal rifle
   factory.
Kolben: butt.
Kolbenring: butt swivel.
Korn: front sight.
Krieg: war.
Kriegsmarine: navy (Third Reich
   period).
Kriegsmaterialverwaltung (KMV): war-
   material directorate, Switzerland.
Kriegsministerium: war ministry.
Kriegstechnichen Abteilung (KTA): war-
   technology section, Switzerland.
Kriminalpolizei: detectives.
Kunststoff: plastic.
Kupfer: copper.
Kupfermantelgeschoss: copper-jacketed
   bullet.
kurz: short.

lackiert: lacquered.
Ladestreifen: charger.
Ladung: charge, loading.
Land: land, district.
Landes-Gendarmerie: rural gendamerie
   or police.
Landespolizei: state police.
Landsturm: 'over-age' army reserve.
Landwehr: the eligible army reserve.
lang: long.
Lauf: barrel.
Legierung: alloy.
leicht: light, lightweight.
Leichtmetall: aluminium.
Leiter: leader.
Leitfaden: instruction, order.
Lieferung: delivery.
links: left(-hand).
Loch: hole, cavity.
Los: lot (delivery).
Luft: air.
Luftwaffe: air force.

Luftwaffewaffenamt (LWaA): air force
weapons office.
Lüttich: Liége, Belgium.

Magazin: magazine.
Mähren: Moravia.
Mantel: (bullet-)jacket.
Marine: navy, naval.
Marinewaffenamt (MWaA): navy
weapons office.
Masseverschluss: blowback action.
Mehrlader: repeater.
Messing: brass.
Militär: military.
Modell: model, pattern, type.
München: Munich.
Mündung: muzzle.
Munition: ammunition, munitions.
Muster: pattern, model.
Mutter: nut.

nah(e): close.
Nahkampf: close-combat.
Nahpatrone: short-range (reduced power)
cartridge.
neuer Art (n.A.): new pattern.
Nationalsozialistische Deutsche
Arbeiterpartei (NSDAP, Nazi):
National Socialist Workers' Party.
Niedersachsen: Lower Saxony.
Niederschlesien: Lower Silesia.
Nürnberg: Nuremburg.

Ober: upper, higher.
Oberkommando der Luftwaffe (OKL): air
force high command.
Oberkommando der Kriegsmarine
(OKK): navy high command.
Oberkommando der Wehrmacht
(OKW): armed forces high command.
Oberkommando des Heeres (OKH):
army high command.
Oberschlesien: Upper Silesia.
Oberste Heeres Leitung (OHL): army

high command, prior to 1918.
Öffung: opening, hole.
Öl: oil.
Öldicht: oil-seal(ed), oil-tight.
Österreich: Austria.
österreichisch: Austrian.

Patrone: cartridge.
Patronenhülse: cartridge case.
Pistole 1904: 1904-model navy Luger.
Pistole 1908 (P.1908 or P.08): 1908-
model army Luger.
Pistolenpatrone 1908 (Pist.Patr.08):
1908-model 9mm pistol cartridge.
Pistolentasche 1908 (PT.08): 1908-
model pistol holster.
Platzpatrone: blank cartridge.
Polen: Poland.
polnisch: Polish.
politisch: political.
Polizei: police.
Prag: Prague, Czechoslovakia.
Prägeteile: stampings.
Präzision: accuracy.
Preussen, Preußen: Prussia.
preussisch, preußisch: Prussian.
Probe: experiment, trial, sample.
prüfen: to examine.
Pulver: propellant, powder.

Querbolzen: cross-bolt.

Rahmen: frame, receiver.
Rand: rim, edge.
Rast: groove, click.
Rauch: smoke.
rauchlos: smokeless.
recht: right(-hand).
Regulierung: adjustment.
Reich: empire, state.
Reichsheer: state army, 1919-33.
Reichskolonialamt: imperial colonial office.
Reichsmarineamt (RMA): imperial navy
office.

Reichsministerium des Innern: interior ministry.
Reichstag: parliament (pre-1945).
Reichssicherheitshauptamt (RSHA): central state security office.
Reichswehr: armed forces, 1919–33.
Reihenfeuer: automatic fire.
Reihenfertigung: mass production.
Reinigung: cleaning.
Repetierlader: repeater.
Riegel: bolt, latch.
Riffelung, Rille: cannelure, groove.
Rinne: groove, channel.
Riss, Riß: crack, split, rupture.
Röhren: barrels, tubes.
Rost: rust.
rostfrei: stainless or non-corrosive.
Rückstoss, Rückstoß: recoil.
Russland, Rußland: Russia.
russisch, rußisch: Russian.
Rüstung: armament.

Sachsen: Saxony.
sächsisch: Saxon.
Sanitätspersonal: medical personnel.
Schaft: (gun-)stock.
Schalldämpfer: silencer.
Schieber: slider.
Schiessen, Schießen: shooting.
Schiessplatz: shooting range.
Schiess-schule: marksmanship or musketry school.
Schlagbolzen: striker, firing-pin.
Schlaufe: swivel, loop.
Schlesien: Silesia.
Schliessen: Schließen: to shut.
Schliessfeder: recoil spring.
Schlitten: slider, sledge.
Schloss, Schloß: lock.
schnell: fast, quick, rapid.
Schnellfeuer: rapid-firing.
Schraube: screw.
Schuss, Schuß: shot.
schussbereit, schußbereit: ready for action.

Schütze: rifleman.
Schutzstaffel (SS): defence guard.
Schutztrupp: protective force.
Schwarzpulver: black powder (gunpowder).
schwenkbar: swivelling.
schwer: heavy.
Selbstlade: self-loading.
sicher: safe, secure.
Sicherheitsdienst (SD): security service.
Sicherung: safety (catch).
Sintereisen: sintered iron.
Sneak: term applied to Lugers made for the German armed forces between the world wars, but with no identifying marks.
Sockel: base.
Sonder: special.
Spannabzug: double-action trigger.
spannen: to cock.
spitz: pointed.
Spitzgeschoss, Spitzgeschoß: pointed ('spitzer') bullet.
Stahl: steel.
Stahlblech: sheet steel.
Standvisier: fixed sight.
Stange: rod, pole.
Stark: strong.
Stift: pin.
Stoss, Stoß: shock, thrust.
Stosstrupp: raiding party.
Streifen: strip, clip.
Stumpf: blunt.
Sturmtruppen: assault troops.

Tasche: pocket, holster.
Technische Abteilung: technical detachment of the Swiss KMV.
Teil: part, piece, component.
Träger: carrier, support.
treffen: to hit.
Treibladung: propellant charge.
Trommelmagazin 1908 (TM.08): 1908-model drum magazine.

Tropen: tropics.
tschechisch: Czechoslovakian.
Tschechoslowakei: Czechoslovakia.

Überzählig: spare.
Übung: practice, training.
umgeändert: modified.
Umschalter: selector, change-over switch.
Ungarn: Hungary.
ungarisch: Hungarian.
unter: below, beneath.
Unterbrecher: disconnector.
Unternehmen: enterprise.
Untersuchung: inspection, examination.
Ursprung: origin.

veraltet: obsolete.
verbessert: improved.
Verbindung: connector.
verborgen: concealed.
Verriegelung: lock.
Verschluss: action, bolt, breech-block.
verstärken: to strengthen.
Versuch: trial, experiment.
Versuchs-Abteilung: trials detachment.
Visier: back sight.
Volkspistole: people's pistol.
Volkssturm: 'assault people', last-ditch
   units.
Vorderschaft: fore-end.
Vorrichtung: device, mechanism.
Vorschrift: instruction.

Waffe: weapon.

Waffenamt: weapons office (inspection
   bureau).
Waffenfabrik: arms factory.
Waffen- und Munitions-Beschaffungs-
   Amt: weapons and munitions
   procurement office, pre-1918.
Walze: cylinder.
Warschau: Warsaw, Poland.
Warze: lug, stud.
Wasser: water.
wasserdicht: waterproof, watertight.
Wechsel: conversion, exchange.
Wehr: defence, protection.
Wehramt: operations section of the
   Reichswehr ministry (post-1918).
Wehrmacht: armed forces.
Wehrmachtwaffenamt (WaA): armed
   forces weapons office.
Werk: factory.
Wien: Vienna, Austria.

Zeichen: sign.
Zeichnung: drawing.
Zeugamt: ordnance office.
Zubehör: accessories.
Zubringer: follower, carrier.
Züge: rifling grooves.
Zündhütchen: primer.
zusammengesetzt: assembled.
Zusatz: supplementary.
Zwilling: twin or double.
Zwinge: clamp, holder.
Zylinder: cylinder.

CHAPTER 1

From the Maxim machine-gun to the Borchardt pistol

1881, the year in which Hiram Maxim sketched out his first automatic firearm, was marked by civil unrest. Tsar Aleksandr II of Russia had been fatally wounded in March by a bomb thrown under his carriage by a nihilist group; US President James Garfield, shot in July by Charles Guiteau, had died in September; and the brief, bloody, inglorious career of William 'Billy the Kid' Bonney had ended in the dust of a New Mexican summer.

By the standards of the time, 1881 had been unusually quiet militarily. The British had undoubtedly suffered greatly at Laing's Nek and on Majuba Hill in the First South African War, but these parochial squabbles had had little effect on military thinking. The Crimean and American Civil wars had receded into memory, and even the angry redrawing of the Balkan map had mellowed. Minor clashes still sparked and flared across Africa, where European nations argued territorial claims at the point of a gun, but without ever questioning long-established rules of engagement.

Little did the New Year revellers realise, as they toasted 1881 to a close, that the seeds of a new type of warfare were germinating not in parade-ground panoply but in the march of technology.

The self-confidence of the entrepreneurial engineer knew few bounds in the 1870s. A visitor to the Great Exhibition in London in 1851 may have marvelled at the decorative arts; but an onlooker at the Centennial Exposition in Philadelphia in 1876, only a quarter-century later, would have gawped instead at a colossal Corliss steam engine – more than forty feet high – which could generate more than 2000 hp.

It had only ever been a matter of time before standardisation of working practices and the development of reliable steam-powered machinery allowed weapons to be made on a grand scale. The advent of effectual machine tools had been an important catalyst, but, though the American inventor-engineer Eli Whitney pioneered mass-production of firearms early in the nineteenth century, military conservatism had stifled development.

Most of the participants in the American Civil War carried small-calibre improvements of the French-designed Minié rifle of the 1840s, relying on

19

expanding ball ammunition to reach prodigious distances. Though the design of the Minié cap-lock was rooted firmly in the tradition of the musket, it not only extended the range of engagement ten-fold but also provided an impetus for mass production. The best of these guns were made with interchangeable components and could be guaranteed to perform efficiently.

However, there were more obvious clues to the future: breech-loading rifles firing metal-cased cartridges, and even the first machine-guns. When the Civil War finished in 1865 most of these were swept into oblivion by a return to the pre-war standards promoted by professional soldiers — few of whom could see that in the maelstrom of non-standard cartridges and proprietary breech systems lay weapons that would change the face of warfare.

With the discarded guns went entrepreneurs who had raised units of their own to fight for the Blue or Gray; inventors who had endeavoured to perfect weapons which shot farther or more rapidly; and many manufacturers who had striven to translate these inventions into reality.

Because it was so easily forgotten that technology often thwarted courage, Custer left his Gatling Guns in Fort Abraham Lincoln as he rode out to his destiny at the Little Big Horn in 1876. In the battle of Plevna in 1877, a Russian army commander mindlessly threw regiment after regiment against the devastating defence offered by Winchester-armed Turks. Even as late as the First World War, high-ranking officers could be found in every army to decry the utility of automatic weapons.

Many men grew rich on the pickings of late-nineteenth century conflict. Colt had died comparatively young during the American Civil War, but Oliver Winchester, once a shirt-maker, amassed a great fortune even though he himself had never designed a rifle. Mauser's star rose swiftly in Germany, whilst Mannlicher attained equal prominence in Austria-Hungary.

From humble beginnings, companies such as Österreichische Waffenfabriks-Gesellschaft (founded in 1863) and Waffenfabrik Mauser (1874) rose to great heights. The magnitude of their profits was matched only by the scales of production, orders for 500,000 or more magazine rifles being common even by 1880. These could only be handled efficiently by mechanising, to the detriment of the labour-intensive methods that had been in decline since the 1850s. The process was facilitated by the creation of specialist toolmakers such as Pratt & Whitney in the USA, Greenwood & Batley in Britain, and Ludwig Loewe & Company in Germany.

Firearms production was soon concentrated in the hands of a very few ultra-powerful companies, which often entered into protective cartels to eliminate damaging competition. Unfortunately, the transactions were not always scrupulously fair. Patronage, bribery and corruption were interwoven so finely that truth may remain elusive even with the benefit of hindsight.

Desperate to gain colonies in a period when much land had already been annexed, the German government subsidised the sale of Mauser rifles and Krupp cannon in an attempt to colonise through commercial dependence. And it was by no means unknown for an agent to represent several interests simultaneously. A prime example of duplicity – perhaps 'triplicity' would be more accurate – may be seen in the case of Xaverien & Company, which successfully delayed submitting a bid by BSA so that a lucrative Turkish contract could be let with Colt. If Colt's offer had been rejected, the work would have gone to another Xaverien client, Remington.

The advent of smokeless propellant

The design of small-arms made enormous strides between 1870 and 1880, with the advent of the magazine rifle and the introduction of mechanically-operated machine-guns such as the Gatling, Hotchkiss, Gardner and Nordenfelt. However, the performance of all these guns was limited by cartridges loaded with black powder – greatly refined, but gunpowder nonetheless. A major advance would clearly lie in propellant which would eliminate not only rapid accumulation of fouling but also the propellant smoke that customarily obscured the battlefield.

The rudiments of smokeless-propellant technology had been appreciated since the 1830s, when Braccono and Pélouze, working independently, had each realised that fibrous substances burned much more rapidly when treated with nitric acid. Initial attempts to harness this power ended in disaster, even after the advantages of steeping cotton wool in nitric acid had been discovered. Guncotton burned with practically no smoke and left no residue, but the pressures it generated were customarily erratic.

After a decade of trial and error, the first satisfactory smokeless small-arms cartridge was adopted with the French Lebel rifle in April 1887. Credit for this quantum leap is usually given to Paul Vieille, deputy director of the government laboratory, though Schultze Powder (with a wood-fibre base) had been introduced commercially some years earlier. Success had hinged on the realisation that fibrous cotton could be transformed into a hard horn-like substance, which was less sensitive than guncotton, burned much more slowly, and could be moulded, chopped or flaked.

Effectual smokeless propellant finally freed gun designers from the limitations of black powder, allowing the perfection of weapons which may otherwise have failed. Among them was the Maxim machine-gun.

The toggle lock

The history of the Borchardt and Luger pistols begins with the perfection of the toggle system. The basics of this were by no means new, as some of the single-shot rifles of the nineteenth century embodied the gist of the idea. Even the reciprocating steam engine was an embodiment of the underlying principle, as it had been known since the days of James Watt that single-cylinder engines could not always be started if the crank pivots and piston rods were exactly aligned.

The successful combination of the toggle-lock and automatic operation was made by Hiram Maxim, the first to transform vague theory into practicable reality. Maxim's considerable genius spanned many fields, but he is best remembered for his machine-gun ... even though his gigantic steam-powered flying machine was more entertaining. Born in 1840 in the isolated community of Sangerville, Maine, Hiram Maxim was of French Huguenot descent. His family had settled in the United States after staying briefly in England, a connection Maxim knew long before visiting Europe in 1881 to attend the Paris Exhibition.

While in Paris (or so Maxim claimed in 1915, in his autobiography *My Life*) he had made the 'first drawing of an automatic gun' and decided to stay in England to continue experiments. The inventor initially hired a room in Cannon Street, London, where the first machine-gun drawings were made, before a move was made to 57d Hatton Garden. In an area teeming with diamond-cutters and dealers in precious stones, Maxim modified a Winchester lever-action rifle so that recoil sucessfully operated the action by way of a spring-loaded butt-plate and several levers. This primitive experiment led to an efficient, if cumbersome, machine-gun.

Protection was immediately sought in Britain, patent 3,493/84 being granted in 1884, and The Maxim Gun Company Limited was incorporated in the autumn of the same year. The guns were to be made in a factory in Crayford, Kent. The well-established Vickers family, Sheffield ironmasters, had invested heavily in the project; Albert Vickers became the first chairman. Another substantial stake was purchased by Ludwig Loewe & Company of Berlin, whose legatee – Deutsche Waffen- und Munitionsfabriken – was to enjoy a lengthy co-operation with Vickers, Sons & Maxim.

Though even his primitive prototype worked well enough, Maxim soon encountered the inertia of the British authorities. Many small-arms experts refused to believe that a gun could fire 500 rounds per minute automatically at a time when only the hand-cranked Gatling, Gardner and Nordenfelt had achieved notoriety. Eventually, a trial was staged for George, Duke of Cambridge, a cousin of Queen Victoria. Commander-in-Chief of the British Army since 1859, the Duke had often stood firm against change; but even this conservative officer was impressed by the Maxim gun. He was followed by so many dignitaries, anxious to tread in royal footsteps, that the fortunes of The Maxim Gun Company Ltd were assured.

The first machine-guns had been crude and ungainly, but sophisticated features – an adjustable fire-regulator, for example – belied their bizarre appearance. The hook-type locking mechanism was quickly replaced by a toggle system, and perfected designs had appeared by 1885.

The toggle action has been likened to a human knee, the hinged bars locking so that they cannot buckle under stress. The principles of operation are much the same in handguns and machine-guns, though differences will be found in the size of individual components and the position of the pivots. Some inventors favoured a compact action, some strove to restrict vertical displacement during the operating cycle, and others sought reliability at the expense of weight. The Borchardt was the first pistol to embody a successful lock of this type.

Panel One

THE OPERATION OF THE BORCHARDT PISTOL

The British periodical *Engineering*, in a review published in May 1895, said that the Borchardt:

...departs considerably from the usual form of such a weapon, the stock being continued backwards to provide for the repeating mechanism. The cartridges are contained in the grip, and as they are fired there is no perceptible difference in the balance of the weapon. The barrel (Figs.1, 2, and 11) is of considerable length, and is capable of sliding in guides in the grip 3 (Figs.4 and 11), together with the receiver 34 (Fig.11). The breech-block 41 is guided in the receiver by means of two ribs, and is held up firm against the force of the explosion of the charge by means of two links 47 and 49 (Figs.4, 7, and 11), which at the time of firing are in line. The link 47 is pivoted to the breech-block, and the link 49 to the receiver. When a cartridge is fired, the barrel is forced backwards by the recoil, the receiver, the breech-block, and the two small links all moving together, the parts being in the positions shown in Figs.3 to 5. But after a very short motion, the roller 52 (Figs.4, 7, and 11) strikes the curved path 19, whereupon the two links are brought into the toggle joint position shown in Fig.9, and the breech-block 41 is drawn clear back from the barrel. In going back it takes the empty shell with it, by means of the extractor, until the shell strikes the ejector 14, and is thrown out. The top cartridge in the magazine is held by the feeding spring 68 to 71 (Figs.10 and 11), ready to be inserted into the chamber on the return of the breech-piece. The lips at the mouth of the magazine allow the base of the top cartridge to project a little into the path of the breech-block, whose return is effected by the springs 31 and 17. The former is fixed to a pin in the grip at one end, and is pivoted to the link 49 at the other end (Fig.8), while the spring 17 limits the movement of the link 49. The effect of these two springs is to move the parts from the position shown in Fig.7 to that in Fig.8, immediately the back stroke is completed.

We have thus seen how the breech is opened, the empty shell extracted, a fresh cartridge put in position and driven into the chamber, and the breech closed. It remains to be seen how the striker spring is compressed and the lock cocked. The front end of the forward link 47 has, on the left side, a projecting nose, which draws back the firing bolt as soon as the opening of the breech takes place. The firing bolt 43 (Fig.3) is a hollow cylinder, with a projecting lug on one side, and a spiral spring (Fig.8) in its interior. This spring takes against the screw plug 42 which closes the rear opening of the breech-block. The lug on the firing bolt is engaged by the nose of the sear 35. The trigger 10 moves in a circular groove in the side and forward of the grip. When it is pulled, the wedge-shaped end presses the front arm of the sear inward, and raises the nose of the sear arm sufficiently to release the firing bolt.

The movement of the breech-block and links is so rapid that the firer cannot release the trigger before they have reloaded the pistol. There is, therefore, a special contrivance to prevent the whole eight cartridges being fired off in a second or so. In order that the sear may not strike solid against the still-raised wedge-shaped end of the trigger, a yielding pin 39 is fitted into the forward end of the sear. This pin rests on the spiral spring 40, and recedes when it strikes against the trigger, and after the trigger has been released, snaps forward behind the wedge-shaped end of the latter so that the firing can be repeated.

The cartridges, eight in number, are contained within a case 61 to 67, which is pushed up into the hollow grip, and snapped there by the spring 8. This case can be withdrawn at any time to see how many remain. Spare cases can, of course, be carried to expedite the loading in the heat of battle. The spring 8 also secures the 'safety' 7 in both positions. This latter is fitted into vertical grooves in the side of the grip. When pushed upwards by the thumb, it locks the sear and the trigger, and prevents every motion of the mechanism.

Fig.2 shows the method of introducing the first cartridge into the chamber. The grip is held in the right hand, and the knob on the link 49 drawn back by the left hand until the breech-block is past the base of the top cartridge. The breech-block is then allowed to return, pushing the cartridge before it. The pistol is now loaded and cocked, and if it is not to be fired immediately, the 'safety' must be pushed upwards to prevent accident.

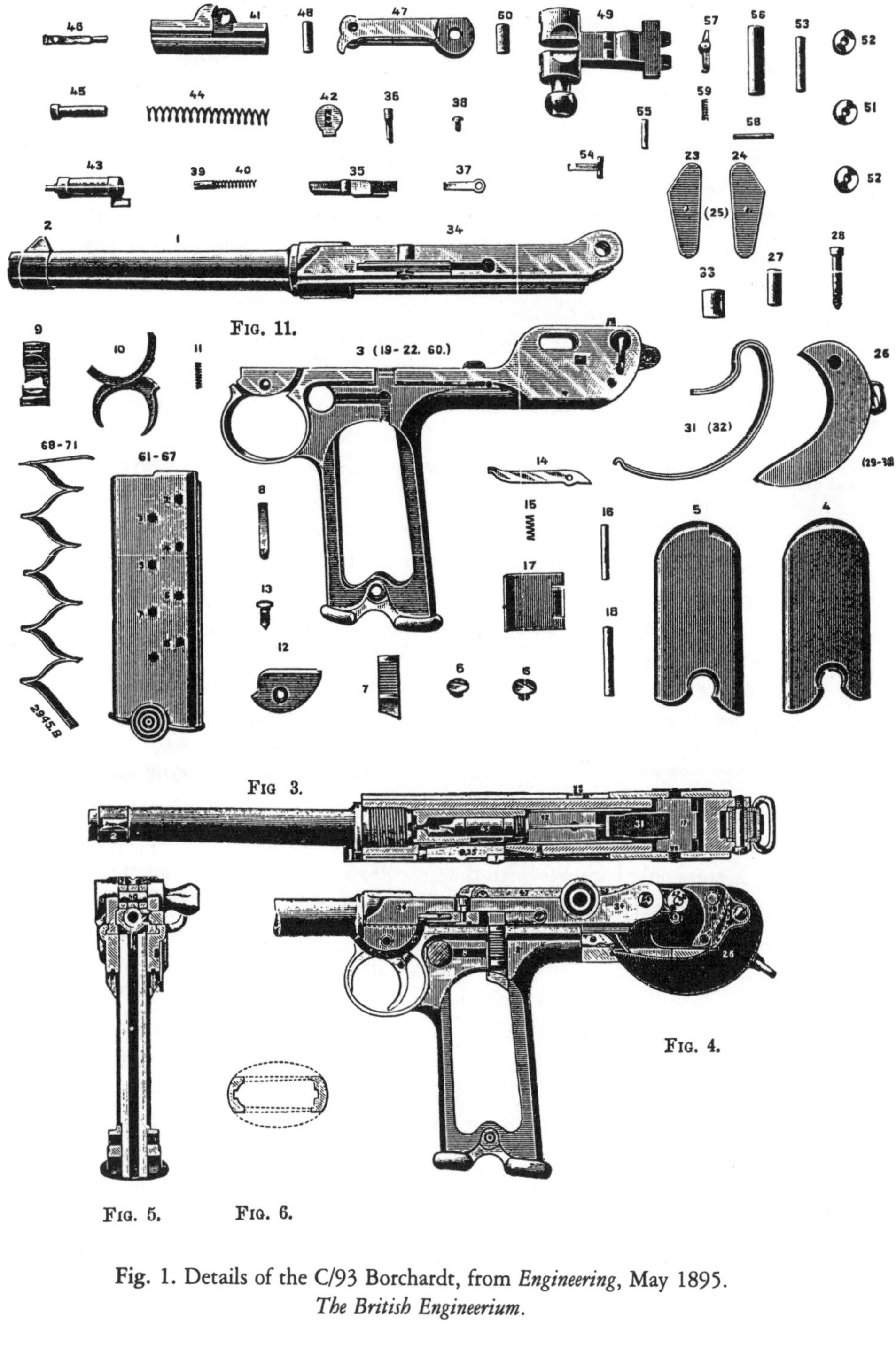

Fig. 1. Details of the C/93 Borchardt, from *Engineering*, May 1895.
The British Engineerium.

Hugo Borchardt

Borchardt was born in Magdeburg on 6th June 1844 but emigrated to the USA at the age of sixteen, shortly before the American Civil War. No details of his movements are known until, in 1865, he was appointed Superintendent of Works for the short-lived Pioneer Breech-Loading Arms Company of Trenton, Massachusetts. Pioneer apparently made breech-loading rifles and five-shot .32 rimfire revolvers, but failed to prosper. Shortly afterwards, therefore, Borchardt accepted a foremanship with the Singer Sewing Machine Company before moving – for only a few months – to Colt's Patent Fire Arms Manufacturing Company in Hartford, Connecticut.

He then went to Winchester, applying for a patent to protect a method of machining lubricating grooves into hard lead bullets. Borchardt's name has also been linked with experimental revolvers exhibited by Winchester at the Centennial Exposition in Philadelphia in 1876, many of which still survive. It has even been claimed that Borchardt played a major part in their development, though the evidence is shaky. There is no doubt that he was involved – for many years, the Winchester museum had a small box labelled in Borchardt's handwriting 'Extractor for Model '76 pistol' – but the basis of the guns seems to be the American patents granted to Stephen Wood in June 1876 and January 1877.

The principal goal of Winchester's revolver-designing exploits was to compete with Colt, who had built a lucrative trade in Model P (Peacemaker) revolvers chambered for the .44-40 Winchester Central Fire cartridge. When the Colt-Burgess lever-action rifle appeared in 1883, however, Winchester revealed a solid-frame rod-ejector revolver designed largely by William Mason. This gun was shown to Colt by Thomas Bennett, Oliver Winchester's son-in-law, ostensibly to seek marketing advice – but mainly to demonstrate that Winchester could compete with the Colt Peacemaker if promotion of the Colt-Burgess continued. The ploy worked very successfully; in 1884, Colt abandoned the Burgess-pattern rifle.

It is sometimes claimed that Borchardt, upset by the failure of 'his' revolvers, left Winchester for Sharps. The chronology is wildly inaccurate, as Borchardt had been appointed superintendent of the Sharps factory on 1st June 1876; if he was disenchanted, it was by the failure of Winchester's management to promote his designs in the mid 1870s. By 1883, he had returned to Europe.

At Sharps, Hugo Borchardt at last achieved a great success: on 26th September 1876, whilst living in Bridgeport, Connecticut, he was granted US Patent 185,721 for a hammerless dropping-block breech-loader derived from the familiar Sharps system of 1848. A patent of addition followed on 23rd July 1878 (no.206,217), both being assigned to the Sharps Rifle Company.

This rifle existed in great variety, despite being in vogue for only a short period. Sharing an identical dropping-block action, they were all made by the

Sharps Rifle Company of Bridgeport. Production totalled about 10,000 military-style weapons and 12,500 sporters, but the demise of Sharps prevented the design attaining its full potential.

Once work on the Sharps-Borchardt had been completed, Borchardt turned his attention to a bolt-action rifle developed by James P.Lee, which Sharps had agreed to manufacture. Borchardt was responsible for the development of tooling, but only a handful of prototypes (sporting and military) had been made when the rickety financial structure of the Sharps Rifle Company collapsed in the autumn of 1880. Liquidation was concluded in 1881.

Borchardt, then residing in Peeskill in New York State, found himself out of work. His last US Patent, no.273,448, was granted on 6th March 1883 to protect a detachable magazine for machine-guns. As Borchardt had already returned to Europe, after failing to find work elsewhere in New England, the patent was assigned to Joseph W. Frazier.

Hugo Borchardt joined the staff of the Hungarian government firearms factory in Budapest, Fegyver és Gépgyár Részvéntarsaság; by 1889, it is claimed, he had risen to the position of works manager or even managing director. During this period, Borchardt would have attended demonstrations of the Maxim machine-gun, and presumably decided to adapt the toggle-lock and recoil actuation to create not only a pistol but also an automatic rifle. Unfortunately, few details of Borchardt's sojourn in Hungary have become public knowledge excepting that he married Aranka Herczog whilst living in Budapest.

In 1891, Borchardt returned to North America to advise Remington on the development of the Lee rifle to compete in the contemporary US Army trials. However, as the Krag-Jørgensen was accepted instead, Borchardt retraced his steps to Europe to perfect his semi-automatic pistol.

The Borchardt pistol

An absence of reliable information prevents a satisfactory development history being given. Owing to the rapidity with which the Borchardt was supplanted by better guns, few commentators writing at the turn of the century paid it much attention. What little is known with certainty generally comes from military test reports, which pay history little heed.

The oldest surviving pistol appears to be no.19, which is claimed to have been presented to Eley Brothers in the mid 1890s and is now in the USA. Gun no.27, owned by a member of the Browning family in Ogden, Utah, also has an interesting – if somewhat apocryphal – story associated with it. According to Val Browning, son of John M., it was left in the Fabrique Nationale factory in Herstal-lèz-Liége by Borchardt himself. The gun bears the marks of Ludwig Loewe & Co, but is largely in the white. The inventor allegedly threw it on the boardroom table after the FN directors refused to manufacture the C/93 in quantity.

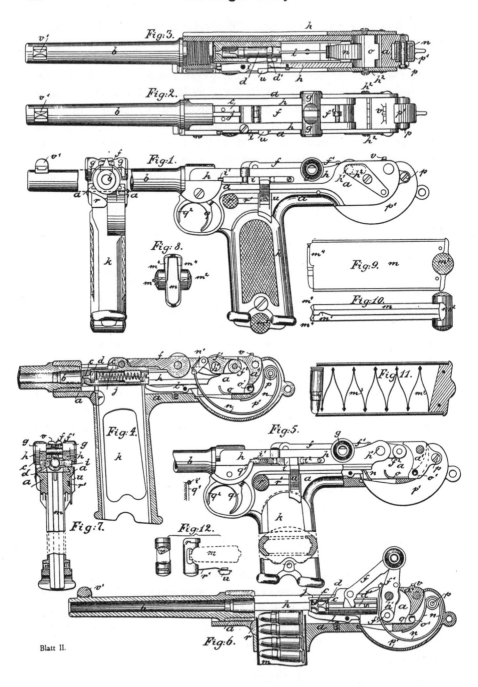

Fig. 2. Drawings of the Borchardt pistol, from German Patent 75,837 of September 1893. *Deutsches Patentamt.*

The date of this event – a tantalising piece of information – has been placed as early as the summer of 1893, but official records are silent. Confronting Fabrique Nationale with a Loewe-made pistol begs a question: if, as has been assumed, Loewe was committed to the project, why should the inventor approach someone else? The most obvious suggestion is that Borchardt, knowing that Loewe was about to transfer exploitation of his pistol to DWM, was keen to regain control. But this would place the meeting with the FN management in the autumn of 1896 instead of three years earlier.

German patent 75,837 was granted on 9th September 1893 to protect the basic pistol construction, and a patent of addition for the method of breaking the toggle, DRP 77,748, followed on 18th March 1894. The crucial question is whether Borchardt, having returned from Hungary, was actually working for Loewe at this time. Most importantly, the patents are granted in Borchardt's name alone. Loewe is not mentioned.

If Borchardt had been an employee of Loewe, it is much more likely either that the gun would have been patented jointly or simply in the name of Loewe alone. This was by no means uncommon in a period when employees did not enjoy the same rights as in more recent times.

Borchardt most probably developed the pistol on his own account, using his proven skill as a machinist to make (or at least commission) a prototype from which the patent specification drawings were prepared. Seeking a financier, he may then have approached Loewe, Germany's leading precision machinist.

Claiming ancestry in a simple partnership founded in the mid 1860s by brothers Ludwig and Isidor, Ludwig Loewe & Companie was incorporated in 1870 to make machine-tools and sewing machines. Thousands of back sights were made for the single-shot Mauser service rifle in the early 1870s, encouraging Loewe to tender successfully to make 70,000 Smith & Wesson-type revolvers for the Russian government. By the end of the 1880s, Loewe had become Germany's leading manufacturer of machine tools. The original Hallmanstrasse site could not accommodate the growing work-force, so a new factory had been built alongside Hütten Strasse in Charlottenburg.

In December 1887, Loewe had purchased the Württembergische Vereinsbank in a superficially straightforward transaction. The bank had loaned money to Waffenfabrik Mauser of Oberndorf, so Loewe, virtually overnight, gained control of Germany's most successful gunmaking business. A huge rifle order was obtained from Turkey in 1887, necessitating production in both Oberndorf and Charlottenburg, but before work began the German authorities offered Mauser a contract for 425,000 of the new 1888-pattern army rifles. Mauser was reluctant to promote a gun designed by an army commission, incorporating features developed by his arch-rival Mannlicher, so a compromise was arranged; all the Turkish guns would be made in Oberndorf, whilst the 'Commission Rifles' would be made in Berlin. Loewe then built a suitable arms-making plant in Martinikenfelde in the Moabit district to fulfil the German army order. The original factory in Hollmanstrasse, Charlottenburg, was subsequently re-equipped to make Maxim machine-guns.

The links between Loewe and Mauser were to have far-reaching repercussions in the story of the Borchardt pistol, and it may be no coincidence that Loewe had become involved in the promotion of the Maxim in Germany. The principles governing the machine-gun and the pistol were essentially similar.

Loewe may have initially accepted an order for nothing but a batch of experimental pistols, perhaps retaining an option on large-scale exploitation. Work on the first Borchardts was certainly under way in June 1893, when a military attaché, Lieutenant Robert Evans of the US Army, visited the Charlottenburg factory. But the exact state of progress at this time is unclear.

Writing in the *American Machinist* of 6th April 1899, in 'Random Notes from Germany on Things Mechanical and Otherwise', Harold E.Hess credited Max Kosegarten of Ludwig Loewe & Company as claiming that the series-made Borchardt pistol was 'in every respect like the first pilot model' submitted by the inventor. This has been questioned, most notably by the late E.C.Ezell in *Handguns of the World* (1981), but comparison of the patent drawings, engravings accompanying sales literature, and photographs in pre-1900 periodicals supports the claim; the differences are comparatively minor.

The patent-specification drawings suggest that the front sight was originally rounded; that the sear spring was once retained by a small screw; and that a small coil spring drove the trigger lever instead of the later leaf. The drawings accompanying the *Reports of the Chief of Ordnance* in 1894 show the rounded front sight, dovetailed into a seat forged integrally with the barrel, as well as the later collar type; they also also share a single-leaf return spring with the gun drawn in the patent specifications. The two-leaf pattern seems to be universal on surviving guns. The earliest magazines had flat undersides, grasping knobs with a concentric-circle design, and the follower spring was made from several short leaves riveted together.

The flat-sided toggle-grip grip shown on the patent specification, with circumferentially milled grooves, was soon replaced by an improved version with a rebound lock set into the right toggle-grip face. A prominent knob protruding leftward undoubtedly facilitated cocking.

The box magazine was soon revised in accordance with German Patent 91,998 of 10th October 1896. The original pattern had been inspired by Borchardt's experiences with the Lee rifle, but relied on the upper surface of the fabricated zigzag leaf spring to raise the cartridges. Experience showed this to be too weak to feed properly, and that the shock of recoil adversely affected the presentation of cartridges to the breech. The cartridge follower in the new magazine was elevated by two coil springs, and the magazine base was noticeably wedge-shaped.

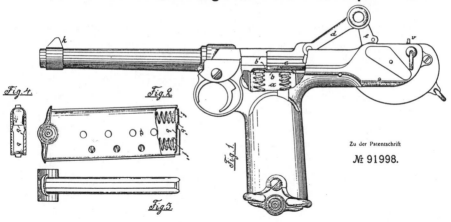

Fig. 3. The improved Borchardt magazine, from German Patent 91,998 of October 1896. *Deutsches Patentamt.*

By 1900, with the emergence of the Borchardt-Luger, the original Borchardt had lost much of the acclaim that had greeted it in the mid 1890s. H.B.C.Pollard, writing just two decades later in his book *Automatic Pistols* (1920), dismissed it as cumbersome and unreliable. But not everyone shared his opinion. In April 1920, whilst reviewing *Automatic Pistols*, a correspondent of *Arms & Explosives* wrote that 'nobody but those who were engaged in the arms trade at that time could appreciate first the incredulity and then the amazement which accompanied the exhibition by Mr H.F.L.Orcutt at his Cannon Street offices of the *hand-made* [my italics] model of the pistol, which was passed round during the time when the tools were being readied for quantity production.'

Henry Orcutt of 145 Cannon Street, London E.C., was Loewe's British agent. Writing in *The Luger Book* in 1986, I suggested that the date of this exhibition would prove the Borchardt to have been the first semi-automatic pistol to encounter tangible success. More recent information indicates that it may not have occurred earlier than Spring 1895 and that, therefore, I can no longer claim that commercial production of the Borchardt commenced in 1893. Tooling may well have begun, but assembly clearly did not get under way for some time.

Though there can be little doubt that the Borchardt was the first semi-automatic pistol to successfully embody a locked breech, the 1894-pattern Bergmann may press it close as the first effectual semi-automatic. Clearly, more information is needed; indeed, it is probable that the Borchardt was not offered on the open market until 1895.

The earliest promotional review to be published in a British professional journal seems to have appeared in *Engineering* in May 1895. The accompanying photographs show a gun with the old-pattern leaf-spring magazine, plain grips, and a large lanyard-ring eye on the back of the return spring housing. This may have been a very early piece, perhaps even a toolroom-made sample to guide series production. As most of the features of the perfected version are already present, however, it is also very tempting to suggest that the gun is no.19 (said to have been presented to Eley Brothers in the mid 1890s) and that the true production run began in the region of serial no.30.

A transverse stock lug was substituted for the lanyard-ring eye when series production began; the eye had already been supplemented with a fixed loop on the left side of the frame, a change that had been made very early in the proceedings. Attaching the stock directly to the spring box by a screwed clamp was a particularly good feature of the Borchardt, providing a much more rigid unit than the later efforts of Mauser, Bergmann and Luger. C/93 pistol no.27, still 'in the white', is known to have been demonstrated to Fabrique Nationale and is currently in North America; it has the stock lug on the operating-spring housing and Loewe marks above the chamber.

Michael Reese pictures C/93 no.127 in *1900 Luger. U.S. Test Trials*, in a case apparently bearing 1893/H.B. in gold. This gun has often been linked not only with Borchardt personally, but also with the earliest American demonstrations. Unfortunately, no proof of these claims has ever been found.

On 21st September 1983, a particularly well-appointed gun was offered in Christie's 'Sale of Modern Sporting Guns and Vintage Firearms'. Made by Loewe, the 19cm-barrelled pistol no.220 was accompanied by 'its original accessories comprising: a wooden shoulder-stock (No.220) and detachable cheekpiece (No.220), with attached leather holster (worn); three spare magazines (each No.220); a wooden dummy magazine stamped "Gesetzlich Geschutzt", housing a brass oiler and a three-piece cleaning rod (with tommy-bar); a brass cleaning-rod with wood-and-steel detachable handle; five small tools (screwdrivers and pin punches); a tinned oil-can with leather cover, and a tin of vaseline (made by Carl Abermann & Co) with leather cover'.

Like many Borchardts, no.220 was accompanied by a baize-lined black leather case with white metal mounts. It was owned by C.B.Westmacott, who, as a junior British Army officer, had apparently purchased it about 1900 for use in the Second South African War. German proof marks were used instead of British equivalents, reflecting that testing barrels from recognised sources – including Germany – did not become a requirement of British Proof Acts until 1925.

One of the most interesting of the surviving Loewe-made guns is no.266, which may have been presented to President Porfirio Diaz of Mexico in 1896 to mark the twentieth anniversary of his assumption of power. The gift supposedly came from Kaiser Wilhelm II, though nothing on the gun proves imperial connections. So could the Borchardt simply have been presented by Loewe to commemorate the adoption of the Mauser rifle for the Mexican army? Diaz subsequently bestowed the pistol on General Pablo Gonzalez, who had been among the first revolutionaries to succeed to high office in Diaz's government.

A pistol owned by the Imperial War Museum in London – Loewe-made, no.415 – has a beautiful non-standard grip which swells to fill the hand. This is a considerable improvement on the standard straight-side type, but was probably added by an enterprising English gunmaker. No other example is known.

At least one automatic Borchardt was made in the mid 1890s. Writing in 'Selbstladegewehre und das System Borchardt' in the periodical *Prometheus* in 1895, Johann Cästner reported that it emptied the eight-shot magazine in 0.3134 seconds, a cyclic rate of 1340rpm. Simple alterations to the trigger or toggle-train allowed continuous fire, but the gun would have been very difficult to control.

The creation of Deutsche Waffen- und Munitionsfabriken

On 4th November 1896, the ammunition-making business of Deutsche Metallpatronenfabrik of Karlsruhe – which Loewe already owned – was renamed 'Deutsche Waffen- und Munitionsfabriken'. On 10th December, the directors of Ludwig Loewe & Company agreed to transfer the Hollmanstrasse and Martinikenfelde factories to DWM, together with 'all rights to guns being made'. The transfer took effect on the first day of 1897. Shares held by Loewe in Mauser, Fabrique Nationale and Fegyver és Gépgyár Részvéntasarság were also transferred to DWM. So, too, was interest in the Borchardt.

At least a thousand sets of C/93 components had been assembled by the end of 1896, all bearing the Loewe name above the chamber and an acknowledgement of Borchardt's original patent on the right side of the receiver. It is not clear whether all the parts-sets that had been made were also assembled; demand had not been great, and the first 'DWM' Borchardts may simply have been assembled from unfinished Loewe-made parts held in store.

A few small changes were soon made. The most obvious is a simplification of the machining on the left side of the frame, where a narrow rib had once continued around the back of the trigger aperture. This was milled flat on DWM-marked guns, and a transverse pin was eliminated below the spring-plate let into the left side of the receiver. Guns of the improved type have SYSTEM BORCHARDT. PATENT, over DEUTSCHE WAFFEN- UND MUNITIONSFABRIKEN above BERLIN, on the right side of the receiver. Series production had probably ended by 1898, even though the 'Automatische Repetirpistole System Borchardt' was still being promoted in 1900. Engravings in DWM manuals, presumably perpetuated from earlier days, seem to show a Loewe-made gun with a DWM 'patent mark' toggle.

The highest authenticated number on a DWM-made gun is 3013, though numbers as high as 5000 are occasionally reported. Most guns have barrels of

190mm, but some shortened to 175mm are known. A plausible report of a factory-original 140mm barrel has yet to be substantiated. According to *Auto-Mag* in August 1983, gun 2915 is said to have Siamese numbers and/or characters on the grip-strap.

The practice of numbering accessories to a gun was erratic, particularly during DWM days; neither 1767 nor 1818, sold by Christie's in July 1984, are numbered on the stock or cheek-piece. The accessories accompanying gun no.1863, ostensibly a DWM product, are all marked L.M.F. (or possibly L.W.F.), which has been read as 'Loewe Metallwaren-Fabrik' or 'Loewe Waffen-Fabrik'. In addition to the standard shoulder-stock, with its attachable holster and optional cheek-piece block, a shaped stock similar to that of the Parabellum carbine has also been associated with Borchardt pistols. A skeleton stock was pictured by Richard Wille in *Selbstpanner (Automatische Handfeuerwaffen)*, published in Berlin in 1896, but has never been found.

The Borchardt cartridge

The 7.65mm Borchardt is amongst the most important of the earliest automatic pistol cartridges, due largely to the use of Walsrode Jagdpulver and efforts made by Deutsche Metallpatronenfabrik to improve manufacturing quality. In an era not known for consistency, 7.65mm Borchardt cartridges often performed extraordinarily well. The US Army trials of 1897 were typical, as only four stoppages were encountered in 2445 rounds.

Georg Luger has been credited with the development of even the earliest Borchardt rounds, though confirmation is still lacking. It is undeniable, however, that Luger took the 7.65mm Borchardt as the basis for the Parabellum patterns. The Mauser company was also appreciative, chambering the earliest of its Feederle-designed pistols for Borchardt-type cartridges. This situation arose simply because Ludwig Loewe & Companie owned a controlling interest not only in Mauser but also in the sole source of ammunition, Deutsche Metallpatronenfabrik; Borchardt apparently disapproved, and bad feeling is said to have existed between the rival designers for some time.

The 7.65mm Borchardt and 7.63mm Mauser cartridges are dimensionally identical, though the Mauser pattern contains a heavier propellant charge which develops a higher velocity as well as higher chamber pressure. True Borchardt cartridges often have one or two cannelures encircling the case-neck. They were originally made only by Deutsche Metallpatronenfabrik of Karlsruhe – subsequently DWM – but later also by Keller & Company of Hirtenberg in Austria.

The C/93 could probably handle the 7.63mm Mauser cartridge satisfactorily, but the main spring would undoubtedly need to be reinforced. In his book *German Pistols and Revolvers, 1871–1945* (1970), Ian Hogg claimed that guns were so treated but the date offered, 1913, may be questionable. He also suggests the possible existence of Borchardts chambering the shorter 7.65mm Parabellum cartridge, though none has yet been found.

The Borchardt in the market-place

Sales literature produced in 1898 by DWM's agent, Hermann Boker & Company of Duane Street, New York City, offered the 'Borchardt Automatic Repeating Pistol and Carbine', complete, with 'three extra magazines, Tools, Oiler, Holster and Strap' for $35. The stock was standard – it came attached to the holster – but the leather case was $5 extra. The wooden dummy magazine, which contained the cleaning equipment, acted as a hold-open whilst the gun was being dismantled, owing to the absence of a mechanical system.

The C/93 excited much interest in North American circles. The *New York Times* for 12th September 1897, for example, recorded that 'A feature of yesterday's practice [at Creedmoor] was the testing of a new magazine pistol, an invention of Borchardt. Col. Butt and Major N.B.Thurston, the latter supervising the day's practice, conducted the tests. Tests at 25, 100 and 200 yards were made, and proved highly satisfactory. At 100 yards Major Thurston fired eight shots in fifteen seconds, and the score showed seven bull's eyes and one centre, a feat hitherto unaccomplished by a guardsman firing an ordinary revolver...'

On 30th September 1897, *Shooting & Fishing* reported that 'A very interesting exhibition was given during the afternoon of the capabilities of the new Borchardt automatic pistol, which has been adopted by the Swiss government. It was shot by Herr Tauscher, and also by several members, one of whom, Mr Francis, secured 39 out of a possible 40 at 50 yards, and made several bull's-eyes at 200 yards. In the rapidity test, the eight shots were delivered in less than half a second.' (This must have been the fully automatic example.)

The C/93 was being redesigned by Luger even as the *Shooting & Fishing* copy was being written. Yet it left a lasting impression on those who saw an automatic pistol operate for the first time.

Borchardt's later career

Hugo Borchardt patented an improved pistol in 1909. Though this shared the general layout of the C/93, the changes were largely concerned with the construction of the trigger and its interaction with the sear: the specifications, British and German alike, do not explain precisely how the gun works. The width of the magazine and the vertical grip suggest that the operating spring cannot duplicate the perfected Borchardt-Luger design, and so a riband-spring must have lain under the rear of the frame. No surviving gun of this type is known.

Borchardt also experimented with toggle-operated rifles – so, too, did Georg Luger – but none has yet been conclusively identified as his work. Thus the life

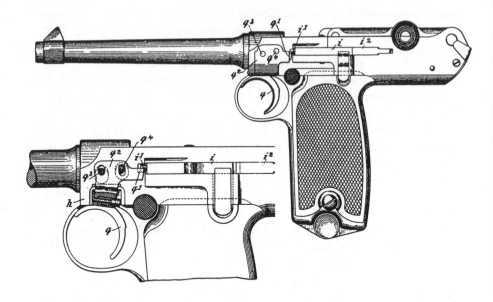

Fig. 4. This illustration of the 1909-type Borchardt pistol was taken from the British patent specification. It is not obvious how the breech is closed, though the return spring is assumed to be a flat leaf beneath the receiver behind the grip.

of a highly skilled engineer passed almost without notice, excepting for the brief period in which the C/93 was in vogue. All that is known for certain is that Borchardt was living at Königgrätzer Strasse 66, Berlin, when his first patents were granted, and at Kantstrasse 31 in Berlin-Charlottenburg when he died of pneumonia on the morning of 8th May 1924.

His inventions included shirt-neck shapers, machines to make ball-bearings, wire-straightening equipment, gas burners and electrical apparatus. As the designer of the first truly successful semi-automatic pistol, Hugo Borchardt deserves a much more prominent place than he currently occupies in the history of modern firearms. Unfortunately, no authenticated portrait of him is known.

The performance of the Borchardt

Reaction to the pistol was usually praise, bordering on incredulity. Between June 1893 and the beginning of 1896, the US Military Attaché in Berlin, Lieutenant Robert Evans, made several visits to the Charlottenburg factory where the pistols were being made. The gun Evans used in 1895 had allegedly fired more than 6000 rounds, yet was still in excellent condition. He managed to fire an entire magazine in two seconds, placing all eight shots on a 46cm-square target placed twenty paces away. According to 'Memoranda on

Attaché's Despatches, 1889–', prepared by the Adjutant-General's Office, Evans reported that the pistol had very little recoil for its power – but also that 'very few' had been completed. It is a great pity, in view of comments made previously about the production status of the Borchardt in the mid 1890s, that he was not more specific.

The US Navy also briefly tested the Borchardt. The *Boston Herald* of 22nd November 1894 reported that:

> The naval small arms board had exhibited before it today a pistol which is quite likely to revolutionise this sort of equipment in the armies and navies of the world.
>
> It is the invention of an American, Hugo Borchardt, now in Berlin, and was shown for the first time in America.
>
> Georg Luger exhibited the new production, and besides admiring it the members of the board could not help expressing themselves as believing that it had a great future before it ... It is after the style of the Maxim mitrailleuse, being automatic in action; receiving its ability to load and extract an empty shell from the recoil of the shot. It is claimed to be the only small weapon capable of doing this continually.
>
> In an exhibition, 100 rounds were fired without a hitch. The exhibitor (Georg Luger) fired 24 shots in 43½ seconds at a range of 100 feet, and all were hits. He was not an expert with the piece.
>
> It weighs 2lb 12½ ounces, is 11 inches in length. The grip is placed at the center of gravity, giving steadier fire. Through it runs the magazine capable of holding eight cartridges, with nickel jacketed bullets of 7.62mm, about the same caliber as the navy revolver of the present day. It has great penetration and an effective range of 500 meters.
>
> A light adjustable stock may be affixed, making for all practicable purposes a carbine for the cavalry. The cartridges are of the Luger rimless type ...

On 19th October 1897, 'in accordance with the instructions of the [US Army] Chief of Ordnance', a Board of Officers was appointed to test a Borchardt Automatic Pistol-Carbine. Captain James Rockwell Jr, Captain Charles Whipple and Lieutenant Tracy Dickson submitted their report to the Chief of the Ordnance Department, Colonel Alfred Mordecai, on 23rd December.

The trials had been attended by Hans Tauscher, 'the inventor's representative', who had partially dismantled the gun and, whilst holding nothing but the barrel and receiver in his hand, had fired a single shot to demonstrate the inherent safety of construction. Tauscher also demonstrated the fully-automatic Borchardt, which had been first shown in the Loewe factory eighteen months previously. According to the report, the 'left end of the toggle joint was arranged to operate the sear so that when the Cartridge was inserted in the chamber and the trigger pulled, shots were fired automatically in about ½ second'.

Tauscher did not attend subsequent tests, which were undertaken by the officers of the Board alone. The first test was simply an examination of the gun, which contained seventy components 'including 7 screws, 18 pins, studs and rivets, 7 flat and 5 coil springs excluding the stock and magazine'.

The first shots were fired to test the action, velocity being 1296.6 ft/sec at 53ft from the muzzle. Field-stripping took forty seconds; reassembly required 2 minutes 20 seconds. The rapidity-with-accuracy test was undertaken at a range of 100ft in conjunction with a 'man-size' target, 6ft high and 2ft wide. With the butt fitted to the spring housing, forty shots were fired from the shoulder in 68 seconds, all but one hitting the target. A repeat of the test improved rapidity – taking only 45 seconds – and registered 35 hits. A freehand test was less satisfactory. Though the forty shots took 38 seconds, merely twelve hits were obtained from 32 shots.

Experiments to determine how fast the gun could be fired gave 32 shots in 22 seconds as a carbine, or 37 shots in first 28 and then 26 seconds 'as a revolver'. The first jam occurred during the second series, as sufficient propellant fouling had accumulated in the chamber to prevent a cartridge seating properly.

Accuracy with the stock attached was truly excellent. The radius of the shot-circle at 25 yards was less than half an inch. At 75 yards the figure was 1.39in; and it had only grown to 15.86in at 500 yards. This was a tremendous achievement for a pistol, even though the commissioners suggested that wind blowing across the range had spoiled the results.

The testers were also impressed by the ability of the pistol-carbine to hit the man-size target consistently, though the projectile retained comparatively little energy at extreme range. Penetration of one-inch pine boards, placed an inch apart – ten at 25 yards – had reduced to 7½ at 75 yards and 3½ at 500 yards.

The extractor fractured during the defective cartridge test, which was otherwise regarded as quite satisfactory. The pistol operated satisfactorily even when the powder charge was reduced from seven to 5.5 grains, an important advantage in an era of unreliable propellant.

The Borchardt was cleaned after firing 402 rounds, with only a single failure. The first endurance trial – 997 rounds in 2hr 37min – produced three jams, all caused by cartridges in which bullets were seated too deeply. A second series of a thousand rounds was completed without a single adverse incident, excepting that a crack developed in one of the magazine bodies. Almost 2000 rounds had been fired, with only four failures, from a gun now often condemned as unreliable. To put this into a proper context, a 'mean rounds between stoppages' figure of 499 would have placed the Borchardt fourth in the endurance trials of the US Joint Services Small Arms Program in the early 1980s

The Borchardt chamber showed little measurable wear after 2000 shots, though the velocity at 53 feet had risen to 1313.9 ft/sec owing to imperceptible wearing of the lands and a consequent reduction in friction.

After dusting, the mechanism failed to close properly after the first shot had been fired but otherwise performed acceptably. The pistol was then tested after rusting. The breech had to be closed manually after the first two shots, but thereafter worked automatically. The gun was dismantled, thoroughly cleaned, and found to be in excellent condition except for wear on the standing breech caused by the toggle roller. 2445 rounds had been fired, with four jams and three breech-closure failures in the dust and rust tests.

The Board concluded that:

The great accuracy with which this pistol was made contributes largely . . . to its certainty of action.

This is really the first marked advance made in the design of revolvers [sic] to which the attention of the Board has been called since the introduction of the metallic case cartridge. The butt stock can readily be attached to the grip and the weapon then becomes a short range carbine.

The ammunition was excellent, except that occasionally a cartridge was found with the bullet forced back within the case against the powder: the bullet is lubricated.

The Board finds: 1st, – That the construction and action of this pistol show a workmanship of the highest order. 2nd, – That the accuracy and penetration of this weapon raise it, ballistically, above the revolver class, but the rapid decrease in penetration as the range increases, due to the lightness of the bullet, restricts its efficiency to ranges not over 500 yards. 3rd, – That the method of obtaining automatic action in this Arm is ingenious, safe, practically certain and comparatively simple. 4th, – That its small calibre, and exceptionally light bullet make its 'stopping effect' questionable, especially for a cavalry weapon. 5th, – That the Borchardt Automatic Pistol-carbine stood all the tests, to which it has been subjected by the Board, in a highly satisfactory manner.

The results of this trial show the Borchardt Automatic Pistol-Carbine to be of the highest excellence as a target arm but, as its suitability for the rough usage of the Military service can be determined only by actual test, the Board recommends that a limited number be purchased and issued for further trial . . .

Colonel Mordecai approved the findings of the report, but lack of funds prevented the purchase of Borchardts for extended trials.

There is no doubt that the gun tested by the US Army had been carefully adjusted to work with selected batches of ammunition, and that this contributed to its outstanding success. Its performance should be contrasted with those of the supposedly improved 7.65mm-calibre Borchardt-Luger in the trials of 1901 (33 assorted jams and misfires in 1734 rounds during the endurance trial alone) and then with the .45 version tried in 1907, which suffered 31 failures in an overall total of 1022.

Borchardt and Luger

It is popularly believed that a decision of Loewe's to let Mauser chamber a new pistol for the 7.65mm cartridge so antagonised Borchardt that he was unwilling to continue development. The key to this particular problem may lie in the genesis of the cartridge.

Patent drawings show that its design had been completed by Spring 1893, as the application was made in early summer. The earliest known examples are all the work of Deutsche Metallpatronenfabrik of Karlsruhe, subsequently incorporated in DWM. But did Hugo Borchardt actually design the cartridge himself? The only pertinent information comes from the review in *Arms & Explosives* cited previously, where it was claimed that 'remarks Borchardt made proved the existence of a certain amount of soreness against Mauser, who, taking the cartridge worked out by Borchardt, found the construction of an improved pistol to fire it an easy matter, for he also had the faults of others to guide his design.'

The relationship between Ludwig Loewe & Co, Hugo Borchardt and – if appropriate – Georg Luger has yet to be explained satisfactorily. Whatever rights the inventor of the cartridge once held were presumably assigned to Loewe as a condition of the contract regulating the exploitation of the Borchardt pistol.

As Loewe held a substantial shareholding in Mauser, valued in 1896 at two million Goldmarks, granting use of the cartridge was a logical step; Deutsche Metallpatronenfabrik (also owned by Loewe) was the only source of ammunition. Retaining a proven cartridge would obviously reduce development time and it may even be that the Feederle brothers – who originated the Mauser auto-loader some time in 1894 – were already using Borchardt-type cartridges in their experiments.

Except for the *Arms & Explosives* review, there is no evidence that Borchardt regarded the use of 'his' cartridge as a grave breach of faith. But it takes no great stretch of the imagination to understand his feelings when the Mauser pistol left a greater mark on firearms history than his own design.

Of course, much also hinges on the participation of Georg Luger in the story of the Borchardt pistol. Luger was undoubtedly reponsible for demonstrating the Borchardt on many occasions in the 1890s, and has been widely credited with refining the C/93 into the Borchardt-Luger.

Writing in the 1930s, Adolf Fischer suggested that Hugo Borchardt – who, unlike Luger, had no military background – had been content merely to create a mechanism that worked, and could not understand the desire of military authorities to make it more combat-worthy. Though this is now widely accepted, it is worth considering an alternative.

None of the individual patents granted to Borchardt or Luger mention either Loewe or DWM as co-patentee, which suggests that the inventors were not on the manufacturers' payroll and that their designs were acquired on a royalty basis. This was by no means uncommon in the engineering circles of the time. Rights to the Borchardt pistol were transferred to the newly-formed Deutsche Waffen- und Munitionsfabriken at the end of 1896, together with Loewe's other gunmaking interests. When the necessity arose to refine the Borchardt pistol, therefore, it was inevitable that the burden of work would fall on Luger. This would have been due partly to his military experience, but probably also to hostility between Loewe and Borchardt arising from the use of the 7.65mm Borchardt cartridge by Mauser.

Theories have also been advanced that Georg Luger designed, refined or perfected the Borchardt cartridge. Had he worked for Deutsche Metallpatronenfabrik instead of Ludwig Loewe & Co, the claims would have more substance. But they are at least worthy of consideration.

CHAPTER 2

Adoption of the Luger in Switzerland: the first real success

Modern enthusiasm for early automatics such as the French Clair, the Austro-Hungarian Schönberger and the German Bergmann-Brauswetter is very misleading. Many of these prototypes survive merely because they were submitted for official trials and were subsequently retained in museum collections. Few were ever exploited commercially, nor did they have lasting effects on contemporary firearms history; many, indeed, had been rejected – disappearing into history only to be rediscovered and hailed as 'significant' in recent times. Many early Roth, Schwarzlose, Krnka and Mannlicher pistols suffered this untimely demise, passing all but unnoticed by the mainstream of late nineteenth-century life.

Even the first Bergmann-Schmeissers were no better. Patented in Germany in early summer 1893, contemporaneously with the Borchardt, they were made in 5mm, 6.5mm, 8mm and possibly other chamberings. Found wanting in military trials in Germany and Switzerland, the Bergmann-Schmeisser was rapidly superseded by an improved design.

Only the Borchardt and the Mauser C/96, with sales of about 2500 and 19,650 respectively, had any appreciable impact on the market for military-type locked-breech pistols prior to 1900. The commercial distribution of rival designs was restricted by expense, unreliability or poor performance, though the perfected blowback Bergmanns and probably also the unfashionable Charola y Anitua had also achieved limited success by the end of the nineteenth century. Not until the small-calibre FN- and Colt-Browning blowbacks appeared was the automatic pistol truly able to challenge the pocketable revolver.

From Borchardt to Borchardt-Luger

When DWM succeeded to the business of Ludwig Loewe & Company, the Borchardt pistol was rapidly being overhauled by more compact, efficient-looking designs. Though few of these possessed the reliability of a properly adjusted C/93, they were much less complicated. If the curious mainspring of the Borchardt broke, the pistol had to be returned to the factory for repair as few provincial gunsmiths were knowledgeable enough to make a satisfactory replacement.

Even though the Borchardt operated satisfactorily when properly adjusted, the lengthy rearward overhang of the spring housing made holstering difficult. This could only be solved by moving the operating spring, which meant substantially altering the basic gun.

The stages by which the Borchardt was transformed into the Borchardt-Luger are still disputed, though a solitary 'Improved Borchardt' or *Übergangsmodell*, serial number 1, replaced the C/93 in the Swiss trials of 1897. Georg Luger had previously indicated that a 'smaller and lighter version' was under development when the Swiss commission drew attention to the ungainly shape of the original Borchardt. Unfortunately, the Improved Borchardt was replaced by the earliest true Borchardt-Luger before the final shooting trials began. The gun was returned to DWM and has since been lost, together with details of its construction.

Great advances have been made since *Luger* was published in 1977, but nothing has dented presumptions made of the progress from the C/93 to the first Borchardt-Luger. Though none of the transitional guns has been found, nor has evidence been forthcoming to refute their existence. The only missing link has come from the period of the Borchardt-Luger.

On 22nd June 1897, the Swiss ordnance department began trials in which guns tested in 1895, a Bergmann and a Mannlicher, were pitted against new submissions from Borchardt and Mauser. The commission convened at the Federal munitions factory in Thun, under the chairmanship of Oberst von Orelli, head of the technical section of the Swiss ordnance department. Its members included Oberst Rubin, director of the Federal ammunition factory in Thun, and Professor Rudolf Amsler.

The committee had intended to test all four self-loading pistols against a 7.5mm Model 82 service revolver. However, as no improvements had been made to the Bergmann and Mannlicher since the trials of 1895, they were omitted to allow thorough testing of the Borchardt and the Mauser.

The Loewe-made C/93, no.95, was demonstrated by Georg Luger. After firing, handling and examination, the Board reported that excessive size and poor balance made the Borchardt a poor substitute for the revolver. The pistol had also been tried by NCOs and men of the cavalry as a light self-loading carbine, but complexity and poor balance still told against it.

The ballistic performance of the 7.65mm Borchardt cartridge, however, was impressive. The 5.5gm jacketed lead-core bullet was propelled by 0.45gm of Walsrode Jagdpulver, attaining a velocity of 410 m/sec and a muzzle energy of 47.3mkg. By comparison, the M1886 revolver cartridge fired a 6.8gm bullet at only 221 m/sec, its muzzle energy being little more than a third of the German design.

Advantageous though the small-calibre high-velocity Borchardt bullet seemed to be, its merits were overshadowed by the size of the pistol – 350mm overall, 1.31kg unladen. Similar complaints were made of the Mauser C/96, and so both pistols were rejected.

DWM then informed the Swiss authorities that an improved Borchardt was ready for submission. On 5th October 1897 this gun, apparently numbered '1', was tried against a Bermann and a Mannlicher. It had a 're-positioned recoil spring', in the grip, and was appreciably smaller than the original trials C/93. Writing in 1971 in *Die Faustfeuerwaffen von 1850 bis zur Gegenwart*, Eugen Heer gives overall length as 272mm and weight as 1000gm.

This pistol is believed to have been the original Improved Borchardt. A few of its features can be surmised by comparing the original C/93 with the drawings accompanying Swiss patent 17,977 of 3rd October 1898 and the surviving Third Experimental Model (Versuchsmodell 1898).

The main spring had been moved from the spring box, beneath the rear of the receiver, into the grip behind the detachable magazine. This enabled the grip to be raked backward, improving balance and allowing a grip safety to replace the sliding Borchardt type. However, the pistol retained the roller to unlock the toggle unit and its action would have been longer than an otherwise

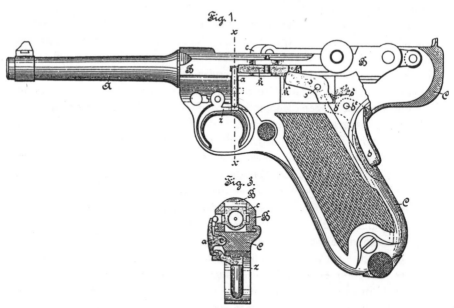

Fig. 5. This is probably the Improved Borchardt of 1897, fitted with safety catches patented in 1898 by Georg Luger. Note that the internal roller has been retained, though the raked grip is an improvement on the C/93. *Deutsches Patentamt.*

comparable Borchardt-Luger. Had the barrel of the Swiss trial gun measured 127mm rather than the figure of '157mm' given by Eugen Heer, the action-length of 145mm would fit the predictions: the C/93 action measures about 165mm whilst that of the perfected Borchardt-Luger is about 115mm.

Unfortunately, it is not known whether the original trial record or, indeed, Eugen Heer's fascinating book, contains a misprint. Thus the identification of the Improved Borchardt with the gun shown in the patent specifications cannot be confirmed. However, the full-length drawings accompanying German Patent 109,481 suggest that the barrel of the transitional pistol was appreciably shorter than the Borchardt type.

As the Third Experimental Model (Versuchsmodell 1898) has a safety, sear and trigger system adapted from – but similar to – this improved Borchardt, the illustration on page 44 probably offers a realistic impression. The 1897 submission is unlikely to have featured any of the improvements to the safety system protected by Luger's 1898-vintage German patent, 109,481 or the later Swiss Patent 18,623 of January 1899.

As several other guns had also been submitted for trials in Switzerland, another Board was appointed in 1898 under the chairmanship of Oberst von Orelli. Six pistols had been received by 5th October: the Improved Borchardt, a Bergmann No.3, a Bergmann No.5, a new Mannlicher, an improved Mauser C/96, and a Krnka-Roth. The improved Borchardt may well have been the one-and-only example fitted with Luger's trigger and safety. Before the firing trials commenced, it had been replaced by the first two true Borchardt-Lugers. One was described as a short-barrel type with a holster stock, whilst the other had a long barrel.

The modifications to the Borchardt are credited to Luger by DWM's fiftieth anniversary history, *50 Jahre Deutsche Waffen- und Munitionsfabriken*, which states that:

> [The] Borchardt pistol's grip had been almost vertical, resulting in an unpleasant hold while shooting. What is more, at the end of the receiver had been a housing, comparatively large, containing the main spring...all this adding to the pistol's length.
>
> Firearms designer Luger, who developed the Parabellum pistol, altered the grip-position in such a way that it corresponded to the natural hold while shooting. He repositioned the mainspring ... in the grip, thus reducing the pistol's length and making it handier.'

By the summer of 1898, Luger had discarded the internal roller and developed a different method of breaking the toggle. Inclined cam-ramps were now machined as part of the standing frame. When the gun was fired, recoil of the barrel and the receiver caused the toggle-grips to strike the cam-ramps. The action is described in greater detail in the accompanying panel, but soon proved to be stronger, simpler and neater than its predecessor – though possibly not as smooth or certain in operation as the Borchardt roller.

Borchardt and the earliest Borchardt-Luger pistols generally exhibited a special lock in the right toggle-grip to prevent the breech-block bouncing back from the breech face at the end of the return stroke. These were commonly encountered in early machine-guns, where the parts were comparatively heavy, but rebound could not occur once the axis of the cross-pin in the toggle-train dropped below the centre-line of the bore. However, the locking mechanism was not discarded until 1905.

The Borchardt-Luger

The pistols submitted to the Swiss ordnance department in November 1898 were the true prototypes of the Luger, developed from the improved Borchardt they replaced. The guns were called 'Versuchsmodell III' ('Third Experimental Model') to distinguish them from the C/93 (first model) and the improved Borchardt of 1897 (second model). They chambered the 7.65mm Borchardt-Luger round, a shortened transformation of the 7.65mm Borchardt pattern to suit the raked grip and magazine. Ammunition development had certainly been completed by the end of 1898, as surviving drawings of the pistol, showing the cartridges, are dated as early as 7th January 1899. Sufficient ammunition had been supplied for the Swiss to begin trials on 1st May.

Luger's first pistol patents date from the end of September 1898, approximately contemporaneous with the appearance of the Third Experimental Model in Switzerland, but months may elapse between application for a patent and the actual grant; design improvements are continuous and evidence based on patents is often unsatisfactory. In addition, Luger applied for patents only after he had perfected his designs in an attempt to extend protection to the farthest possible date.

The key period in the transition from the Borchardt to the Borchardt-Luger has now been reached, but the surviving trials pistol in the Bern small-arms factory collection, bearing the serial number 5, must be conclusively identified as an 1898-vintage Third Experimental Model and not the improved Fourth Model of 1899.

Accepting that the fundamental change to the toggle system had been made by the autumn of 1898, despite the dismissible 'evidence' provided by the patents, the Third Experimental Model would have had a standard Luger cam-ramp action. The trial reports concur that the old internal roller system had disappeared.

The solitary survivor retains some characteristics of the improved Borchardt of 1897, as the trigger not only perpetuates a riband-spring but also pivots ahead of the trigger-plate; in addition, the same removable side-plate permits access to the safety mechanism. However, the rear part of the frame has been greatly shortened by eliminating the toggle-roller and its internal track. This gun, therefore, represents the first true Borchardt-Luger; in spite of its transitional appearance, all the basic operating principles of the perfected Swiss Ordonnanzpistole 1900 are clearly established in its action.

Changes made in 1899, important though they may seem to be, are largely superficial. The most significant features that separate the Borchardt from the Borchardt-Luger – the position of the mainspring and the method of opening the toggle – are both incorporated in the Third Experimental Model.

The 1898-type pistol foreshadowed the appearance of the later Borchardt-Lugers, excepting that the rear frame was machined differently. The manual safety lever was added a year later. A short grip safety was fitted on the left side of the frame and a removable side-plate, on the left side of the gun above the grip, gave access to the safety bar. At 990gm, the pistol was considerably heavier than later pistols of similar barrel-length and calibre. A spring lock in the right toggle-grip prevented the breech-block rebounding from the face of the chamber on the completion of the loading stroke. The gun has plain-bordered chequered grips, but is unmarked except for serial numbers.

Firing trials ended in Switzerland on 28th November 1898, having included a rapid-fire test of two series of fifty rounds, an accuracy test in which three targets were fired at at a range of fifty metres, and an endurance test in which 400 shots were fired without cleaning the mechanism. The Borchardt-Luger performed with hardly a misfire or jam, and showed itself to be the most accurate of the submissions. The Swiss liked the gun, rating it easily the best of the competitors. The Bergmann No.5 and the Mauser C/96 had failed; the Krnka-Roth was disliked owing to charger-loading and inadequate safety features; and the Mannlicher (which had been placed third on the basis of numerical scoring) was preferred to all but the Borchardt-Luger. The worst feature of the Mannlicher was its magazine, ahead of the trigger, which had to be loaded from a charger through the top of the action.

It is assumed that at least five Third Experimental Model Borchardt-Lugers were made, three to serve as developmental prototypes and two to be delivered for trials in Switzerland. The surviving gun, no.5, has a 14cm barrel; no.4 had a holster-stock and a short barrel, possibly 12.7cm.

The Third Experimental Model convinced the Swiss that the Borchardt-Luger had great potential, though changes were still required. The most important was to be the addition of a lockable grip safety system to prevent accidental discharge. Luger's Swiss Patent 18,623 of 2nd January 1899 illustrates some improved designs, though there is no evidence that they were satisfactory. This patent also shows a toggle with flat grips, perhaps even with the single raised rib featured by both the original Borchardt patent drawings and the so-called Erste Originalpistole.

In February 1899, Luger personally delivered blueprints of an improved design to Oberst von Orelli, president of the Swiss trials board, to show that progress was being made. These are clearly marked 'Selbstladepistole Borchardt-Luger'.

In 1975, a colour picture of a unique pistol was added to the fourth printing of Harry Jones' book *Luger Variations* (volume one), captioned as the *'Erste Original-pistole (Baujahr 1899) "System Borchardt-Luger" – Modell, das zum Serien-nachbau diente. Vorrichtung und Lehrenbau: Deutsche Waffen- und Munitionsfabriken'* ('Original Borchardt-Luger system pistol, made in 1899. Pattern to guide series production. Designed and developed by DWM.') Owing to uncertain provenance and characteristics that seem closer to the perfected guns of 1899–1900, it is difficult to regard this as the 'first Luger' – an honour which I believe should rightly belong to the Third Experimental Model of 1898.

The Jones gun is externally similar to the pre-production pattern of 1900, though its flat-faced toggle grips have a single annular rib. However, the surviving gun from the November 1898 Swiss trials has the dished toggle-grip perpetuated by the later 'old model' guns and its toggle-train is clearly original, even though the parts differ sufficiently from those of the post-1899 Borchardt-Lugers to prevent interchangeability. Another obvious visual characteristic of the Third Experimental Model is the square interface between the two toggle links – subsequently radiussed to minimise the effects of wear, but which distinguished between the prototype and perfected Borchardt-Lugers.

The Erste Originalpistole shares the squared interface and is apparently unmarked, except for SYSTEM/BORCHARDT-LUGER inlaid in gold on the front toggle link. This corresponds with the title on the blueprints shown to Oberst von Orelli by Georg Luger in February 1899; in addition, the toggle-grips match those shown in Luger's Swiss Patent 18,623 of 2nd January 1899.

The provenance of the Erste Originalpistole has excited great controversy. The principal problem concerns the design of the toggle grips, as there seems no good reason for DWM to regress from the dished pattern used in 1898. Perhaps the gun was created in the early twentieth century for exhibition purposes, on the basis of a redundant Fourth Experimental Model prototype/pre-production gun. The distinctive toggle may have replaced a damaged or worn-out component, as the concentric-circle would have been easier to make in the tool room than the perfected knurled-edge dished type. This would not have mattered if the gun was to be confined to an exhibition show-case.

The final Swiss trials

After discussing the results of the previous year's exploits, the Swiss decided to hold a third series of trials on 1st–4th May 1899. A prize of 5000 francs was at stake and a new committee, substantially that of the previous year, convened at Thun.

An improved Borchardt-Luger had been submitted by DWM, in accordance with drawings Georg Luger had shown Oberst von Orelli six weeks previously. The principal change was the addition of a manual safety lever on the left side of the frame – where a panel, so characteristic of later guns, had been milled out to receive it – and the breech-block had been redesigned to make its action smoother. This Fourth or 1899-type Experimental Model (Versuchsmodell 1899) replaced the Third Experimental Model of 1898.

The committee also considered the Krnka-Roth and the Mauser C/96, but neither had progressed beyond the previous submissions and so were refused additional trials. A Browning-system gun had appeared from Fabrique Nationale, and a written submission by the German inventor Albert Hauff was also made.

The principal trial was a straight contest between the Borchardt-Luger and a new or Third Model Mannlicher. The Second Model, or 1896-patent 'M1903' Mannlicher, had performed with such distinction in earlier trials that the examining board was anxious to extend the same opportunities to its 1898-patent successor.

Luger's two pistols, differing only in barrel length, were successfully submitted to firing trials on 2nd May. The Board recorded the guns as 'improvements over the Modell 1898 III Borchardt-Luger'; the safety catches had been modified and the weight reduced by 75gm or 90gm depending on the barrel length. Luger, who was present at the trials, stated that the 7.65mm pistols could be altered to any calibre between 7.3mm and 8mm simply by changing the barrel and extractor. If the 7.65mm case-rim design was retained, even the extractor could be left in place.

The Third Model Mannlicher (a simple blowback) was rejected when it failed to challenge the Borchardt-Luger satisfactorily. DWM was asked to supply at least twenty guns, for 400 Swiss francs apiece, and sufficient ammunition (costing 3000 francs) to permit full-scale field trials to be undertaken in the autumn of 1899. Luger agreed to try to reduce pistol weight below 850gm and apparently took both trial guns back to Berlin. One of these may have formed the basis of the Erste Originalpistole described above.

The twenty field-trial Borchardt-Lugers arrived in Switzerland in November 1899, but, unfortunately, none of them has been conclusively identified. The most plausible candidate is illustrated by Christian Reinhart and Michael am Rhyn in *Faustfeuerwaffen II: Selbstladepistolen* (1976), with the cautionary comment that it could alternatively be one of ten presented to the personnel of the trials commission in 1900.

It seems reasonable to accept the gun as a survivor of the field trials, as it has the square toggle-link interface characterising the Jones 'Baujahr 1899' gun. The design of the interface apparently changed at gun no.21; no.26, a survivor of six submitted to the British Small Arms Committee in November 1900, has a radiussed interface, though it also displays a hand-engraved Federal Cross above the chamber. The British records note that guns no.23 and no.25 were also tried, suggesting that the six were numbered either 21–26 or 23–28. The Borchardt-Lugers tested in Britain must have been made some time previously, as guns no.35 and no.36 had been delivered to the Netherlands in March 1900.

The hand-engraved enrayed Federal Cross chamber mark on no.19, together with hand-struck serial numbers and Georg Luger's script 'GL' monogram on the back toggle link, has been used to support the theory of presentation, but the surviving British test gun also displays these characteristics even though the two tested in the Netherlands did not.

Panel Two

EARLY BORCHARDT-LUGERS

Assuming that the existing 1898 Jones, Swiss and British trials guns are accepted not only as genuine but also still in their original condition, the progression below probably represents the perfection of the Borchardt-Luger.

i) The Third (Swiss) Experimental Model of 1898. At least two guns were made, as no.4 and no.5 were teted in Switzerland; the latter still survives in the collection of the Federal small-arms factory in Bern. It has been suggested that the guns numbered 1-3 were retained in Berlin, though it is possible that no.1 and possibly also no.2 were the Improved Borchardts.
ii) The Fourth (Swiss) Experimental Model of 1899. Two examples of this pattern were delivered to Switzerland at the end of April 1899, but returned to Germany at the end of the trials. Though they originally had dished toggle-grips, one gun may subsequently have been given flat-face toggle grips with a single circumferential rib. This would have created the so-called Erste Originalpistole pictured by Harry Jones in the 1975 reprint of *Luger Variations* (volume one).
iii) The Swiss field-trials guns, 1899. Twenty of these were delivered in November 1899, with conventional dished or cut-away toggle grips. They differed from the Fourth Experimental Model in purely minor respects; the trigger, sear and other components were refined, and changes to the machining (notably inside the frame) reduced weight. Gun no.19 still exists in Thun, whilst the survival of no.9 and no.17 has also been reported. The principal distinguishing characteristic is the square toggle-link interface.
iv) The pre-production model, 1900. Beginning at about no.21, the final manufacturing pattern was perfected. Exactly how many of these guns

existed is not known, though numbers probably reached 50. Six are known to have been tested in Britain (nos.21–26 or 23–28), and two in the Netherlands (nos.35 and 36); one of the Dutch guns had a 15cm barrel and could accept a shoulder-stock. The principal improvement concerned the toggle hinge, which was changed to radiussed pattern to prevent fractures. The guns had double concentric striker springs and a striker-spring retainer with a 28mm tapered shank, the maximum shank diameter being about 3.3mm. The head of the safety lever was long, flat and chequered.

v) The perfected model, 1900. This was a minor improvement of the preceding pattern. The double concentric striker springs were replaced by a single one, intended to minimise misfiring, whilst the spring-retainer shank was about 26mm long with a maximum diameter of 3.9mm. The well-known DWM trademark was added to the toggle-train at about gun no.60, and the plain-bordered grips were replaced shortly afterward by an entirely chequered design. The safety lever remained flat headed (two differing patterns), until an improved fluted dome-head type appeared after the first deliveries of Swiss Ordonnanzpistolen 1900 had been made.

The first twenty Swiss pistols were issued to a number of units – including the Walenstadt marksmanship school – with a request that reports should be made by March 1900. During this period, a prototype lightened pistol (835gm without its magazine) arrived from DWM. On 30th April, the Federal parliament was advised to accept the Borchardt-Luger, and, on 4th May 1900, the gun was adopted for the Swiss army as the 'Pistole, Ordonnanz 1900, System Borchardt-Luger'. It was to replace the 10.4mm Model 78 and the 7.5mm Model 82 revolvers, but never entirely replaced the latter except as an officers' weapon.

Oberst von Orelli informed the Swiss ordnance department on Christmas Eve 1900 that the first 2000 guns were expected to arrive in Switzerland at the beginning of 1901; each was to cost 57.50 Swiss francs (46 Reichsmarks), which rose to 62 francs once customs duties had been added.

The Swiss Ordonnanzpistole 1900

The first Borchardt-Luger to achieve military status – indeed, one of the first semi-automatic pistols to be issued anywhere in the world – was issued to staff officers, commissioned cavalrymen and some senior NCOs.

The first batch of series-made pistols was delivered on 2nd April 1901, but about a hundred trials guns had already been purchased for training. These had non-standard serial numbers, hand-engraved Federal Crosses above the chamber and narrow magazine housings; like the first few hundred of the bulk deliveries, their special magazines had flat follower buttons.

Panel Three

THE ACTION OF THE BORCHARDT-LUGER PISTOL

The perfected Borchardt-Luger, renamed 'Parabellum' in 1901, had most distinctive lines. Its characteristics were described in detail in many periodicals of the early 1900s. The following description was published in *Engineering* on 3rd April 1903.

After considering the potential lack of stopping power – a consideration that was then uppermost in the British mind – the article went on to state that:

It will be seen that the pistol carries eight cartridges, contained in a removable case 35 (Fig.6) inserted in the stock (Figs.1, 2, 5, and 9). Several of these cases may be carried in a pouch ready for use, or a single case may be replenished from time to time. The cartridges are pressed upwards by spring 35b surmounted by a carrier 35c (Fig.2). In Fig.2 there is a cartridge in the barrel of the pistol ready to be fired. When the trigger 20 is pulled, the firing-pin 12 in the breech-block 2 is released, and, its point striking the fulminate in the base, the charge explodes. The barrel, with its breech-block and mechanism (Figs.7 and 8), slides in guides in the stock (Figs.4 and 9); it is held forward by the recoil spring 11 (Figs.2 and 5), its forward motion being limited by the stop r and the catch 24 (Figs.2 and 5). The effect of the recoil is to drive the barrel backwards against the pressure of spring 11 (Fig.5). This motion is restricted to a short traverse of about three-eighths of an inch. The object of this motion is to trip the toggle joint which controls the breech-block. This joint is composed of two links 3 and 4 (Figs.2, 5, and 10), 3 being pivoted at one end of the breech-block, and 4, at its other end, to an extension of the barrel, called by the makers the 'bifurcated receiver,' shown in detail in Figs.7 and 8. The two links of the toggle joint are connected by a pin 6 (Fig.10), and the rear link is expanded on each side to form two projections C.X, which act the part of cams, coming in contact with two inclines on the stock (Figs.1 and 9). When the mechanism is in the firing position shown in Fig.1, the middle pin of the toggle joint lies slightly below the line joining the two other pins 5 and 7 (Fig.5), and consequently the breech-block is solidly supported against the force of the explosion. When the barrel and the breech-block move back, the extensions C.X catch against the cam paths [C.II] Fig.1), and the toggle joint is bent upwards, so that the inertia of the breech-block 2 forces it into the bent attitude shown in Fig.5. It will, however, be noticed that there is a heel at the end of the rear link of the toggle joint, which comes against the middle of the stock, and limits the travel of the breech-block to the position shown in Fig.5. When the parts are thus arranged, it is evident that the spring in the cartridge holder will force up the top cartridge until it lies partly in the path of the breech-block 2 (Fig.5) and, as that returns, the cartridge will be driven forward into the chamber of the barrel, as shown in Fig.2, the breech-block following it and closing the breech.

These actions naturally take place in a very small fraction of a second, the initial movement of the barrel, the tripping of the toggle joint, its complete doubling up into the position shown in Fig.5, and then the return of the breech-block, and the straightening out of the toggle-joint by action of the spring 11, which has been compressed from the position shown in Fig.2 to that in Fig.5 during the travel of the breech-block, take place so rapidly that it is practically impossible to follow them with the eye. As an additional safe-guard, to prevent the toggle joint opening accidentally, it is provided with a spring catch 17.I (Fig.4) which hooks over a guide on the stock when the toggle joint is straightened, and can only be released by sliding off the end of this guide. This release takes place when the barrel recoils to the end of its travel; but as there is the powerful spring 11 always holding the barrel forward, its release cannot take place accidentally . . .

The pistol . . . is provided with a safety sear 29 (Figs.1 and 11) which lies in the division between the thumb and the first finger of the user. This sear is operated by a spring, and so long as it is extruded from the stock the pistol is absolutely safe against explosion. But the moment the man aims with the pistol, taking a firm hold of the stock, he necessarily squeezes the sear inwards, removing the safety catch from the mechanism, and leaving himself free to pull the trigger; indeed, it is almost impossible to pull the trigger without first releasing the sear. This trigger mechanism is difficult to follow by means of drawings and, indeed, it takes some minutes to grasp it . . . , not because it is complicated, but because the parts are arranged so neatly and compactly that they easily escape notice. When the breech-block 2 is moving forward to the breech, the toe n of the link 3 of the toggle motion (Figs.5 and 10) draws back the striker 12 (Fig.2) in the breech-block and as the breech-block goes forward, this striker is caught on the point n.II of the trigger-bar 18 (Fig.3) which stands out from the inner side of the bifurcated receiver, and catches an extension n.I of the striker. As the breech-block continues to move forward, the striker is held back and the spring is compressed. The trigger-bar is a straight bar (Fig.12) which is mounted in the side of the bifurcated receiver. The little pin on the left-hand side of it goes under the finger of the bellcrank lever 22 (Figs.4 and 13), the other arm of which fits into the jaw on the trigger (Figs 2, 5, and 14). This little pin 18.I (Figs.3 and 10) is not made solid with the trigger bar, but can retreat into the bar, and is pushed out by a spring, which is a very important part of the mechanism and gives great control over the firing. When the breech-block goes back into the position shown in Fig.5,

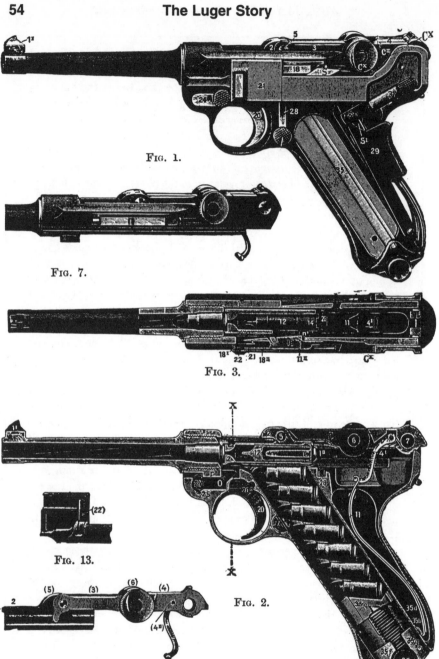

FIG. 1.

FIG. 7.

FIG. 3.

FIG. 13.

FIG. 10

FIG. 2.

Fig. 6. Details of the Borchardt-Luger, from *Engineering*, April 1903.
The British Engineerium.

the trigger bar (Fig.12) leaves the bellcrank (Fig.13), as this latter is stationary with the stock. Therefore whether the trigger 20 is held back or not makes no difference, as the connection between it and the striker is completely broken. On the return of the breech-block . . . , the spring is compressed by a projection on the striker 12 coming into contact with the end of the trigger bar 18 (Figs.3 and 12). This trigger bar is inserted in a recess in the side of the bifurcated receiver (Figs.7 and 8), and partakes of the motion of the pistol barrel. As the barrel goes back it leaves the bellcrank, and as the barrel goes forward it again returns to the bellcrank; but at this moment the bellcrank is held pressed down, because the firer has not had time to release his finger, and hence the pin 18.I cannot get underneath the end of the lever 22.I to be pressed down at the next shot. The pin 18.I is therefore pushed into the recess in the trigger bar 18, and remains there until the pressure of the finger on the trigger 20 is relaxed. The spring 20.I then forces back the trigger, the lever 22 rises, the pin 18.I slips underneath it, and then all is in readiness for the next shot – that is, if the sear 29 is pressed down. This sear is shown in detail in Fig.11. The hook S can be seen in Fig.1. It rises up beside the end of the trigger bar 18 (Figs.1, 7, and 12) in such a way that when pressure is applied through the intermediary of the trigger on the end 18.I, the other end cannot be moved to release the trigger, as long as the part S stands in the position shown in Fig.1. This arrangement can also be followed in Fig.3, where the trigger bar 18 is clearly shown, and the catch S can be seen rising up through the bifurcated receiver. Further, as long as the piece S is in the position shown in Fig.1, it is evident that the pistol barrel cannot move backwards, and that the whole mechanism is completely locked. A further safety appliance is provided in the catch 31 (Fig.1), the tail of which can be moved in the path of a projection on the sear 29 (Fig.11), completely locking it. When this catch 31 is in use there are therefore two safeguards against accidental explosion, one of which can only be removed intentionally and purposely, while the second, 29, is automatically removed when the pistol is raised into the line of fire for use, and automatically replaced as soon as this attitude is abandoned.

The reader will have gathered that this pistol is a wonderfully ingenious piece of mechanism. It can be taken completely to pieces in less than a minute, and no tool is needed, except to withdraw the screws of the butt side-pieces . . .

It has been suggested that guns numbered below about 900 all had unrelieved feedways, but, if this was so, many were subsequently converted to the later design. The knurled section of the safety lever was shortened from 14mm to 10mm when the serial numbers had reached 800-900, the change being approximately contemporaneous with the alterations in the magazine and magazine housing. The feedway of later guns was relieved to accommodate a raised follower button, protruding from the body-side, which allowed the magazine follower to be retracted with greater ease. Rolled-in national markings and narrow 'old pattern' triggers – about 8.5mm wide – were standard, though most of the pistols in the 4000–5000 group (but not 5001A–5100A) had 15mm-wide triggers, virtually as broad as the trigger-guard.

The safety-lever knurling was replaced by fluting in the 1800–2000 series, as it was already being used on most other Borchardt-Lugers, and the grip safety was widened at about the same time. Shortly before the First World War, survivors of the initial narrow-magazine deliveries were rebuilt by the Swiss federal arms factory to the standards of the perfected Ordonnanzpistolen 1900 and numbered from 5001A to 5100A.

Modern investigative techniques have confirmed that, far from being new, these guns were thoroughly refinished. A new serial number was struck over an earlier three-digit 'E'-prefix identifier, showing that they had been used as training pistols (Exerzierwaffen). The 'new' guns must have originated after the first Ordonnanzpistolen 1906 had been ordered, otherwise the 'A' number-suffix would have been unnecessary and the numbers of the new model would simply have begun at 5101.

Panel Four

VARIATIONS OF THE SWISS 1900-MODEL LUGER

In *Die Geschichte der Parabellum-Pistole in der Schweiz*, Reinhard Kornmayer recognises four separate Ordonnanzpistole 1900.

Type 1 was numbered from 1 to approximately 2000 and distinguished by a narrow trigger and narrow grip safeties; Type 1A (1–750?) had a 14mm knurled-section safety lever, whilst Type 1B (750?–2000?) had a raised 10mm section.

Type 2 was numbered from about 2000 to 3900, plus the rebuilds 5001A–5100A. These guns all had narrow triggers, fluted safety levers and wide grip safeties.

Type 3, numbered from about 3900 to 5000, had characteristically wide triggers, wide grip safeties and fluted safety levers.

Type 4 Parabellums were German commercial guns with four-digit numbers; standard crown/B, crown/U and crown/G proof marks; and Federal Cross chamber marks. They were otherwise identical with Type 2.

According to Christian Reinhart and Michael am Rhyn, writing in *Faust-feuerwaffen II: Selbstladepistolen*, the first 2000 pistols were finished and numbered in Berlin. Fifteen hundred were then shipped to Bern in the white, unfinished and unmarked except for the DWM toggle-link monogram, to be numbered and blued in the federal arms factory. This explains why their serial numbers are stamped with different dies. The last 1500 of the 1900-pattern Swiss Borchardt-Lugers were assembled in Bern from German-made parts.

All but a few of the earliest trial submissions bore the DWM monogram trademark on the toggle-link, a rolled-in Federal Cross above the chamber, German proofs, and Swiss inspectors' marks.

The earliest cartridges ('Ord.Pist.P.00') were made in the Karlsruhe factory of Deutsche Waffen- und Munitionsfabriken, production in the federal ammunition factory in Thun commencing only after the Ordonnanz Pistolen-patrone Modell 1903 ('Ord.Pist.P.03') was adopted on 7th August 1903. The brass bottle-neck case was loaded with the 1903-pattern bullet (Geschoss 03), which weighed 6gm and had a plain steel-jacketed lead core. The propellant charge was .33gm of a nitrocellulose-base smokeless powder prior to 1906, subsequent rounds containing a .31gm load. Muzzle velocity was about 350 m/sec.

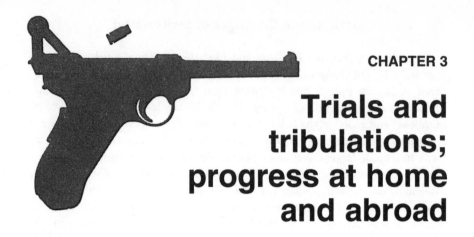

CHAPTER 3

Trials and tribulations; progress at home and abroad

By 1890 many military authorities had realised that advances in small-arms design had overtaken service revolvers. Though mechanically-operated repeating pistols had been championed by – amongst others – Bittner, Rieger, Passler & Seidl, Krnka, Schulhof and Laumann, the genre was unsuitable for military service. All it achieved was to pave the way for the first true semi-automatics.

While the Borchardt-Luger was being prepared for series production, Deutsche Waffen- und Munitionsfabriken AG attempted to interest many military agencies. Georg Luger often personally represented the company at the trials; he had served in the Austrian army reserve in 1865–72, apparently enjoyed travelling, and understood the soldier's mind sufficiently well to facilitate negotiations.

The Borchardt-Luger pistol was soon renamed the 'Parabellum' after DWM's telegraphic code name; the relevant trademark had been registered in April 1900. It competed regularly against other pistols. Every inventor believed that his design was the best, which was inducement in itself to submit guns to trial, whilst the lure of adoption by a leading military power attracted the best-established manufacturers.

The backing of a large and powerful gunmaker usually ensured that a gun would be given a fair trial, and, most importantly, allowed changes to be made to satisfy testing commissions. This alone ruined the chances of many weapons which had been submitted privately, few of whose promoters had the facilities to make rapid revisions.

The principal goal of the promoters of semi-automatic pistols was military adoption, though commercial licensing was also attempted whenever possible. Any suitable design would be touted throughout Europe, the Far East and South America, until the First World War ended commercial speculation.

Against the better-established guns were ranged an assortment of lesser designs. Chauvinism played a large part in many pre-1914 trials and indigenous inventors would always submit guns to trial, even if their ideas had never been actively sought. Many guns were turned away unfired; others were tested briefly, found wanting, and discarded. The few that proved effective were sometimes offered additional trials, but pistols of this type rarely challenged the products of the arms barons.

Some countries proved to be more chauvinistic than others, but the results were rarely beneficial even though the side-effects were sometimes unexpected. The British dallied far too long with the Gabbett-Fairfax 'Mars' before adopting the cumbersome and unreliable Webley & Scott automatic in 1912 — at the expense not only of the Luger (whose calibre was, admittedly, too small for the British) but also the Colt-Browning.

The Austrian trials included guns submitted by Salvator & Dormus and Kromar, as well as an assortment of Krnka-Roths, whereas the Germans had tried the Schlegelmilch, the Hellfritzsch, the Mieg, the Fischer, the Vitali and some Frommers.

Mannlichers were among the most important rivals of the Luger, though successful only in Argentina, where the high price and the considerable complexity of the principal German pistols allowed Österreichische Waffenfabriks-Gesellschaft to find a niche for the 1905-type blowback.

The earliest Mannlicher, patented in Germany in December 1894, was a quirky blow-forward design. A 6.5mm version competed unsuccessfully in Switzerland against the Borchardt, but only about 200 were ever made. An improved pistol was introduced some months prior to the grant of a German Patent in January 1898, but very few were made before the revival of the design as the 'Model 1903'. Superficially resembling the Mauser C/96, it was locked by a flimsy pivoting strut connecting the bolt and the rear of the receiver.

The perfected Mannlicher, patented in Germany in October 1898, was an elegant blowback made first by Waffenfabrik von Dreyse in Sömmerda (Model 1900) and then by Österreichische Waffenfabriks-Gesellschaft in Steyr (Models 1901 and 1905). The M1905 was adopted by the Argentinian army, but other trials highlighted the weakness of the charger-loaded design. The Germans only allowed the pistols to participate to test their suitability for purchase privately by the officer corps. Only about 10,000 guns of this type were sold over a ten-year period.

The locked-breech Browning pistols were much more efficient competitors for the Luger than the Mannlichers, though the blowback patterns — made in Europe by Fabrique Nationale d'Armes de Guerre — were adopted in Sweden and the Netherlands. The master patents were granted to John M.Browning in the Spring of 1897, then improved by stages until the .45 pistol was adopted by the US Army in March 1911.

The earliest Brownings relied on two 'parallel motion' links, which, as the mechanism recoiled, disengaged lugs on the barrel from recesses in the underside of the slide as the mechanism recoiled. The system was reliable enough to beat the Luger and the Savage in the US Army trials of 1906–7. In 1909, however, Browning replaced the twin links with a simpler and more robust single-link system.

Colt-Brownings were usually less accurate than the Lugers, but were more reliable and undoubtedly stronger. One gun fired 6000 rounds without misfires or parts breakages, a performance no Luger would ever match.

Military trials

DWM had great hopes of the Luger, especially in countries where the Mauser rifle or Krupp field-gun had been adopted; but there were others in which the Germans had practically no chance of success – where a trial, no matter how successful, would be met with nothing more than polite acclamation.

Belgium and Italy, for example, had healthy firearms industries of their own. However, though the Italian navy had accepted Mauser C/96 pistols in 1899 – the first official adoption of a semi-automatic – the army showed no inclination to follow its lead. The US Army gave the Luger a fair chance in 1901, but the trials of 1906/7 were biased against guns other than the Colt-Browning by the selection of a Colt cartridge.

The French had tested the Luger officially, whilst considerable numbers were sold commercially prior to 1914 by Manufacture Française d'Armes et Cycles of Saint-Étienne. But deep-seated rivalry, bitter memories of the Franco-Prussian War of 1870–1 and the loss to Germany of the provinces of Alsace and Lorraine, all prevented the acceptance of a German handgun in the French army.

Austria-Hungary's was largely a Teutonic army, but historical traditions of firearms production in Bohemia led the army to the designs of Karel Krnka and Georg Roth. There is no evidence that the Luger was ever considered seriously, and even the Mannlichers were unsuccessful.

The 7.65mm Luger in military trials

The refinement of the Borchardt-Luger and its adoption in Switzerland – its first great success – have been considered in detail in the previous chapter. However, though a thousand 7.65mm guns were purchased for the US Army, and adoption for the Dutch army was rescinded only at the very last moment, experience in Belgium, Britain and throughout Scandinavia was less encouraging:

Belgium In 1898, seeking a replacement for the Nagant-type officers' revolver, the Belgians convened a committee at the state-owned arms factory in Liége to test the leading handguns of the day. These included Nagant and Pieper revolvers, together with 'large and small' Browning, Bergmann, Borchardt, Mannlicher and (Krnka-)Roth pistols.

The Borchardt was replaced by the Luger before trials began, though not before the committee had expressed dislike of the older design. The guns were all rejected excepting the Belgian-made Brownings, the Luger and the Mannlicher – results which paralleled those customarily obtained elsewhere. The war department then scheduled a second series of trials, and a second trials board met at the Liége arms factory late in 1899 under the chairmanship of Général Donny.

The small Browning was preferred owing to its simplicity, light recoil and low cost, though the fact that it was made locally by Fabrique Nationale d'Armes de Guerre was no disadvantage. The Luger was accurate, but breech-closing problems had been encountered and the 7.65mm cartridge was considered to be too powerful for a service handgun.

No special Belgian-marked Lugers survive, as the trial pistols – perhaps only two of them – bore nothing but serial numbers. The Browning was finally adopted for officers on 3rd July 1900, and subsequently for the gendarmerie, some cavalrymen, sections of the artillery, and officers of the Garde Civique.

The Netherlands Research undertaken by Guus de Vries and Bas Martens, published in 1994 in *The Dutch Luger*, has revealed that the earliest trials were undertaken in March 1900, when two pre-production Lugers, no.35 and no.36, were pitted against the Mauser C/96, a Bergmann No.5, and 'Roth no.67'. Luger no.36 had a longer breech-block and a more powerful mainspring than its companion, as it had been adjusted to fire cartridges with a differing combination of bullet weight and propellant loading. One of the guns had a lug on the butt heel and was accompanied by a holster-stock.

The trials showed that the Lugers were more accurate than their rivals, average dispersion of gun no.36 being 4.1cm vertically by 2.8cm horizontally at 25 metres, and 58.5 × 29.7cm at 200 metres. The firers managed thirty-two shots from a Luger in thirty seconds, compared with twenty-two shots for the Mauser C/96 and twenty-one for the Bergmann No.5 and the Roth.

Luger no.35 had fired 240 rounds without misfiring, though no.36 had encountered problems with its hold-open system. The Dutch regarded these results as very good, particularly as the Roth had failed to eject 164 of 235 shots automatically, so an endurance trial was arranged for Luger no.35. The first 500 shots were attended by only one misfire; then came immersion in water, fine sanding and complete burial in the sand – tests totalling 275 shots without incident.

The pistol was then subjected to sand and water, after which all eight shots of the first full magazine and the first four shots of the succeeding eight had to be fired by closing the toggle manually. Work stopped, the magazines were cleaned, and thirty-six rounds were fired normally. The rust test was reasonably satisfactory, only the first and third shots of fifty requiring manual assistance to close the breech. The gun was then thoroughly cleaned and oiled, and pro-

ceeded to work normally until the magazine stopped feeding satisfactorily. This
was speedily rectified, allowing the trials to continue until more than 3000
rounds had been fired.

The Mauser, Bergmann and Roth were then rejected in favour of the Luger,
an order for ten long-barrel (12cm) guns – with leather holster-stocks – being
approved on 29th June 1900. Luger delivered them personally on 11th October
1901.

The ten guns were issued to the cavalry, but the opinions voiced were as
conflicting as they would be in the better-known US Army trials held in 1902.
Consequently, the Dutch authorities decided to continue research. On 9th
September 1903, however, the war minister approved the purchase of ten
7.65mm 'M1902' Mannlicher pistols (with a hammer-blocking safety lever on
the slide) and ten new short-barrelled 7.65mm Lugers, the latter being identified in accompanying literature as 'Model 1903' and numbered between
10087 and 10100.

One gun – probably no.10098 – subsequently received a cartridge counter
devised by First Lieutenant Jan Vethake, which comprised a mica-covered slot
cut through the left grip into the magazine well and a red-painted magazine-
follower button to show how many rounds remained.

The Luger comprehensively defeated the Mannlicher pistol and the Dutch
service revolver in the trials, though individual opinions were still divided. On
23rd December 1904, therefore, the Dutch ordered 174 Borchardt-Lugers for
full-scale field trials in the knowledge not only that 9mm-calibre guns were
being tested in Germany, but also that important changes had been suggested
in the return-spring assembly. Thus the order placed with DWM was for 109
7.65mm guns with 10cm barrels, sixty-five comparable 9mm guns, and ten of
the 9mm 'improved model'. The development of the latter is discussed in
Chapter Six.

The 7.65mm guns were delivered in March and July 1905, followed by the
9mm examples in August 1905. Surviving records note that some of their serial
numbers ranged from 22219 to 22361, but that the special guns were numbered in a separate series – 10127[B] being the only gun referred to by number.
Pistol 10130B still survives in a private collection.

Though the trial reports contained the usual contradictory elements, a
contract for 917 guns was given to Deutsche Waffen- und Munitionsfabriken
on 14th December. Before work could begin, however, hostility in the Dutch
parliament forced the rejection of the Borchardt-Luger in favour of retaining
the indigenous service revolver. This soon left the army embarrassingly short of
handguns.

Germany Experiments had been undertaken by the Prussian rifle-testing
commission (GPK) as early as 1891, and procurement of revolvers had been

suspended shortly afterwards whilst the merits of 'repeating pistols' were assessed. Early trialists included the Borchardt, the Mieg, the Mauser and the 'Spandauer Selbstladepistole M 1896'. A few lightened double-action revolvers were even made in the Erfurt rifle factory in 1896–7, but had no lasting effect on German military pistol history.

Initially, the Mauser-Selbstladepistole C/96 seemed to have the best channce of success. It had been designed by the three Feederle brothers in 1894–5, though the relevant German patent – 90,430 of 1895 – was sought in the name of Peter-Paul Mauser alone.

Operated by short recoil, the action was locked by a propped-up block beneath the bolt. The gun was ungainly compared with the Luger, and its cartridge, though undeniably powerful, was nothing more than an adaption of the original Borchardt type. However, special attention had been given to construction and the C/96 pieces interlocked without screws. Trials soon revealed that cartridges frequently jammed in the breech, but Mauser's newest rifle design had just been adopted for military service and his reputation was high enough to overcome the earliest objections.

The first experiments with the Mauser pistol, dating from 1896, had been successful enough for 145 to be ordered for field trials. Delivered in June 1898, they were issued to the infantry school of musketry in addition to the Garde-Jäger zu Pferde and the Leib-Garde-Husaren-Regiment. On 22nd December 1898, the rifle-testing commission informed the war ministry that the semi-automatic pistol was preferred to the service revolver; it was more accurate, more poweful and had a flatter trajectory. But there had been too many malfunctions and feed jams to permit immediate adoption, and the stock and holstering arrangements were unacceptable.

Yet 124 additional Mauser pistols were ordered in January 1899 to facilitate wider issue, and 17,050 live, 8070 blank and 2480 dummy 7.63mm cartridges were supplied by the Spandau munitions factory. The guns were distributed to infantry, cavalry and field-artillery units. The state army of Württemberg acquired forty-eight pistols of its own, Saxony merely sent observers to the Prussian tests, and Bavaria awaited developments before committing the state's resources.

Reports of the trials with the C/96 were eventually submitted to the war ministry in November 1900. The existence of the Luger had been noted for the first time in the preceding September, when a new Mannlicher had also been brought to the attention of the authorities. Representative examples of each design were submitted in December 1900 and April/May 1901 respectively.

The first serious challenge to Mauser's ascendancy now occurred, because the rifle-testing commission reported on 18th February 1901 not only that trials with the C/96 had been discouraging, but also that widespread issue could not be recommended. Spent cartridge cases or the new round in the breech had jammed between the rear of the barrel and the front of the chamber; two or more rounds had fired at a time; the hammer often failed to remain cocked after the breech mechanism had returned, necessitating re-cocking; the action sometimes failed to stay open after the last round had been fired and ejected; and the action had occasionally failed to open at all after firing.

By the summer of 1901, however, the 'improved' Mausers were proving far superior to those acquired in 1898–9; one had even fired two series of 500 rounds, without oiling or cleaning, and no misfires had been encountered. The rifle-testing commission recommended persisting with the C/96, but subsequent submissions also performed badly and the reputation for jamming was enough to prevent the Mauser C/96 challenging the supremacy of the Luger. However, though the Germans had decided to adopt the latter by 1904, pending a few minor alterations, Mauser persistently stalled proceedings by asking for 'new designs' to be considered. This delayed the introduction of his DWM-made rival for four years.

The C/96 remained in production until the beginning of the Second World War, the large military sales of the Luger prior to 1914 permitting Mauser to exploit commercial markets vacated by DWM. John Breathed and Joseph Schroeder, writing in *System Mauser* in 1967, recorded that 46,509 Mausers had been sold between 1896 and 1905; the 100,000th example was sold c.1911. DWM claimed to have sold 156,900 Lugers by this time, but probably only by including some incomplete contracts for the German armed forces.

In the spring of 1901, DWM supplied the GPK with a few 12cm-barrelled Swiss-type 7.65mm Lugers. The authorities reported late in August that the Mauser C/96 and the Luger were still being considered, though the Mannlicher had been dismissed in June as unsuitable for military service. Mauser was asked to supply two modified C/96 pistols in a quest for better reliability; one was to have a short barrel, though otherwise identical with the trials guns obtained in 1898–9, but the other was a 'reduced-weight type for officers'.

Increasing disaffection with the C/96 led to greater interest in the Luger, which was light, handy and efficient. However, concern was expressed about the delicacy and complexity of the Borchardt-Luger, the comparative lack of power in the standard 7.65mm cartridge, and the difficulty of determining the state of cocking. The GPK eventually reported that Luger was:

... unable to reduce the number of parts (59 compared with 37 in the Mauser pistol). Only the grip safety has been eliminated, resulting in alterations to the positive safety. The Commission has, however, *initiated several improvements* [author's italics] in order to prevent vital parts breaking and to increase the reliability of the pistol... The fact that one cannot see whether the pistol is cocked or not, has turned out to be disadvantageous...

Plate 1 Borchardt C/93 no.2203, assembled by DWM in 1897. Note the curious housing behind the toggle, which held the return spring. *Henk Visser*.

Plate 2 Georg Luger (1849–1923), pictured shortly before the First World War. *Reinhard Kornmayer*.

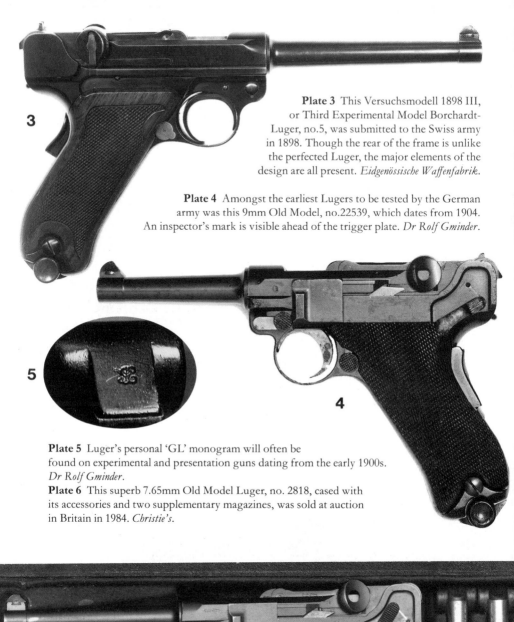

Plate 3 This Versuchsmodell 1898 III, or Third Experimental Model Borchardt-Luger, no.5, was submitted to the Swiss army in 1898. Though the rear of the frame is unlike the perfected Luger, the major elements of the design are all present. *Eidgenössische Waffenfabrik.*

Plate 4 Amongst the earliest Lugers to be tested by the German army was this 9mm Old Model, no.22539, which dates from 1904. An inspector's mark is visible ahead of the trigger plate. *Dr Rolf Gminder.*

Plate 5 Luger's personal 'GL' monogram will often be found on experimental and presentation guns dating from the early 1900s. *Dr Rolf Gminder.*

Plate 6 This superb 7.65mm Old Model Luger, no. 2818, cased with its accessories and two supplementary magazines, was sold at auction in Britain in 1984. *Christie's.*

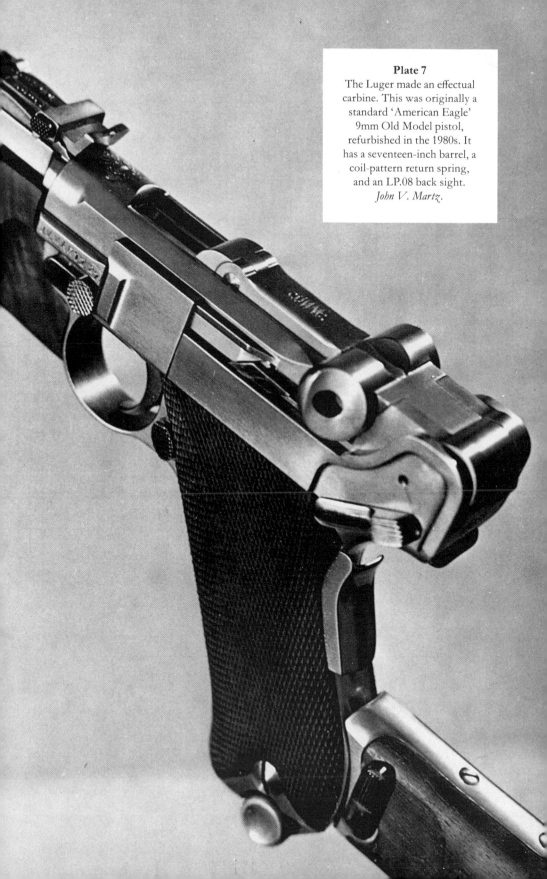

◁ **Plates 8, 9** This view of Luger no.10023B (8), an experimental 9mm example dating from *c*.1903, emphasises the original full-width trigger guard. 9mm New Model 'Swiss Commercial' Luger no.788 (9), however, displays the later narrow guard.

◁ **Plate 10** Men of II.Torpedo-Division, fresh from infantry-training, pose for the camera in May 1911. The fine array of navy Lugers and accessories is noteworthy.

Plate 11 Pistole 1904 no.3173a, an original 1906-type gun with an altered safety catch, is shown here with a holster, a board-type shoulder stock, a shoulder strap, and spare magazine pouches. One pouch clearly displays the mark of its manufacturer, H. Müller & Company of Offenbach am Main. *Per Jensen.*

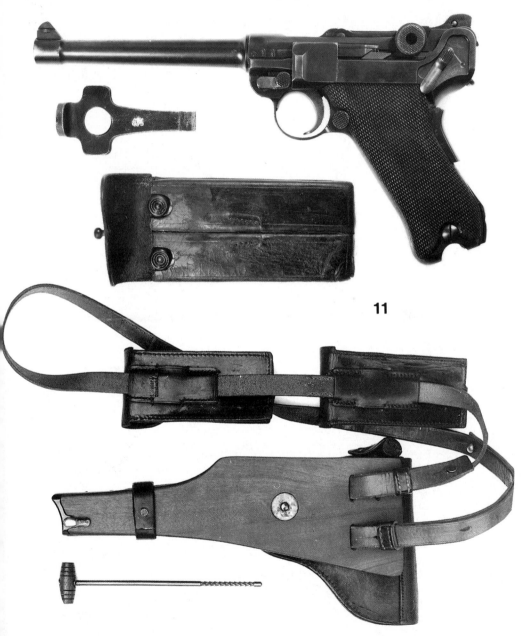

11

12

14

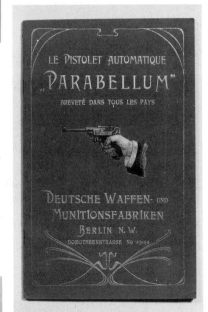

15

13

Plates 12, 13 The advent
in 1904 of the combination
extractor/loaded-chamber
indicator was accompanied by
a major redesign of the breech-
block. The photographs show
the difference between the Old
Model flat variety (12) and the sculpted New
Model (13). *Dr Rolf Gminder.*

Plates 14, 15 Typical of the literature produced
to accompany the Luger pistol were these
manuals, which were produced in many languages.
The two shown here probably date from about 1907. *John Pearson.*

Plate 16 Showing evidence of hard use, this Bulgarian Luger,
now no.1267, was originally a 7.65mm 12cm-barrelled gun supplied
about 1907. It has been converted by substituting a 9mm-calibre 10cm
barrel, apparently in the early 1940s. *Dr Rolf Gminder.*

16

17

Plate 17 The receiver/barrel
assembly of this gun, 9mm
New Model Luger no.869, clearly
displays the crossed-rifles chamber
mark associated with the 'Russian
Contract'. These guns are believed to
have been supplied for commercial purposes,
as they bear no signs of military ownership.

18

Plate 18 The .45 Luger supplied for the US Army
trials of 1907 was an imposing gun, but was narrowly
beaten by the Colt-Browning. *Joseph J. Schroeder.*

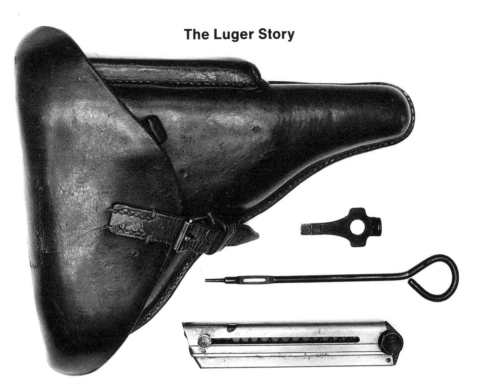

Plate 19 This holster for the Pistole 1908 was made in 1916 by R. Max Philipp of Niederschönhausen/Erzgebirge. The cleaning rod and the spare magazine are carried in pouches on the spine, whilst the dismantling tool is carried within the flap. *Per Jensen.*

Plate 20 The first of the 1908-pattern German army pistols, made in Berlin by DWM, lacked a date above the chamber whilst the proof- and principal inspectors' marks lay on the left side of the frame ahead of the trigger-plate. *Dr Rolf Gminder.*

Plate 21 Soldiers of Bavarian Landwehr-Infanterie-Regiment Nr.3 pose at Gazon l'Hôte in April 1916 with two captive Frenchmen. Note that one of the Germans (centre, left) has a P.08 in a converted Reichsrevolver holster. *Bayerisches Kriegsarchiv, München.*

Plates 22, 23 Lugers were used by the Landes-Polizei in German South-West Africa prior to 1918. These men of the Landesausstellung in Windhoek (22) were pictured about 1910; though the identity of their handguns has not been established, they would have re-equipped with Pistolen 1908 within a few years. The inset (23) shows a typical grip-strap marking. Virtually all survivors were made in Erfurt in 1911. *James Hellyer.*

Plate 24 This machine-gunner of Reserve-Infanterie-Regiment Nr.103, raised in Saxony, wears a holstered Luger and a carrying strap for the 1908-pattern Maxim machine-gun. *George Bush, Jr., via Anthony Carter.*

△ **Plates 25–7** The proof- and principal inspectors' marks on three Pistolen 1908 – (25) 7716a made by DWM in 1909; (26) 6225a made by DWM in 1913; and (27) assembled by Spandau in 1918. Note that the Spandau example has a DWM-made receiver, identified by the crown/T/bar, crown/S, crown/S inspectors' marks, but that there are two additional marks – a string of five in total.

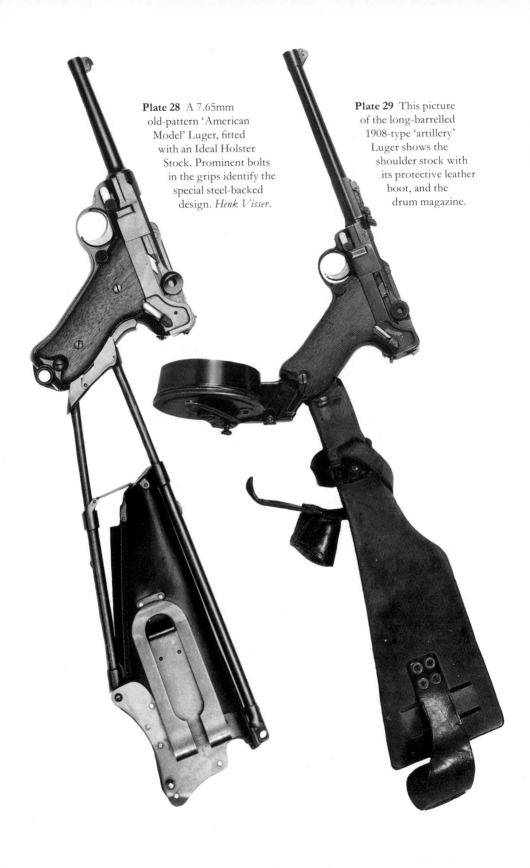

Plate 28 A 7.65mm old-pattern 'American Model' Luger, fitted with an Ideal Holster Stock. Prominent bolts in the grips identify the special steel-backed design. *Henk Visser*.

Plate 29 This picture of the long-barrelled 1908-type 'artillery' Luger shows the shoulder stock with its protective leather boot, and the drum magazine.

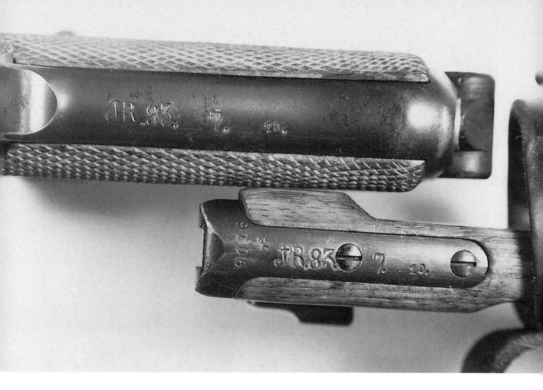

Plate 30 A detail of the front grip-strap and stock-iron of a typical LP.08, showing the matching unit mark 'J.R.83.7.10.' – the seventh company of Infanterie-Regiment von Wittich (3.Kurhessisches) Nr. 83. *Mark Jarrold.*

Plate 31 Many of the drum magazines, or TM.08, shown here with a loading tool and a detachable sheet-metal dust cover, were made by Gebr. Bing of Nürnberg. The older magazine has a sliding winding lever, whereas the improved later pattern has a lever that swings outward. *Hans Reckendorf.*

31

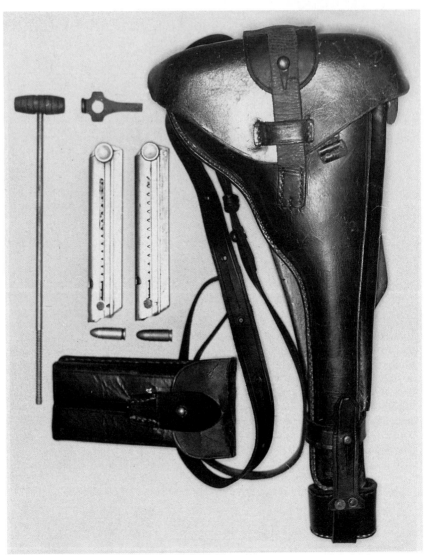

32

33

16 scharfe Pistole patronen 08.
Gefertigt am 13. Juli 1917. Dm.
P. P. R. (270) 1. d. 16. Zdh. 17. Dm.
Hülsen Dm. Gesch. Dm. og.

◁ **Plate 32** The holster and shoulder-stock unit of the LP.08, with accessories. The holster was made by Mühlenfeld & Co. of Barmen in 1918. *Per Jensen.*

◁ **Plate 33** A typical 9mm ammunition box, dating from July 1917. The information shows that the components were made – and the rounds loaded – by 'Dm.'. This is believed to be DWM's Karlsruhe factory, formerly Deutsche Metallpatronenfabrik. *Hans Reckendorf.*

△ **Plate 34** Pictured in France in 1915, this machine-gun crew of Füsilier-Regiment Königin (Schleswig-Holsteinisches) Nr.86 poses with its Maxim. Note the gun-carrying strap and Luger holster on the belt of the soldier at the rear. *Anton Fuchs, via Joachim Görtz.*

▽ **Plate 35** Men of the first machine-gun company of '25.Bayr.Inf.Regt.' are pictured here in the summer of 1916. Being machine-gunners, most of them carry Pistolen 1908.

Plates 36, 37 The stern portion of the wreck of *U51* (36), being scrapped in Bremerhaven. The four Navy Lugers retrieved from *U51* were badly corroded, many of their smallest parts having crumbled away. This particular example (37) is dated '1916' – being virtually brand-new when the submarine was sunk. *Ehrhard Schreiber.*

The highlighted phrase is particularly significant, as the transition from the old to the new model Luger is a vital part of the production history. But to whom should credit be given? The most obvious claimants are Luger himself and the men of the rifle-testing commission. Writing in the British periodical *Guns Review* in 1974, however, the late Dick Deibel advanced an alternative theory in his article 'The "Dutch" Luger', claiming that the coil-type mainspring was suggested by the staff of the principal arsenal of the Netherlands, the Artillerie-Inrichtingen in Hembrug. This is discussed in greater detail in Chapter Six.

Another Mannlicher was submitted in December 1901 and finally, on 12th April 1902, a third series of field trials began. These were undertaken with fifty-five improved six- and ten-shot Mauser-Pistolen C/96; a similar quantity of Lugers, forty of which lacked grip safeties; and fifteen Mannlichers, being tested expressly as officers' weapons.

Trials continued intermittently until the summer of 1903. In December, the rifle-testing commission reported to the war ministry that the Luger was the best of the submissions – even though it lacked a loaded-chamber indicator and occasionally failed to close satisfactorily.

The problems of poor stopping power had been investigated by altering the bullet shape. In March 1903, DWM loaded the standard 7.65mm case – which the company numbered 471C – with a truncated bullet, 261A, but the experiments did not meet expectations and a 9mm cartridge was substituted.

By February 1904 the German authorities had asked Georg Luger to improve the pistol. The guns tested in 1902–3 were undoubtedly originally 7.65mm 1900-pattern guns, though the barrels of many may have measured only 10cm. The old-style dished toggle and the toggle-lock were both still present at this time. Though forty of the pistols were delivered without grip safeties, DWM could simply have omitted these components from otherwise standard guns.

The pistols were taken from regular production and displayed commercial-type numbers, such as 22329. Though many of them have been subsequently converted to 9mm, they can be identified by a distinctive crowned Fraktur 'D' inspection mark on the front left side of the receiver.

A claim is regularly made that Luger pistols were carried by officers present at the defence of the German legation in Peking, during the Boxer Rebellion of 1900–1, but these guns were apparently Mausers. None of the Lugers that have been offered as evidence – *eg* no.8597 – were made until the troubles had finished. However, some were undoubtedly taken to the Far East in the early 1900s by officers serving in the Kiautschou protectorate.

Great Britain The earliest mention of the Luger pistol – usually called simply 'Borchardt' by the British – appears in the Minutes of the Proceedings of the Small Arms Committee for 24th April 1900. Some time previously, perhaps early in March, Trevor Dawson of Vickers, Sons & Maxim had introduced to the committee 'Herr Alexis Riese, Director of Deutsche Waffen- und Munitionsfabriken of Berlin, accompanied by the improver of the "Borchardt" pistol [Georg Luger]'. Riese stated that manufacture of the pistol, 'a new prototype', would not begin until production machinery had been revised.

On 31st May 1900, the Secretary of the Small Arms Committee asked Vickers, Sons & Maxim to supply six guns and 3000 cartridges for trials; Luger was to be asked if difficulty would be encountered in producing a .45 version. On 13th October, Vickers replied that:

> . . . we have now ready the six pistols, together with ammunition. . . In order to explain the action and several points of the pistol clearly to the Committee, we should be glad to have an appointment, so that we can bring the inventor [sic], with a view of answering any special questions which they may wish to put, and to put the Committee in possession of all details connected with the general system.

The Small Arms Committee agreed to see Luger and Vickers' representative, presumably Trevor Dawson, on Monday 22nd October 1900. Luger does not appear to have attended, though the new pistols were certainly delivered. All six were issued to the Chief Inspector of Small Arms (CISA) whilst arrangements were made for Luger to represent DWM in subsequent trials.

The pistols were tested in the Enfield small-arms factory shortly afterward, the relevant report appearing on 9th November 1900. It was forwarded to the Director-General of Ordnance and thence to the Small Arms Committee. The Luger, it said, was:

> . . .well made, is of good design, and handles comfortably. The breech bolt is strongly secured to the sideplates by means of a toggle joint and a stout axis pin; there is no liability of its being blown out into the firer's face. . . An important advantage that this pistol possesses. . .is the fact, when the eight rounds contained in the magazine have been fired, that the magazine can be replaced by a full one and fire resumed in four or five seconds. . . The pistol may safely be carried ready loaded as there are two safety arrangements both of which act properly. One is automatic and is disconnected by gripping the stock, the other is operated as required by the thumb of the right hand. The pistol is easily stripped for cleaning or inspection without the aid of tools, it may be entirely dismantled with the aid of the small drift and screw-driver supplied. The latter is only required for the screw fastening the wood grips. There is no danger of a bullet remaining in the barrel on account of a light charge,and another cartridge being automatically loaded up and fired. Cartridges loaded with 1½, 2 and 2½ grains of powder used, fired the bullets out of the barrel but did not load up the next cartridge.

The pistols have fired about 120 rounds, without a missfire or any failure. On one occasion the pistol was heavily dusted with sand before firing without interfering with the automatic action. The accuracy of the pistol was quite satisfactory, and the penetration was very good, as shown. . . : Webley Mark 4 revolver, 9 boards. Russian Revolver, 11-12 boards. Roth automatic pistol, 5-7 boards. Steyr automatic pistol, 7 boards. Borchardt[-Luger] automatic pistol, 14-15 boards. Each board was a ½-inch thick piece of deal, spaced at 1-inch intervals.

The bullet might be improved, for after passing through 15 ½-inch planks it was not set up. The steel envelope in which the lead core is contained would probably wear the rifling unnecessarily much. The recoil in this pistol as in the other automatic pistols is but little felt.

The pistol, on account of its having no cylinder, packs flatter in the holster than a revolver.

In conclusion, this is a good serviceable weapon, and is much to be preferred to any of the other revolvers or automatic pistols we have had for trial. The only point I have not been able to ascertain is the wounding power of the bullet. Penetration tests into boards or clay blocks do not give a fair idea of this. I consider that this pistol is worthy of an extended trial.

The calibre of the Luger was given as .299, the depth of the four grooves being .004 and the land width measuring .177. The rifling had right-hand twist, making a turn in 9.84in. The barrel was 4.8in long, sight-base being 8.46in. Overall length on the centre-line was 9.31in; maximum height was 5.3in; and the gun weighed 29.4oz without its magazine. An unladen magazine weighed 1.96oz.

The 7.65mm cartridge was 1.18in long and weighed 162 grains, complete with a 92.5-grain projectile; the charge contributed 5.25 grains to the total. Muzzle velocity had proved to be 1148 ft/sec, resulting in a maximum range of 1967 yards at an elevation of 27°30'.

The Small Arms Committee recommended trials to determine the effectiveness of the 7.65mm bullet, compared with the .455 service-revolver pattern. Two pistols were sent to the School of Musketry at Hythe, two were dispatched to the Royal Laboratory in Woolwich, one was returned to the Superintendent of the Royal Small Arms Factory at Enfield Lock, and the sixth was retained on behalf of the Director-General of Ordnance.

On 17th January 1901, the Superintendent of the Royal Laboratory wrote to the Secretary of the Small Arms Committee stating that nothing had been done with the Luger, as it was imperative to decide the best method of determining stopping power. The Chief Inspector of Small Arms bemoaned the absence of a reliable method of gauging the 'hitting qualities' of pistol bullets, so it was decided that trials between the Luger pistol and Webley revolver would be used to develop appropriate testing procedures.

The Small Arms Committee minutes for 20th May 1901 noted an earlier report of experiments undertaken on live animals in the School of Musketry. These had been analysed by Lieutenant-Colonel James of the Royal Army Medical Corps. James, concluding – understandably – that the jacketed 7.65mm bullet was less lethal than the .455 Webley pattern, was supported by the Professor of Military Surgery, who informed the Director-General of the Army Medical Service that:

> . . .the only wound of a non-vital part which may be depended on to immediately stop a man determined to come on at all risks, a Ghazi or other Eastern fanatic, for instance, is one which fractures the bones of the leg or thigh. Deformable bullets. . .sometimes cause enormous destruction of soft parts at short ranges, but, setting these aside, no bullets … can be expected to stop the rush of a determined man when they traverse unimportant soft tissues only. Great energy in a bullet by no means guarantees great stopping power; but size and weight of bullet combined with energy tend towards producing it. Since the days of the old round bullet, the energy put into small arms projectiles has steadily been increased, while their diameter has been lessened; and with the latter condition their stopping power has steadily diminished.

The Commandant of the School of Musketry reported that the Luger had performed faultlessly on the target range, where the absence of recoil and ease of reloading had contributed to marked superiority over the Webley service revolver.

The Small Arms Committee then decided to try all the pistols that had been submitted in open competition. On 7th October 1901, the final report arrived from the Captain of the navy gunnery school, HMS *Excellent*. Each gun had fired 250 rounds. The Mauser C/96 reportedly had no advantages, jammed continually, had a bad feed; and, if the gun was loaded and cocked, fired when the safety catch was moved from 'safe' to 'fire' without touching either the trigger or the hammer. The blowback Browning was light and compact, with a simple mechanism; but its grip, pull-off, sighting arrangements and ineffectual cartridge were all criticised. The Luger possessed the advantages of the Browning together with excellent sights – though recoil was considered to be 'rather heavy', contradicting the opinion of the School of Musketry. The stopping power of the Webley was liked, but it was heavy and less handy than either the Browning or the Luger.

The Mauser C/96 and the Browning were rejected as unsuitable for military service, but the Luger, which still had its champions, was retained for further experiments.

The six trial guns delivered in October 1900 came from the pre-production series. The pistol surviving in the Ministry of Defence Pattern Room collection in Nottingham, no.26, bears a hand-engraved Swiss Federal Cross above the chamber and shows evidence of appreciable hand-finishing. As guns nos.23 and 25 are known to have been used in the trials, the British guns, assuming they were numbered consecutively, would have been 21–26, 22–27 or 23–28. These Lugers were amongst the earliest to feature the perfected radiussed toggle-hinge interface. Their flat safety levers and plain-bordered chequered wooden grips greatly resemble the drawings accompanying British Patent 4,399 of 1900.

United States of America   On 9th March 1901 the Board of Ordnance and Fortification met Hans Tauscher, the American representative of DWM, to order two Luger pistols and 2000 7.65mm cartridges.

Despatched from Tauscher's New York City office on 11th March, the consignment arrived at Springfield Armory three days later. On 18th March, a Board of Officers – Major John Greer, Captain John Thompson, Captain Frank Baker and Captain Odus Horney – convened to meet Tauscher. The calibre of the pistols was .301in; weight was 1lb 13oz unladen; the barrel measured 4.625in; the magazine held eight rounds; and the propellant charge of 5.2 grains fired the 93.5-grain bullet at 1154 ft/sec, measured at a distance of 53ft.

Owing to great familiarity with the pistol, Hans Tauscher field-stripped it in less than four seconds and then replaced the pieces in 12.5 seconds. The entire weapon was dismantled in 1 minute 19 seconds, though reassembly took more than three minutes.

The velocity determination trial gave figures ranging from 1120 ft/sec to 1154 ft/sec. The best results in the rapidity trial with were obtained by Captain Horney who, though he had never handled a Luger, hit the man-size target twenty-four times from thirty shots fired in a little less than a minute.

More than thirty misfires and jams occurred during the 1734 rounds fired in the endurance tests. Trouble had arisen in the first 500-round series from insufficient striker protrusion; and cartridges had jumped out of a dented magazine as the breech-block ran back, jamming in the feed-way when the breech closed. As the pistol had not been cleaned since arriving in the USA, its exterior was oiled after 300 rounds.

Hans Tauscher, dissatisfied with the performance of the Luger, asked to modify the striker before the endurance test was repeated. There were six misfires in the second 500-round series, when defective cartridges failed to force the breech-block backward to the limit of its opening stroke; the front under-edge of the returning block caught in the cannelure of the top cartridge in the magazine and jammed the action.

The hold-open, which supposedly retained the breech-block once the magazine was empty, was too soft to function efficiently and was removed after 200 rounds had been fired in the third series. 534 rounds were then fired without incident, except for a single failure when the pin holding the toggle-lock worked loose.

The Luger passed a dust test without difficulty, but the action was so thoroughly rusted after twenty-four hours in the steam room that it was too stiff to eject any of the ten rounds fired. Tauscher asked to apply a light coating of oil externally, after which nearly eighty rounds were fired without difficulty.

Certainty of action was tested with reduced-charge cartridges – 4 to 5 grains in quarter-grain increments – but the pistol fired them all with equal ease.

The trials board recommended purchasing a larger quantity of Lugers for field trials. Lieutenant-Colonel Frank Phipps, representing the committee, appeared before the Board of Ordnance in New York City on 4th April 1901 to press the claim. An appropriation of $15,000 was subsequently made for a thousand guns and 200,000 7.65mm cartridges, which were to be delivered as soon as practicable to New York Arsenal on Governor's Island in the Hudson River.

The consignment was shipped from Germany in August, 800 guns arriving in America on 26th October to be followed by the remainder three days later. They were sent for inspection in Springfield Armory, from where, on 31st December 1901, one gun and its accessories were sent to Rock Island Arsenal so that manufacture of a thousand holsters could begin. The leatherwork was completed on 23rd January 1902.

Michael Reese, in the revised edition of his *1900 Luger. US Test Trials*, suggests that issues – on the scale of five guns per troop – were made in November 1901 to men of the first fifteen cavalry regiments (3rd, 6th and 9th Cavalry excepted), some of whom were stationed in Cuba. Simultaneously, guns were also dispatched to more than sixty troops in the Philippine Islands.

The balance of a hundred guns was initially retained at Springfield Armory, though some Lugers were subsequently dispersed. Ten may have gone to the US Academy at West Point, fifteen to The Presidio in San Francisco, ten to Fort Hamilton in Brooklyn, and forty to Fort Riley in Kansas, leaving barely twenty-five guns in Springfield.

Though the Luger had been deemed important enough to merit full-scale trials, the field reports were discouraging. The pistols were usually greeted as an improvement on other semi-automatics, but most units expressed a preference for revolvers. Captain M.W. Rowell, commanding D Troop, 11th Cavalry, stationed at Gerona in the Philippine Islands, reported on 21st October 1902 that:

... relative to the five (5) Luger Pistols, Cal. 7.65 m.m., which were received for trial November 23, 1901... In my opinion, this pistol should not be adopted for use in U.S. Cavalry, nor should it be carried by officers except by permission of their company and squadron commanders... My reasons for this opinion are as follows:

1. Very great danger of accidental discharge. This danger exists in all pistols, but with this type it is increased. The danger is always present, even with fairly well trained troops and it becomes greater with partially trained men or with horses not thoroughly broken, conditions which now exist and which will recur from time to time in the Cavalry...

2. The mechanism while comparatively simple for so complicated a machine will not stand the wear and tear of service. Exposure to rain, dust and mud on field service will render the pistol unserviceable.

3. Caliber too small. It is thought that no caliber less than .45 will produce a sufficiently powerful "stopping effect" or "shock" at the short ranges...

4. With reference to this pistol as a secondary arm it is not seen that either rapidity of aimed fire or a greater number of cartridges than six or seven or even the ability to reload the magazine are really essential ... safety, sure action, and heavy caliber are in my opinion the three imperative features and it is believed that these objects are all best fulfilled by the best pattern single action cal. .45...

5. This pistol, with respect to its magazine features, appears to infringe the use of the carbine... I can conceive of no circumstances worthy of mention in any class of warfare, where a reloaded revolver magazine will be necessary...

I have had no opportunity to conduct exhaustive mechanical tests of this pistol and can make no recommendations for its improvement beyond recommending that it can be provided with such mechanism that in automatically cocking itself on discharge it also automatically locks itself at the same time [sic] thus removing the chief source of danger...

Most reports were similar combinations of good and bad, reflecting the conflicting views of individual cavalrymen. Surviving pistols were recalled to Springfield Armory in 1905 and, a year later, the remaining 770 were purchased by Francis Bannerman & Sons at a public auction. Each Luger had cost the US Treasury $14.75, plus 88¢ for each extra magazine, though the sale recouped $8250 of the original $15,630 investment.

Michael Reese notes that only guns nos.6167, 6361, 6601 and 6602 are mentioned individually in the surviving field trial reports – all by Second-Lieutenant Orlando Palmer of the 7th Cavalry, stationed in Cuba – whilst *Martial & Collectors Arms (MARS TM-157)*, published in 1971, lists the 770 guns acquired by Bannerman & Sons as 6167–96, 6282, 6361–7108 and 7147.

The Springfield Armory Museum possesses 6196, 6282, 6885 and 7108; the Museum at West Point owns 7014; and the John M. Browning Museum in Ogden, Utah, has 6399 and 7031. Most, if not all of these have been US Army trials guns. Serial numbers from 6151 to 7150 are conventionally attributed to the US Trials Lugers. No.6152 was apparently presented to government inspector William F. Read, who had been responsible for accepting the Lugers into US Army service, but it is suspected that the distinctive 'WFR' monogram over the receiver was added some time after delivery – either when the Lugers were withdrawn to store or when they were sold to Bannerman.

Scandinavia   Though the Borchardt-Luger was extensively tested in northern Europe prior to the First World War, the results were disappointing. This seems to be partly due to the high cost of the pistol compared with existing revolvers, partly to claims made by local inventors – especially in Denmark – and also to poor reliability in very cold climates.

The Danish army school of musketry tested the 'Borchardt-Lugers Rekyl-pistol, Parabellum' in 1902, having previously examined 1899 and 1900-pattern Browning blowbacks. The only Luger acquired was a 1900-pattern 7.65mm example with a 12cm barrel. On 3rd February 1902, the school of musketry reported on comparative trials of the Luger, the 1900-type Browning and the standard M1880 army officers' revolver. The long range, flat trajectory and good penetration of the 7.65mm German bullet were greeted with great enthusiasm.

About 450 rounds were fired without much incident, minor breech-closing difficulties being cleared by striking the front toggle-link with the palm of the hand. However, like many others, the Danish authorities regarded the closure of the breech by residual spring-pressure as a potential weakness of the Luger design. Nothing further was done for more than a year.

The school of musketry tested a 1902-pattern 9.5mm (.38) Colt-Browning in April 1903, reporting that the gun worked acceptably even though it was clumsy and poorly balanced. The first Danish-designed Schouboe was submitted as the 'Dansk Rekylriffl Syndikats 11.5mm Rekylpistol' in 1906. Often simply known as the 'DRS' – its maker's trademark – the Schouboe was a large-calibre blowback firing curious metal-jacketed hollow wood-core bullets at high velocity. This supposedly gave the benefits of large cross-sectional bullet area whilst retaining an ultra-simple operating system.

A trial between the Browning, the DRS-Schouboe, and the Luger acquired in 1902 resolved in favour of the German pistol, but it progressed no farther in Denmark. Only the DRS-Schouboe of the original triumvirate participated in subsequent trials, but was soundly defeated in 1908-9 by the Bergmann-Bayard.

In April 1903, the Swedish quartermaster-general, seeking a pistol to replace obsolescent service revolvers, instructed the school of musketry in Rosersberg to test suitable designs. Triallists included two 7.65mm DWM-made Old Model Lugers; two 7.65mm 1900-model and two experimental 9mm 'försöksmodell 1903' FN-Brownings; two 9.5mm Colt-Brownings; two 7.63mm Mannlicher pistols; four fully-stocked 7.65mm Mannlicher 'Karbinpistoler'; two 8mm

Frommers; and a solitary 6.5mm Hamilton-Pistol, submitted on behalf of Gustav Hamilton by J.Thorssin & Son of Alingsås. Swedish and Russian Nagant revolvers served as control weapons.

The Luger returned the highest figure in the velocity-determination trials, with an average of 333 m/sec comparing with only 223 m/sec for the Swedish m/87 revolver. A firing trial at disappearing half-figure targets at a distance of 15 metres was won with the Browning No.2 and a forty per cent hitting rate. The remaining results ranged from thirty-two per cent (Colt-Browning and Frommer) to only eleven per cent for the Browning No.1. The Luger scored twenty-three per cent, surprisingly low in a trial of this type, but subsequently proved to be the most accurate when fired from a rest.

One of the Lugers fired 1430 rounds in the endurance trial, breaking the extractor after 800 and recording several minor jams and misfeeds. The Browning No.1 had eight misfires and a feed-jam in 1240 rounds, whilst the Colt-Browning encountered only four failures in 1550. The Mannlicher pistol survived 1375 rounds with four failures, whilst one of the Browning No.2 pistols expended 1340 rounds with only three misfires and an extractor failure after 790.

Testing continued until 2000 rounds had been fired from each gun. Persistent parts breakages dogged the Hamilton, whilst the Frommer had been rejected after more than thirty jams in 390 shots.

Excepting the Hamilton and the Frommer, which had been withdrawn, the pistols all passed the rust test, and four – the Luger, both FN-Brownings and the Mannlicher – successfully negotiated the sand and dust test. However, whereas the Luger and the Mannlicher worked stiffly until oiled, the Brownings had functioned flawlessly.

The Luger and the FN-Browning No.2 (fm/03) were retained for supplementary trials, the others being distributed amongst army departments. One Luger and a hundred 7.65mm cartridges were sent for trials as an officers' weapon, whilst the other was given to the state rifle factory in Eskilstuna for metallurgical analysis. Testing continued until the German guns were finally withdrawn on 19th July 1904. The FN-Browning No.2, or fm/03, preferred for its simplicity and reliability in adverse conditions, was adopted in 1907.

Writing in *The Luger Pistol*, Fred Datig quoted a letter written in 1906 – by Hans Tauscher – stating that Norway had recently adopted the Luger. In reality, nothing more than a trial had been undertaken. A single 7.65mm Old Model pistol was tested in 1904 against other semi-automatics. The authorities were not convined that any of the weapons were reliable enough to replace the standard Nagant-type service revolvers, and so the defence department, preferring to await better designs, discontinued the trials in 1905.

After experimenting with a selection of weapons from 1907 onward, the commission unanimously approved the Colt-Browning – even though Sunngaard-Hansen, Dreyse and Schouboe pistols were re-tested in 1911. Three hundred Colt-Brownings were purchased in 1912, and a licensed Norwegian copy was introduced in 1914.

CHAPTER 4

The advent of the 9mm cartridge

When the Borchardt-Luger was being tested by the Swiss army in 1899, Georg Luger had stated that – changing nothing but the barrel and extractor – the pistol would chamber any cartridge of suitable length, as long as the calibre lay between 7.15mm and 8mm. It is not known whether any attempts were made to develop alternative chamberings until, responding to criticism of the poor hitting power of the 7.65mm bullet, Luger produced a 9mm version.

The first 9mm Parabellum cartridge-case, DWM no.480, was made simply by enlarging the neck of its 7.65mm predecessor. It apparently had a slight bottle-neck, one example of this type being pictured in volume one of *Handbuch der Pistolen- und Revolver-Patronen* (1971) by Hans Erlmeier and Jakob Brandt. Unfortunately, no details of the ammunition used in the earliest trials have been found, and the cartridges themselves are extremely rare.

No details of the individual guns have yet been extracted from the German trial records. This is unfortunate, as the submission of the first 9mm pistols to the rifle-testing commission in 1904 may indicate that the date conventionally ascribed to the 9mm Old Model Lugers – 1902 – is too early. The British records suggest that the perfected 9mm prototype was not readied until the beginning of 1903, and the first authenticated bulk delivery of 9mm guns (the fifty US army guns fitted with Powell's Cartridge Indicating Device) did not leave Berlin until April 1904.

The serial numbers of the earliest 9mm-calibre pistols were in the region of 10000, the prototypes being taken from the commercial production lines, modified, and given B-suffix numbers. Most of the surviving guns are numbered in the 10023B–10069B group, though there are oddities such as Luger's seven-shot 10077B and 10158B, presented to Manuel Mondragon.

Britain On 7th March 1902, a letter from Vickers, Sons & Maxim was forwarded by the Director-General of Ordnance to the Small Arms Committee. 'Having communicated with our friends [DWM],' it said, 'we find that, although there are certain difficulties to be met with in producing an automatic pistol with a larger calibre than the one adopted for the Borchardt[-Luger] weapon, they are at the present time experimenting with a new weapon which they hope may give satisfactory results'.

The Small Arms Committee merely noted the information, but Vickers must have been sent a copy of the Small Arms Committee's final requirements. These asked for the calibre, bullet weight and muzzle velocity to exceed .40, 200 grains and 1200 ft/sec respectively. On 18th December 1902, Vickers sent another letter to the Director-General of Ordnance:

> We find it practically impossible to submit a Borchardt[-Luger] pistol fulfilling the requirement specified... By actual experiment it is found that the maximum calibre which could be given to the Borchardt[-Luger] pistol is 9mm, firing a bullet weighing 8 grammes. Such a pistol with its ammunition could be submitted for trials in the third week in January next [1903], and we would respectfully ask you to agree to try this pistol, as, in many respects, we feel confident that it would be found satisfactory, both as regards accuracy of fire, rapidity of fire and stopping power. Although the bullet is somewhat smaller than that which you have specified, we beg to state that the muzzle velocity is higher, and consequently the muzzle energy of the bullet will be as great as in the case of a weapon firing a heavier bullet with a larger calibre, and, on that account, possessing only a lower muzzle velocity...

The Small Arms Committee refused to entertain the submission, preferring to investigate the Gabbett Fairfax 'Mars' which – at least on paper – met all the basic performance criteria. Though the Small Arms Committee still received reports from the Military Attaché in Washington DC, describing the contemporaneous US Army trials, the disqualification of the Luger was unlikely to be rescinded.

The British records of January 1903 are particularly valuable as they provide the earliest authenticated appearance of the 9mm pistols. Unfortunately, the records do not include specific details of the cartridge. Infuriatingly, therefore, it is not known whether the original bottle-necked cartridge had already been replaced by a straight-tapered pattern.

It is suspected that the earliest 9mm guns chambered for straight-case ammunition were unreliable. Prior to this era, guns chambering neckless cartridges generally indexed on the case rim. It is worth speculating, therefore, whether the earliest 'straight case' Luger cartridges (the missing DWM case no.480B, perhaps?) were semi-rim patterns inspired by the contemporaneous Browning patterns. These may have fed badly from the magazine, which was raked far more noticeably than in any of the Brownings. The problem was eventually solved by indexing a rimless cartridge (case no.480C) on the case mouth, a suitable shoulder being added inside the chamber. This was not patented in Germany until 16th February 1910 – no.237,192 – but had been in use since 1905 or earlier.

Unfortunately, the ease with which Borchardt-Luger pistols can be rebarrelled or re-chambered complicates the story; the first 9mm guns could easily have been revised for straight-case ammunition within a year of creation, making the changes difficult to date.

Germany   The rifle-testing commission was still experimenting in 1903–4 with the fifty-five 7.65mm Lugers acquired in April 1902. By March 1904, however, tests were being conducted 'to improve on the mortality, namely (1) by means of a large calibre, and (2) by means of bullets of a special substance'. In April 1904, the testers informed the war department that 'a report on a 9m/m Luger [pistol] will be forwarded in the near future'. By May 1904, an 'improved Luger-pistol (Parabellum), calibre 9mm, [had] been submitted with a flat-nose bullet'. Whether these entries can be used to date the appearance of the perfected 9mm pistol is still disputed.

United States of America   The US Army Board of Ordnance and Fortification met in New York on 16th April 1903, under the chairmanship of Lieutenant-General Nelson Miles, to consider an offer made by Hans Tauscher to submit experimental 9mm Lugers for trial.

On 6th May 1903, Brigadier-General Ripley, the Chief of Ordnance, informed the Secretary for War that:

> Mr. Luger, inventor of the Luger Automatic Pistol, had reached New York...with several small arms of his invention, and ammunition which he desires to submit to the War Department for such tests as the Department may desire to make... I recommend that the Secretary of the Treasury be requested to direct the Collector of Customs at the Port of New York, to permit these arms and ammunition to be forwarded ... to Springfield, Mass., through the Commanding Officer, New York Arsenal, or otherwise as he may decide, and that they may be sent to the Commanding Officer, Springfield, Mass., for such tests as his office may direct...

This letter has been used to support claims that Luger had brought fifty 9mm pistols from Germany personally. However, as these did not appear until 1904, the guns accompanying Luger were several prototypes with 'B'-suffix serial numbers.

At the end of June, the Board of Ordnance and Fortification asked Springfield Armory for a report on trials undertaken 'to enable it to select the most suitable length of barrel to be used with the 50-9mm. Luger Automatic Pistols to be exchanged'. On 2nd July, Colonel Frank Phipps, commanding the Armory, replied that 9mm-calibre pistols had been submitted with 3.$^7/_8$ in, 4.$^{11}/_{16}$ in and 5.$^{13}/_{16}$ in barrels (10cm, 12cm and 15cm). The style of the chambering – necked or straight – is not known. Two of these have been identified as 10030B and 10060B, with a special 12cm barrel and a standard 15cm barrel respectively. On 7th November 1913, according to Fred Datig (in *The Luger Pistol*), a short-barrel gun was sold from Springfield to Dr Earl Fuller of Utica, New York State.

Cartridges loaded with .35gm charge of Rottweiler nitrocellulose propellant generated 1033 ft/sec in the 10cm barrel, 1077 ft/sec in the 12cm version, and 1102 ft/sec in the 15cm pattern – compared with 1095 ft/sec, 1127 ft/sec and 1172 ft/sec for the experimental .38gm load. The recoil of the heavier charge was greater, but could not be justified by the minimal increase in performance.

The final Springfield report was considered by the Board of Ordnance on 30th July 1903, resulting in recommendations that fifty old 7.65mm guns should be exchanged for fifty new 9mm Parabellums, and that a cartridge-indicating device credited to George H. Powell should be added. This had been approved by the Cavalry School at Fort Riley on 18th June. Supplementary cartridge-performance and bullet-penetration tests were authorised, as results obtained at Springfield seemed to contradict those undertaken by the commission of 1901. Finally, $35,000 was appropriated to purchase 25,000 9mm cartridges, though the exchange of guns ensured that no additional charges would be made.

On 13th August 1903, Colonel Phipps was requested to send Luger the prototype gun fitted with the cartridge indicator. This may indicate that the short-barrelled 9mm B-series prototype went back to Germany, though the device could equally have been built into a surviving 7.65mm trials pistol.

Tauscher was informed of the decision on 17th August, but no deliveries had been made by October even though ammunition experiments were under way. In December, Colonel Phipps informed the Chief of Ordnance that Tauscher 'states under date of 4th inst. that the 50 9m/m Luger pistols cannot be expected until some time in February, the delay being caused by the work of attaching the Powell cartridge-indicating device.'

This refutes claims that the indicators were fitted after the pistols had arrived in the USA, though the prototype was probably converted in workshops in Fort Riley. The guns arrived in New York Arsenal on 20th April 1904 and were dispatched to Fort Riley two days later. Apparently numbered 22401–22450, they were divided equally between the Light Artillery and Cavalry boards.

On 10th April 1907, twenty-four survivors were returned to Springfield. No records of official trials have yet been discovered and it is clear from a letter written on 10th June 1908 by Captain W.A. Phillips, addressed to the commanding officer of Springfield Armory, that experiments were never undertaken there. Phillips described the Powell Device as:

...an indicating pointer attached to the follower in the magazine and sliding in a slot on the left side of the magazine. In the left grip is set a transparent celluloid strip about $3^1/_4$" long covering corresponding stops in the grip and magazine. There is a scale of black numbers numbered from the top 1 to 7, painted on the inside of the rear half of the celluloid strip, and then covered with metallic paint so that the numbers show black on a silver field. The end of the indicator on the magazine follower shows through the celluloid strip opposite a number showing the cartridges remaining in the magazine ... it is believed that the left grip would be injured by the rough usage of service.

CHAPTER 5

The Luger in the commercial market

Exemplified by the 1900-pattern Swiss service pistol, the 12cm-barrelled Luger has an elegance unsurpassed by later weapons of similar type. Its mechanical features were protected by a series of patents – among them British Patent 4,399/00 of 7th March 1900 and US Patent 753,414 of 1st March 1904, which incorporated the essence of a series of individual patents granted in Germany.

These pre-1914 pistols were beautifully rust blued, a time-consuming practice commonly abandoned after 1918. Once it had been assembled and inspected, a gun was dismantled and polished (though even the early DWM products show tool marks in the safety-lever recess) before a suitable blueing chemical was swabbed onto its exterior. The parts were then laid aside to rust. Once the desired intensity had been achieved, the parts were boiled to neutralise the chemical reaction, dried, and scoured with small wire brushes. The process was repeated until a deep rich blue was obtained. Then, after boiling in water, the parts were air-dried, treated with oil and set aside. Blueing salts that crystallised in internal cavities were removed, then the parts were cleaned and polished for the last time. The pistol was reassembled, given a protective coat of grease, inspected, and transferred to the storeroom.

Several individual components were finished by heating them to pre-determined temperatures, oxidising and colouring the surface whilst simultaneously making it rust-resistant. The extractor, ejector, spring-lock, locking bolt, trigger, magazine-release catch and manual safety lever of the original riband-spring Luger were usually heat-treated. Variations in temperature from batch to batch often caused changes in the colours of individual parts, but they customarily assumed a straw-like hue.

Commercial success

Commercial production began simultaneously with work on the Swiss contract, though the latter initially took priority. Owing to the variety of transitional 'semi-production' phases, the manufacturing pattern does not seem to have been settled until the summer of 1901.

Even before the pattern had been finalised, the original squared toggle-link interface had been substituted by a rounded one and the DWM monogram was added on the toggle-link. The safety lever originally had a shallow chequered head, but this ineffectual design was replaced by a short, high, fluted pattern projecting farther from the safety recess. This was much easier to operate with the thumb than its predecessor had been.

Two surviving carbines bear two-digit numbers, both with original DWM-marked toggles. As early as February 1900, DWM had applied to register 'Parabellum', trademark no.43353 being granted on 21st April 1900. By the end of the year, the gun had been renamed 'Selbstlade-Pistole Parabellum, System Borchardt-Luger'. Blueprints thus marked, shown by Christian Reinhart and Michael am Rhyn in *Faustfeuerwaffen II: Selbstladepistolen*, date to as early as 15th-20th December 1900.

Dr J.H.Mathews recorded rifling details of one early gun in his monumental *Firearms Identification*; 7.65mm Old Model Luger no.513 had four-groove left-hand twist making a turn in 9.7in. Land width was .089, land diameter measured .3014, and groove diameter was .3120. There is, however, some doubt about the origin of the barrel – which apparently bore a small Federal Cross, though the gun bore German commercial proofs. A later gun, no.2648, had four-groove right-hand rifling making one turn in 9.8in, with a land width of .108, a bore diameter of .3016 and a groove diameter of .3115.

The standard Luger, known as the 'Old Model' after the introduction of the New Model in 1906, had a grip safety that could be locked by the upward movement of the manual safe lever, a rebound-lock set into the right toggle-grip, and chequered walnut grips. The toggle grips were distinctively dished, or partly cut away.

Many unusual guns were made in the 10000–10100 group. Several in the 10003–10014 range, for example, have 175mm barrels and unique six-position sliding back sights on the toggle – quite unlike the earlier carbines, which have five-position sights. Fixed-sight 175mm-barrelled guns were also made, numbered 10010–10044 with gaps, and were often offered with special push-button stocks. These guns were featured in Spanish-language promotional literature dating from 1904 and may have been specifically developed for trials in South America. The experimental stocks accompanying guns tested in the Netherlands in the early 1900s have not been identified.

The perfection of the Luger in Europe caused lawyers acting for John M.Browning and Colt's Patent Fire Arms Manufacturing Company to file a Bill of Complaint alleging that the Borchardt-Luger infringed Browning's patents – specifically US no.580,294 of 1897. The assertion that the Luger was illegal unless licensed by Colt and Browning now seems ridiculous, as Browning probably infringed Maxim on the same basis. Colt's case was not substantial enough to prevent the US Courts deciding in favour of Luger and DWM in

---

Panel Five

PROOF MARKINGS ON TYPICAL OLD MODEL LUGERS

Commercial guns invariably display standard German proof marks. No comprehensive proof existed in the German empire until the acceptance of the proof law of 1891; a proof house had been established in Solingen in 1861, but it was thirty years before imperial practices were regulated.

Realising that the absence of legislation was hindering exports, the Germans dispatched commissions to London, Birmingham and Liége to study Anglo-Belgian procedures. Draft laws were presented to the Reichstag on 30th November 1890, receiving imperial assent on 18th May 1891, but the implementation regulations, or *Ausführungsbestimmungen*, were not approved until 22nd June 1892.

Proof marks were finally used for the first time on 1st April 1893, in Oberndorf am Neckar (mark: a stag's antler); Suhl (a shield bearing a sole and an axe in saltire); Zella St.Blasii (a heart and fir tree); and Frankfurt an der Oder. The Frankfurt establishment was subordinated to Suhl, and may have used the same mark.

An optional 'crown/N' nitro-proof mark was added on 23rd July 1893 and used until the laws were modified in 1911, but is rarely encountered on Lugers made prior to 1918. The most common marks are 'crown/B', 'crown/U' and 'crown/G' on the barrel, together with 'crown/B' and 'crown/U' on the left side of the receiver ahead of the trigger-plate, on the breech-block, and on the toggle link. The barrel mark is usually accompanied by '172,28' (7.65mm) or '118,35' (9mm) – the bore measurement gauged on the basis of the number of lead balls to the pound.

The widespread distribution of smokeless powder necessitated changes in the regulations, and, from September 1911 in Zella St.Blasii (1912 in the other proof-houses), the nitro-proof changed from 'crown/crown/N' to simply 'crown/N', the marks being found on the barrel, the front left side of the receiver, the breech-block and the front toggle link. Many guns made between 1912 and 1918 have the so-called 'lazy N', which lies horizontally on the receiver-side; post-war examples are generally vertical.

May 1908, but the case was not initially dismissed as an appeal lodged on behalf of Colt was not rejected until November 1909.

In the intervening period, with the US judiciary unwilling to grant an injunction preventing its sale, the United States of America greeted the Luger with enthusiasm, typified by the award of a Grand Prize in its class at the 1904 St Louis Exposition. Many guns had an 'American Eagle' – the obverse of the

Great Seal of the USA – rolled into the receiver above the chamber. This was a feature of the thousand trial guns delivered to the US army on 26th and 29th October 1901, which were allegedly numbered in the 6151–7150 group; but Harry Jones, in *Luger Variations*, recorded examples numbered as low as 2004 and 2011.

Distribution of Lugers was entrusted to Hans Tauscher of New York City, who always referred to them by the designer's name. By 1907, the North American market was taking more than half of DWM's commercial output. Though quantities are hard to define, at least 7000 guns had been made by the autumn of 1901 in addition to the 2000 that had been delivered to Switzerland.

The Parabellum was successful enough to encourage the manufacture of holsters and accessories in the USA. The extraordinary Ideal Holster-Stock was designed by Ross Phillips of Los Angeles and patented on 14th June 1904 (US 762,862), though the application had been submitted in September 1901. The rights to the design were assigned by Phillips to the Ideal Holster Company. An additional patent granted in Britain, 22,654 of 1901, illustrates a telescoping stock with an aperture sight on the attachment block.

The stock comprised a leather holster with tubular steel reinforcements, and was locked into recesses in the special steel-backed grips by a sliding catch. It was originally conceived for Colt and Smith & Wesson revolvers, but adaptions were subsequently made for the Luger and Colt-Browning pistols The hooks on the attachment block of the Luger version were shaped so that the grip safety could still be depressed with the stock in place.

DWM stopped numbering the right side of the dismantling-catch spindle in the region of pistol 7000: it is missing from both US Army trials gun no.7078 and standard commercial no.7255.

The provisions of the US Firearms Act of 1890 were extended at the end of 1902 to identify imported goods. 7.65mm Old Model Luger no.7976 is not appropriately marked, but no.8156, an otherwise standard 7.65mm Old Model, displays GERMANY on the front of the frame, immediately below the serial number. This additional stamping, however, may appear on the frame side.

Once the 9mm Luger had been perfected, a few guns were sold commercially – probably in 1904, in the brief period between the perfection of the cartridge and the development of the so-called M1904 and the New Models described in Chapter Six. The serial numbers apparently began at about 22001 and ran erratically up to 25050, gaps being filled by carbines and standard 7.65mm Old Model guns.

The 9mm Lugers retained the grip- and lever-safety system, and perpetuated both the toggle-lock and the dished toggle-grips. The earliest or first-pattern receivers and frames characterised the original 7.65mm Old Model Luger, whilst the second version appeared about 1904. The two differ slightly in overall length, measuring 136.5mm and 134.5mm respectively. The reduction in length meant that the second, or 'short frame' as it is now universally known, curves upward much more abruptly ahead of the locking-bolt spindle.

The two frames were used concurrently for some years; 9mm Old Model pistols may display either type, even though the short version is more common. The 1904-type navy Lugers retained long frames until the middle of the First World War, even though they chambered 9mm cartridges.

A change from 4- to 6-groove rifling was also made in 1904, but both patterns were initially intermixed. In *Firearms Identification*, J.Howard Mathews records the rifling of a typical early 9mm Pistole 1904 as 6-groove right-hand twist, with a land width of .790, a bore diameter of .3482 and a groove diameter of .3580.

Some later 9mm Old Models, assembled contemporaneously with the first navy pistols, had New Model (flat) toggle-grips with the lock inlet in the right side. Others incorporated Georg Luger's combination extractor and loaded-chamber indicator, patented in Germany on 22nd May 1904 (no.164,853).

A few 7.65mm Lugers were made with a short barrel, and sometimes also with a short frame. These unique 'fat barrels' are almost parallel-sided, with virtually no taper, and lack a ridge where the front sight band appears on later guns. Their transitional nature means that many minor variations will be found. Some ally Old Model frames (with the riband main spring) with New Model receivers and breech-blocks featuring the 1904-patent extractor. Some extractors are marked CHARGÉ, but whether they are genuinely the 'French Test Trial' guns identified by so many enthusiasts or simply intended for the French commercial market is still contested. Some guns retain the three-piece rebound lock in the toggle; others do not. It is impossible to catalogue these hybrids precisely. Some were probably genuine factory experiments; others represent intermediate stages of production between the Old and New Model Parabellums; and a few may even have been assembled to rid DWM of old parts.

Sales of Old Model Lugers continued after the advent of the New Models in 1906. The highest number observed on an Old Model 7.65mm 'American Eagle' pistol is 23362, after which a block of serial numbers was allotted to the modified short-frame guns in 7.65mm and 9mm. However, Old Model carbines may be numbered as high as 24672 with the occasional straggler; one is reputedly numbered 50069, which would date it to c.1909.

The Luger's greatest rival was the Mauser C/96, introduced commercially some years earlier, which had outsold the DWM design commercially until the outbreak of the First World War. In 1905 alone, 8011 C/96 pistols had been sold – though this had been a boom year, owing to the Russo-Japanese War, and sales had been declining steadily from a peak of 12,304 in 1899. DWM's preoccupation with German military contracts undoubtedly helped Mauser greatly.

The scarcity of the differing Old Models is difficult to assess, owing to differences of opinion over the commencement of numbering. It has been suggested that about a hundred pre-production pistols were followed by Swiss Ordonnanzpistolen 1900 numbered from 01 upward, but that DWM only began commercial production – at no.2001 – after 2000 Swiss pistols had been delivered. This seems to ignore the fact that the initial Swiss order was for 5000 guns and it seems much more likely that the serial-number ranges, Swiss and commercial, always operated concurrently. It is probable that the commercial sequence simply continued that of the pre-production guns.

The experimental pistol of 1903

Most Luger pistols shared a common toggle system, even though the design of the retraction grips and the breech-block varied. However, Georg Luger did make at least one attempt to develop a differing action.

The experimental design that was the subject of US Patent 851,538, granted on 23rd April 1907 (more than three years after the application had been filed), was basically an Old Model Luger, complete with plain bordered chequered grips and a riband main spring. The toggle-train, however, was unique. Its dished retraction grips, partially cut away at the rear, had a rhomboidal flange running diagonally downward, forcing a change in the rear of the frame. Breaking the toggle by camming the retraction grips upward with frame-ramps was superseded by a projection on the toggle striking the small shoulder on the frame.

Luger had obviously given the matter much thought, as the patent states that:

It is obvious that, with this arrangement, the jerking strain which arises from the co-action of the parts p and q [the new cam system] is directly taken up exclusively by the forward link forming a massive piece with the side-projections a^1 and shoulders or projections p. Only the forward-link pin v takes part in this direct strain, while the middle joint c is not subjected to the direct jerking or arresting action. This relieving of the central pin . . . is of decided advantage, and another advantage resides in avoiding multiple link connections, by which the jerking action would necessarily be transmitted in the event of shifting the cam projections on the rear link. . .

Above all, the effect of a certain uniform retardation during the folding action, which effect is necessary especially for the reliable function of the folding, results from the present arrangement, as the side pieces a^1 and the shoulders p, respectively, of the forward link a, which take up the sudden impulse, remove all vibration and the impinging motion is counteracted by the braking inertia of the middle pin and rear link parts, which are unaffected at the outset by the jerking action and need only be moved upward directly by the forward link. . .

Luger was clearly attempting to improve the smoothness of the action whilst reducing the strain on the parts. However, the revised design is neither as elegant as the standard gun nor as easy to make. It was an interesting departure from standard DWM practice and at least one gun may have been converted as a test-piece. But it made little mark on the history of the Luger pistol. The true 'Model 1903' was a standard 10cm-barrelled 7.65mm Old Model submitted for trials in the Netherlands in the summer of 1904.

The carbines

Several carbines survive from the earliest days of the Borchardt-Luger. Gun no.58 exists in the USA, whilst another, 9103C, was pictured by Ian Hogg in *German Pistols and Revolvers, 1871–1945*. These guns had an auxiliary recoil spring in the fore-end, guided around a spigot-like frame extension, where it was compressed during recoil between a lug on the underside of the 30cm barrel and the standing frame. The case (DWM catalogue no.471A) of the special carbine round was chemically blackened to indicate that chamber pressure would be fifteen to seventeen per cent greater than normal. An elegant chequered walnut fore-end was held to the frame extension with a transverse wedge, though a spring-loaded wedge-lock was soon discarded.

The rear toggle link of some early guns carried a unique five-position tangent sight, graduated for 100, 300 and 500 metres with unmarked intermediate positions for 200 and 400. The design of the sight was changed when it was moved from the reciprocating toggle-link to the barrel ahead of the receiver, improving accuracy by isolating movement in the action.

The revised carbines are regarded as the perfected Old Model (or '1902' pattern) and are understandably much more common than the original DWM prototypes.

The oldest presentation gun seems to be the Luger once owned by Mexican dictator Porfirio Diaz, though its reputed number, 55C, presents problems; unless it has been radically altered, the gun clearly represents the perfected pattern rather than the prototype. It is distinguished by a 300-metre back sight on the barrel, has a 'PD' monogram over the chamber, and is accompanied by a brass-mounted case of red morocco leather.

Deutsche Waffen- und Munitionsfabriken made a few presentation carbines in 1902, numbered between about 9105 and 9115 with a 'C' ('Carabiner') suffix letter. The unique dimensions of their butt-heel lugs prevented their stocks interchanging with later commercial examples.

Carbine no.9109C was presented to Hiram Maxim, its chamber being marked H.S.M./MARCH 15/1903 in gold; Luger's 'GL' monogram appears on the rear toggle link. The date has been claimed as Maxim's birthday, though this was actually 5th February.

Borchardt and Luger owed Maxim a considerable debt, having adapted his system of recoil operation to their own purposes. A deal had been struck in the early 1890s between the Maxim Nordenfelt Guns & Ammunition Co Ltd and Ludwig Loewe & Co, allowing Loewe, and later DWM, to act as agents in negotiations with the German government. Thus Maxim, Borchardt and Luger would have been brought into close contact.

Carbine no.9112C was given to the unidentified recipient 'H.C.R.', and, in *1900 Luger US Test Trials*, Michael Reese reproduces a letter from C.L.Graff – Hans Tauscher's attorney in New York – which mentions delivery of fifty cartridges for 'President Roosevelt's Lueger [sic] carbine'. Unfortunately, part of the date is missing and all that can be made out is '24, 1902'.

A pamphlet produced by Tauscher in 1906, shortly after he had moved to Thomas Street, New York, remarked that:

> ...the Luger Automatic Carbine is similar in construction and action to the Luger Pistol. It is a Repeater, shooting 8 shots and automatically reloading after each shot as long as any cartridges remain. The cartridges are held in a magazine held in the pistol grip, and the empty magazine can be removed and a full one inserted with great rapidity ... the barrel is longer than in the pistol, giving greater distance between sights. This, together with the carbine stock, which enables the arm to be held with as great, if not greater, steadiness than a rifle produces wonderful accuracy in shooting. The calibre is the same as the pistol [7.65mm], but the cartridge is loaded with a greater charge of powder, developing a range of 500 yards and much greater penetration. The stock is easily detachable, and the carbine can be carried in an ordinary size traveling bag.
>
> 116 SHOTS PER MINUTE! It is owned and used by the most renowned people the world over – President Roosevelt, President Diaz of Mexico, the King of Italy, and, almost exclusively, for all kinds of game, by His Majesty the German Emperor, William II...

Unfortunately, the Kaiser's carbine has never been identified. The serial numbers of the perfected Old Model carbines are generally listed as 21599–21992 and 23401–24792, but neither sequence is likely to have been continuous and will also contain standard-length pistols.

CHAPTER 6

The New Model Luger pistols

By 1903, Luger had been forced to respond to worries expressed by many armies about the comparatively poor 'stopping power' of the lightweight small-diameter 7.65mm bullet. By opening out the existing necked 7.65mm case to accept a heavier 9mm-diameter bullet, without losing much velocity, the design satisfied the German army experts – even though the British and the US authorities remained unenthusiastic.

In March 1903, Hauptmann Plass, a Bavarian observer of the trials being undertaken in Prussia by the rifle-testing commission, reported that experiments were under way with bullets 'of larger calibre' and 'different types of . . . material'.

The third series of field trials in Germany, undertaken with 7.65mm guns, had only finished in mid-summer 1903 and suggestions that credit the rifle-testing commission with the introduction of a 9mm cartridge do not seem defensible. But the GPK may have been the first agency to test the perfected 9mm straight-sided DWM 480C cartridge case. The phrase 'bullets of special material' simply indicates flat-nose ammunition, which is corroborated by a reference in a report of the proceedings made by a Bavarian army observer in March 1904.

Tests were already under way by this time to improve 'wounding efficiency' by increasing the calibre or using bullets of special material. Luger, the commission recorded, had 'submitted an improved pistol'. Unfortunately the surviving material holds no clues to the improvements. However, the new guns probably had the combination extractor and loaded-chamber indicator, patent protection for which had already been sought, and possibly also the new chequered flat-face toggle grips.

In June 1904, the rifle-testing commission reported that the Luger, as the pistol was actually being called at this time, had been improved sufficiently to justify adoption. But Mauser had learned of his rival's supremacy and intended to 'submit his improved self-loading pistol in a larger calibre in August'. The Luger, therefore, would 'not be officially adopted for the time being'.

As the authorities whiled away the summer of 1904, awaiting yet another

Mauser pistol, the imperial navy began its own trials. On 1st August, by order of the imperial navy office, the Baltic station was issued with five '9mm Selbstlade-Pistolen Modell 1904'. The order records that:

> For a field test with self-loading pistols, five such pistols are placed at the disposal of the high command, each of which is fitted with a holster-stock, three magazines, one cleaning rod, one screwdriver, three dummy cartridges and a manual. The imperial dockyard, Kiel will distribute the pistols to such land-based naval units as will be indicated by the high command. Shipboard tests will be conducted on ships of the active battle-fleet, and also on the gunnery test ship.
>
> The Selbstlade-Pistole Modell 1904 is to replace the revolver. It will serve to arm all such personnel of a landing party that are not armed with rifles, i.e. officers, petty officers, signalmen, engineers, stretcher-bearers, etc. For this purpose, it is intended to arrange for higher pistol quota than the previous revolver quota, namely for each battleship about 100 pistols.
>
> By using a self-loading pistol with a shoulder-stock, even personnel with little training with handguns will be placed in a position . . . to engage the enemy in close combat more successfully than with a mere handgun. . .
>
> Apart from some minor modifications, the Selbstlade-Pistole Modell 1904 corresponds technically to the Parabellum pistol, the battleworthiness of which had been proved by extensive army field tests. . .'

The trials were intended to determine how the pistols should be carried; how much ammunition should be issued to individual ships or men of landing parties; and whether the grip safety mechanism was desirable. Trial reports submitted to the navy office by 20th September 1904 agreed that the pistol was far superior to existing revolvers and much handier than the rifles. Suspecting that the results of the trials would be favourable, the authorities had apparently already asked the war ministry to order 2000 1904-model navy pistols from Deutsche Waffen- und Munitionsfabriken. No formal adoption of the navy Parabellum has yet been traced, though an 8000-gun contract was delivered to DWM on 12th December 1904.

On 12th May 1905, a date often mistakenly offered as official adoption, the navy office informed the command of the Baltic naval station, Kiel, that:

> . . .development of the self-loading pistol . . . is to be considered as successfully finalised. The suggestions resulting from the test have been incorporated in the design as far as possible.
>
> The pistol receives the designation 'Selbstlade-Pistole 1904'. It corresponds to the model as tested, apart from minor modifications.
>
> Delivery of the . . . pistols cannot be expected to occur until March 1906, after which fitting out of front-line units is planned to be effected immediately.

This seems to indicate that the design was only stabilised in the spring of 1905, but information concerning the guns tested in mid-summer 1904 is still lacking. It has been suggested that the five pistols issued in August 1904 were 15cm-barrelled Lugers of the experimental prototype series dating from 1902–3, with B-suffix five-digit numbers. This seems unlikely. The precision of the 'Model 1904' designation suggests that they were made especially for the navy. The guns undoubtedly had 15cm barrels, but would also have had standard toggle-locks and the new combination extractor/loaded-chamber indicator. However, the earliest examples may have had a multi-position back sight instead of the two-position sliding pattern that characterised the later guns. The return springs would have been the original riband type.

Surviving correspondence between the navy office and DWM suggests that none of the 8000 guns ordered in December 1904 were delivered before March 1906. Yet eighteen Lugers numbered between 3 and 44 had been issued in August 1905 to personnel of the East African expeditionary force, despatched to crush the Maji-Maji rebellion in German East Africa. A similar quantity of pistols had gone to South West Africa, where the Herero-Nama revolt was being quelled, but their numbers are not recorded.

In July 1906 the marine infantry inspectorate submitted a discouraging report to the high command about the performance of the 9mm Lugers. The soldiers had expressed a preference for rifles carried by native bearers, and the officers had often purchased smaller pistols for self-defence. The excessive weight of the Luger and the awkward grip safety had also attracted disapproval.

One of the eighteen original guns sent to East Africa had been lost; eight had excessive rusting in the bore; one hold-open latch had broken; one hold-open latch and spring assembly had disappeared; and an entire toggle lock had vanished. The guns all had 15cm barrels; the unique two-position sliding back-sight on the back toggle link; a grip safety; and a three-piece rebound lock set into the right toggle-grip. The safety levers were originally of the 'up-safe' pattern and the riband main springs operated the toggle through an intermediate bell-crank lever.

Surviving guns of this period are numbered between 36 and 1148. The authenticity of all but the lowest-numbered of them has been contested by many enthusiasts, myself included. A claim that the navy acquired at least 1250 of these riband-spring Lugers originated many years ago, and any challenge has been consistently opposed.

The order placed with DWM in December 1904, which called for the delivery of 8000 navy Lugers by March 1906, may have been placed before the existence of the coil-spring pistol became known. In January 1906, owing to unexpected difficulties, DWM was informed that the secretary of state, imperial navy office, would 'accept a delay in the delivery of the Selbstladepistolen 1904, Order W.II.1 1835 of 12th December 1904, new deadlines to be: 2500 pistols not later than the end of March, 2400 more pistols in April, 3100 more pistols not later than the end of May. Any further delay in delivery will not be tolerated.'

To pay for these guns, a capital sum of 350,000 Marks had been allotted in the navy budget approved for the 1905 fiscal year (which ran from 1st April 1905 to 31st March 1906). However, surviving papers indicate that 32,720 Marks had been spent on guns, ammunition and accessories prior to 1st April 1905; none of the 8000 coil-spring guns had been delivered, so how was this money spent?

If the existence of the coil-spring prototype was known, the sums may have bought large numbers of riband-spring guns for training purposes. Alternatively, if the existence of the coil spring was not known, the riband-spring guns may simply have represented the first consignment of the 8000 pistols ordered late in 1904. The former explanation is preferable, as the order number given in the navy office letter addressed to DWM in January 1906 – W.II.1 1835 – had been allotted in December 1904. A revised or re-negotiated order would almost certainly have had a new number.

Surviving correspondence between Deutsche Waffen- und Munitionsfabriken and the navy office does not specifically identify the reasons for slow progress, but it is probable that either the coil-pattern return spring or the cartridge-locating method had taken longer to perfect than anticipated.

Issue of the first manual was announced in the *Marine-Verordnungsblatt* on 15th February 1906 as the 'Leitfaden betreffend die Selbstladepistole 1904'. Property marks were introduced on 2nd November 1907, when 4.2mm unit identification letters were ordered to be stamped on the butts. In February 1910, the navy office accepted an earlier suggestion by the torpedo inspectorate that a 2.5mm-high weapon number should be added. The earliest butt markings, therefore, were applied in two stages.

The 1910 directive also confirms that none of the shoulder stocks had previously borne the distinctive marking-discs, the unit identifiers being stamped directly into the woodwork. It may still be possible to locate an original stock, but so many were altered that 'first issue' items will be very scarce indeed.

The advent of the coil spring

In *Die Pistole 08*, published in 1985, Joachim Görtz suggested the perfection of the Luger by 1906:

> The chamber had been redesigned by Georg Luger with the extractor acting as a 'loaded-and-cocked' indicator... The main spring had been changed, and the first steps had been made to reduce the number of pistol parts. Considering...that all this had taken its time, one can only assume that Luger had started re-designing his pistol immediately after the G.P.K. had talked to him in 1901.

Yet the trials undertaken by the navy in the summer of 1904, leading to the adoption of the Pistole 1904, were undoubtedly conducted with riband-spring guns; and the first bulk deliveries of navy pistols were of similar pattern. Improvements made in guns submitted to the German army in 1904 may only have concerned the omission of the rebound lock, the style of the toggle-grips, or the addition of a cartridge-locating stop ring within the chamber.

The DWM factory designation 'Model 1904' referred not to the guns tested by the German navy in 1904–5, but instead to the so-called 'New Model' during its formative period. Its major distinguishing feature, a coil-pattern return spring, was not exploited militarily or commercially until the beginning of 1906.

To the intense annoyance of German enthusiasts, much of the evidence – admittedly almost all circumstantial – suggests that the coil spring originated in the Netherlands. On 23rd December 1904, less than two weeks after the German navy had placed its 8000-Luger order with DWM, the Dutch ordered 174 guns in 7.65mm and 9mm chamberings. Ten of the 9mm pistols were to be of a special 'Dutch Model'. According to the contract:

> [the] main spring construction, the breech-block, the extractor etc., will be altered according to the latest agreements... On the left side of the frame, an arrow and the word 'RUST' ['safe'] must be placed...near the safety catch. Toggle-lock and toggle-lock catch will not be installed. The sights will be made somewhat wider; the grip screws somewhat shortened; the position of the trigger if possible improved.

These Lugers were delivered early in August 1905, the only serial number mentioned in the trial records being 10127 – possibly with a 'B' suffix.

In his pamphlet *Automatische Handvuurwapenen*, published in 1912, First Lieutenant S.J.C.Oly of the school of musketry claimed that the staff of the Artillerie-Inrichtingen at Hembrug redesigned the Luger 'including the substitution of the original leaf main spring by a much stronger and more efficient coil spring', in addition to making changes to the breech-block and the extractor. Unfortunately, even the painstaking research of Bas Martens and Guus de Vries in archives in the Netherlands, published in *The Dutch Luger* in 1994, cannot prove this claim beyond doubt.

It can still be argued – rightly or wrongly – that the term 'Dutch Model', to which such great significance is being attached, may have been given by DWM simply to an improved Luger being tested for the first time in the Netherlands.

Blueprints found in the Artillerie-Inrichtingen have been cited in support of Oly, but the only date they now display is 1936, substituted for the originals when they were renumbered. Sixteen of the total of seventeen sheets are signed by Georg Luger and clearly labelled 'Selbstlade-Pistole Modell 1904'; the coil-spring system is accurately depicted, as are the combination extractor and loaded-chamber indicator patented by Luger in 1904. The drawings also show a flat-headed 9mm bullet in a case headstamped K DWM J 480C. The first sheet is entitled 'Pistool Parabellum 9 m.m. (Hollandsch model)'. Its Teutonic origins are suggested by the style of the handwritten lettering and, as all but the first sheet are in German, the drawings were probably taken from stock held in Berlin. A special master-sheet was presumably added to suit the Dutch. Old Model drawings supplied to Argentina in this era followed the same practice, and several other 'Model 1904' blueprints are known.

However, even accepting that the drawings were all produced by DWM gets no nearer the truth. If the Dutch origins prove to be incorrect, the only other leading claimant (excepting Georg Luger) is Bavarian soldier Adolf Fischer. Development of two straight-pull rifles had brought Fischer to the attention of the Bavarian war ministry in the 1890s, and he had even offered a semi-automatic pistol to the military authorities in 1899. The pistol was unsuccessful, but gained its inventor a coveted posting to the Prussian rifle-testing commission. His career has been explored in detail by Joachim Görtz in *Die Pistole 08*.

In a letter written to his departmental head on 24th October 1904, Fischer claimed that 'suggestions made by me to improve on the original design [of the Luger] have been forwarded by the commission to the ministry with a request to be approved. This pistol has already been adopted for the navy. A decision has not yet been taken by the army. Regarding two different types of pistol bullets suggested by me, tests are still being conducted.'

Though its validity cannot be challenged, this interesting letter contains nothing of real substance. Fischer probably did play an important part in the perfection of the Luger, but whether this included the substitution of the coil-pattern mainspring for the original riband is impossible to judge on the basis of the meagre existing information.

Fischer repeated some of his claims in *Artilleristische Rundschau* and *Zeitschrift für das gesamte Schiess- und Sprengstoffwesen* in 1929–30 but, as he was nearly seventy, it is difficult to decide what emphasis should be put on them; Luger, who may have known the truth, was dead. Unfortunately, Fischer never defined his 'improvements' and left endless scope for speculation.

The truth may be simply that the Prussian rifle-testing commission, the Dutch, and possibly other military agencies, suggested that a 'better' spring was required. Virtually every trial board fretted over the 'weak closure' of the toggle system, yet none said in detail how it was to be changed. It is wise to keep an open mind on the detailed transition from Old to New Model Lugers.

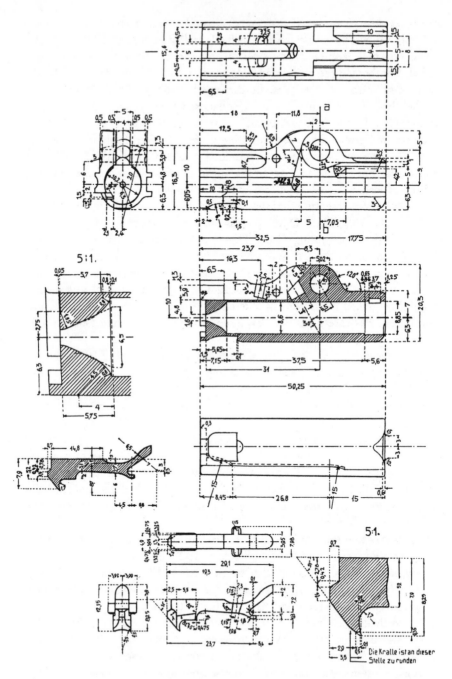

Fig. 7. The 1904-patent breech-block and extractor/loaded-chamber indicator, from official German army drawings. *Joachim Görtz.*

The New Model

The earliest authenticated reference to the coil-spring guns is the contract placed with DWM by the Dutch government on 23rd December 1904, though they were not delivered until August 1905. The Swiss authorities did not learn of the existence of the 'New Model' guns until the autumn of 1905, according to Eugen Heer in *Die Faustfeuerwaffen von 1850 bis zur Gegenwart*. The war-material directorate (KMV) was forced to re-test the pistol and report to its superiors before the Ordonnanzpistole 1906 could be accepted. The final submission was made on Christmas Day 1905, prior to which two 'Modell-waffen' had been tried.

It is a shame that none of the surviving Dutch blueprints retains its original date. Even if this still failed to resolve the problem, at least the chronology of the New Model would be clarified. The design of the pistol had clearly been perfected by the end of 1905; though series production had yet to begin, features such as the coil spring and the combination extractor/loaded chamber indicator had become an essential part of Luger design.

The earliest coil-spring guns were made in the DWM toolroom, by dove-tailing a special bracket into otherwise standard Old Model frames. This was necessary to support the bell-crank lever needed to transmit the pull of the coil spring to the toggle link. Several surviving guns have been altered in this manner, including 10070B, with Luger's 'GL' monogram on the toggle link; 10130B, a survivor of the guns delivered to the Netherlands in August 1905; and 6023, a curious hybrid built on a modified Old Model frame. Doubtless others remain to be identified, but the chronology of even the survivors (10130B excepted) is difficult to gauge.

Adoption in Germany

Once the rifle-testing commission had completed the third series of field trials in the spring of 1904, adoption of the Luger was all but settled. However, Mauser had sufficient influence to postpone the decision while a 10.4mm 'large-calibre' pistol was tested. This was supposed to have appeared in August 1904, but it had still not been submitted by August 1905.

A Frommer was considered in December 1904, and an Italian Vitali was rejected in March 1905. Tests with a Frommer and a Mauser were pursued throughout 1905, though the Luger was still favoured. By October 1906, it was being reported that trials of a 'completely redesigned' Mauser pistol would be undertaken when the gun was submitted; and the Frommer had shown itself 'nearly equal to the Luger' in December.

Joachim Görtz has drawn attention to priority given to the procurement of Mauser rifles and Maxim machine-guns in this era, adoption of a pistol being much less important. The deliberately protracted nature of the trials may have contributed to the tardy adoption of the Luger as much as the malign influence of Mauser.

Finally, in March 1907, the army adopted the 9mm Luger for the four experimental infantry machine-gun detachments formed in August 1906. On 23rd May 1907, these detachments were reorganised as machine-gun companies. Each required ninety-three Pistolen 08 in 1910 (later reduced to eighty) and had seven Maxim machine-guns. The first official Parabellum manual, *Leitfaden betreffend die 9mm Selbstladepistole (Luger)*, dates from this period.

Three survivors have been identified from the formative period of the machine-gunners: nos.118, 171 and 183 are all short-framed 9mm New Model pistols with 10cm barrels and grip safeties. Each bears a single military inspector's mark on the left side of the receiver ahead of the trigger-plate.

It has been estimated that about 375 guns would have equipped the first machine-gun units; allowing for reserves, therefore, DWM may have supplied 500 as an expedient, providing additional guns to be tested. A 9mm 'officer's model' Frommer and a lightweight 9mm Mauser pistol were promised for the summer of 1907. The latter may have been the first of the C/06 series, with a detachable box magazine and two laterally pivoting locking bars in the receiver; the C/06 had a raked grip, whereas the C/06-08 had a vertical pattern and the magazine ahead of the trigger.

Comparative tests undertaken by the rifle-testing commission throughout the late summer and autumn of 1907 merely confirmed the superiority of the Luger. In February 1908, therefore, the '9mm self-loading pistol Luger with flat-nose steel-jacketed bullet' was recommended for adoption to replace the existing 10.6mm revolvers. The orders were formally signed by Kaiser Wilhelm II on 22nd August 1908.

While the army prevaricated, the imperial navy, accepting on the basis of previous trials that the Luger was the best semi-automatic pistol obtainable, conducted its own brief tests in August–September 1904. As most of the reports had been favourable, an 8000-gun contract had been awarded to DWM on 12th December 1904. Production, however, was initially very slow.

The Selbstladepistole 1904 was officially renamed 'Pistole 1904' in February 1907, coinciding with an acceleration of warship production in Germany inspired by the commissioning of HMS *Dreadnought*, which reduced the effective value of the numerical superiority of the Royal Navy by eclipsing elderly battleships and large armoured cruisers. Plans that had been laid before parliament in September 1905, calling for about 6,900 navy Lugers, had clearly been overtaken by events in Britain. A revised scheme, prepared in secrecy and initialled by Admiral von Tirpitz on 4th June 1909, called for the issue of about 12,675 guns (excluding the needs of the detachments serving in the Far East).

The 8000-gun order given to DWM in December 1904 had been completed, so another contract must have been prepared. Had this been for 12,000 guns, then the total of 20,000 Lugers would agree with claims made by DWM in 1911 – even though delivery extended into the opening weeks of the First World War.

The Tirpitz Plan listed the small-arms required by each ship, from the newest dreadnoughts to navy auxiliaries. A typical modern battleship, SMS *Helgoland* for example, carried ninety-nine Lugers and 410 1898-pattern Mauser rifles for a crew of 1113 men. Cruisers were designed for colonial service, sea-lane protection or raiding, and carried unusually high quotas of small-arms; typical was SMS *Gneisenau*, with ninety-three Lugers and 225 1898-pattern Mauser rifles for a complement of only 764 men. Destroyers had twenty to thirty pistols, depending on their size; whilst even a U-boat could carry twenty-four. A detailed list of the individual shipboard issues will be found in *The Navy Luger* (1988) by Joachim Görtz and John Walter.

Deliveries of the standard long-frame coil-spring Pistolen 1904 continued until about 1913. With effect from 22nd June 1912, however, the operation of the safety lever – which had previously moved upward to block the sear – was changed to prevent unintentional release. The precise nature of the change is not specified in surviving papers, but it was undoubtedly the introduction of 'down-safe' operation.

A projection on the tip of the manual lever could be rotated behind a shoulder on the grip-bar to lock the mechanism in place. Unfortunately, when the manual lever locked in its upper position, it could be caught on the holster when replacing the gun. This sometimes pushed the manual catch downward, unlocking the grip safety and freeing the gun to fire. As this feature was clearly undesirable, the mechanism was reversed, making it more difficult to re-set the manual lever accidentally. All navy Lugers were to be changed so that their safety system, despite the additional grip mechanism, resembled the 1908-pattern gun adopted by the army. Work was apparently entrusted to Kiel dockyard, guns on overseas stations being recalled when appropriate and replaced by modified examples.

The GESICHERT safety-recess markings were also altered – some by welding, betrayed by colouring on the inside of the frame, but mostly by milling the lettering away.

In January 1914, the navy office informed Kiel that, as the grip safety of the Pistole 1904 was to be discarded, dockyards were forbidden to 'disengage the grip safety' until the necessary orders were promulgated. This may indicate that two separate changes were to have been made; the mechanism was 'revised' with effect from June 1912 – changing it to down-safe operation – and then 'disengaged' altogether, possibly by removing the interlock between the grip and manual safeties so that the components functioned independently. However, no confirmation of the predicted second change has ever been found.

CHAPTER 7

The .45 Luger and the US Army trials of 1907

The US Army Board of Ordnance and Fortification decided to investigate handgun design in 1906. Many submissions had previously been rejected because their ammunition was unacceptable, so the authorities decided to accept only guns chambering the .45 M1906 round.

Advertisements were promptly despatched to inventors, manufacturers and manufacturers' agents, telling them of trials scheduled for October 1906. The specification demanded a magazine capacity of at least six rounds; a muzzle velocity of 800 ft/sec or more, with bullets weighing at least 230 grains; a locked breech with a 'solid bolt-head'; vertical ejection; and a loading mechanism that would function with jacketless bullets.

The trials had already been postponed when Hans Tauscher admitted that the .45 Parabellum could not be delivered in time:

To Brigadier-General William F. Crozier, Chief of Ordnance, U.S. Army. 16th November 1906.

General, re: New Model Luger Automatic Pistol, cal. .45. Referring to your valued favor ... informing me of the postponement of the competitive tests of automatic pistols and revolvers until December 3rd, I have the honour to advise you that, although Mr. Luger cheerfully used all his available time which he could possibly spare from his pressure of work ... to construct a .45 cal. pistol (which was practically completed when I left Berlin beginning of last month), I just received the regrettable news from my firm that since then Mr. Luger has been ill for several weeks and will not be able to complete his experiments with the 5,000 .45 cal. cartridges from Frankford Arsenal... Consequently, he will be unable to arrive here in time for the competitive tests of 3rd December and he, therefore, urgently begs for a postponement of these tests until end of January or beginning of February 1907.

Some of the problems had undoubtedly arisen from the poor quality of ammunition supplied from the USA, forcing DWM to make 850 11.35mm cartridges from existing 11mm Bergmann no.490 case-dies. Few of these rounds survive, as at least 797 were expended in the trials. They were essentially similar to the experimental 'Cartridge, Caliber .45, Model of 1906' and were loaded with 230-grain bullets supplied from Frankford Arsenal. The cartridges, which do not seem to have been headstamped, attained a muzzle velocity of 729–790 ft/sec with a 6.2-grain charge.

On 28th December 1906, under the chairmanship of Colonel Phillip Reade, representatives of the infantry, cavalry, artillery and ordnance convened at Springfield Armory and agreed to defer trials. The Board eventually returned to Springfield on 20th March 1907 to begin work in earnest.

Revolvers submitted by Colt and Smith & Wesson were immediately rejected; not only was a pistol to be favoured, but the products of both companies had been issued since 1889 and their mechanical characteristics were well known. Unsuitable calibre or ammunition proved to be the downfall of the Glisenti, the Schouboe and the Krnka-Roth, but an interesting variety of weapons still remained.

The Luger, the Colt-Browning and the Webley-Fosbery 'automatic revolver' were made by large companies with prior experience of handguns; the Savage was submitted by an established gunmaker with no previous experience of automatic pistols; the Bergmann-'Mars', though comparatively well known, was made under sub-contract in Suhl; whilst the White-Merrill and the Knoble were entered by individuals without large-scale backing.

The pistols of William Knoble of Tacoma, Washington, were rejected after the preliminary examination: 'careful examination and several efforts to fire these weapons showed that they were so crudely manufactured as to render any test without value, smooth working being impossible'.

Special German-made ammunition for the .45 Bergmann-'Mars' had been impounded by the US Post and Customs Authority in New York. Attempts were made to fire Frankford arsenal rounds, but the Bergmann hammer did not have sufficient force to ignite them consistently. Thirteen misfires occurred in twenty rounds, and so the Bergmann was promptly – if a little unluckily – disqualified.

Submitted on behalf of Joseph C. White of Chelsea, Massachusetts, the White-Merrill at least managed to fire 211 rounds. However, it had worked so hesitantly that 'the test was discontinued. The conception of a loading lever which permits loading by the pistol hand is commended, but its practical application was not entirely satisfactory'. The effort required to cock the mechanism against the powerful return spring was regarded as too great to operate efficiently.

The fascinating Webley-Fosbery passed virtually all of the tests, only to be rejected on the grounds that the concept of an automatic revolver was 'not desirable for the military service. The only gain of importance being the more gradual take-up of recoil. The difficulty in reloading the arm on horseback after six shots have been fired, is the same as in any other revolver. The introduction of the automatic feature adds to the complication and weight of the weapon, and double-action is not present'.

Only the Luger, the Colt-Browning and the Savage remained in contention after the first series of tests, but none had proved to be entirely satisfactory.

The handling characteristics of the Luger were greatly liked, as the raked grip facilitated instinctive shooting. The automatic and manual safeties, the loaded-chamber indicator, accessibility of parts and the vertical ejection of the toggle-lock system were also praised, but breech-closing problems and the strength needed to cock the action were major drawbacks.

The Colt-Browning relied on pivoting links below the muzzle and breech to unlock the action by dropping the barrel parallel to the slide during the recoil stroke. The barrel was surprisingly long for such a compact design, but there was no automatic safety system. Some of the components were poorly designed, others were inaccessible, ejection was lateral, and two hands were required to withdraw an empty magazine.

The Savage was the most interesting of the trialists in many ways. Based on a patent granted to Elbert Searle on 21st November 1905 (no.804,985), the action was locked by rotating the barrel laterally through about five degrees. This rotation was initially opposed by the torque of the departing bullet engaging the rifling, though the strength of the lock has often been disputed. The Savage is, therefore, often classed as a delayed blowback.

Though wholly lacking in pistol-making experience, the Savage Arms Company competed gamely with two of the world's leading manufacturers in a stringent trial. The trial pistols performed effectually enough with the .45 M1906 round and were particularly easily dismantled; however, they lacked an automatic safety and the grip was uncomfortable.

The Luger was the most accurate of the trialists, achieving a group-radius of only 1.3 inches at a range of twenty-five yards, but was prone to minor stoppages. By the end of the first series of trials – accuracy, rapid fire, reduced and excess charges – 641 rounds had been fired with fourteen stoppages. Most of the mishaps had occurred with Frankford Arsenal cartridges, which developed an erratic average velocity of 809 ft/sec compared with a more constant 763 ft/sec for DWM-made ammunition.

The dust test was hazardous, jamming the Luger four times in fourteen shots, and a repeat with the magazine left in place during dusting process fared no better. The rust test proved the pistol's undoing just as it had done in 1901, as all fourteen rounds had to be fired by closing the action manually. A coating of oil, applied externally, subsequently restored normal operation.

A total of 1022 rounds were fired, with thirty-one assorted jams and misfires. By comparison, the Colt had recorded twenty-seven stoppages in 959 rounds, and the Savage suffered fifty-one in 913. The Luger had performed best in the endurance trial (eight stoppages compared with twenty-four for the Colt), but the Colt-Browning had been victorious in 'dust and rust'.

The trials Board concluded that:

> ...the Savage and Colt automatic pistols possess sufficient merit to warrant their being given a further test under service conditions... The Luger automatic pistol, although it possesses manifest advantages in many particulars, is not recommended for a service test because its certainty of action, even with Luger ammunition, is not considered satisfactory because the final seating of the cartridge is not by positive spring action, and because the powder stated by Mr. Luger to be necessary for its satisfactory use is not now obtainable in this country.

Colt and Savage were each given orders for 200 pistols. On 18th May 1907, Brigadier-General William Crozier, Chief of Ordnance, informed the US Army Adjutant-General that Colt had promised delivery for early 1908. Savage, however, had declined the order owing to lack of production capacity. The proposal had been made, therefore, 'to purchase 200 Luger automatic pistols...and information is desired as to whether they should be issued to the troops already designated for the test of the Savage pistols. The date of delivery of the Luger pistols ... will probably be about the same as for the Colt.'

On 10th June 1907, Hans Tauscher was asked to quote for the supply of 200 'Luger Automatic Pistols, caliber .45' and 100,000 cartridges. His reply of 12th August asked $48.75 for each Parabellum, two magazines and some spare parts, and $20 for each thousand cartridges. General Crozier sanctioned the official order on 28th October 1907.

Everything seemed to be proceeding smoothly until, on 16th April 1908, Tauscher informed Crozier that he could not accept 'the order for 200 Luger Automatic Pistols and 100,000 cartridges, etc. Thanking you for this order and the kind consideration shown me in this matter, I regret all the more the withdrawal of the Luger pistol from the competition, as this pistol (cal. 9m/m and 7.65m/m) has hitherto been adopted by the German army and navy and six other governments.'

Learning of DWM's withdrawal, the Savage Arms Company agreed to supply 200 guns for the field trials after all, and the .45 Luger was forgotten. However, neither the Savage nor the original Colt-Browning proved acceptable until the latter had been redesigned to eliminate one of the actuating links. The revised pistol eventually became the .45 M1911.

It has often been alleged that the trials were deliberately manipulated in Colt's favour, but the Board seems to have undertaken work with scrupulous impartiality; apart from the luckless Bergmann-'Mars', which was a victim of circumstances, the foreign weapons were given every chance. Relations between Colt and DWM were strained, as the former was pursuing a lawsuit alleging that the Luger infringed Browning's patents, but the case had not been heard at the time of the trials.

There is no evidence that Colt had a malign influence on the conduct of the trials, excepting in the most indirect way. The .45 M1906 cartridge had been adapted by the US Army authorities from the .45 Auto-Colt pattern of 1905, giving Browning more time to perfect his pistol – about eighteen months, compared with the five or so accorded to DWM and the Savage Arms Company.

The entirely untried Savage had the greatest problems, but was almost a triumph; even though the .45 Luger was new, the operating characteristics of its toggle-link system had been investigated for more than seven years.

The tone of the 1907 report implied that the Luger had little chance of adoption, regardless of its participation in the field trials, so DWM sensibly declined the order of a mere 200 .45 guns at a time when large orders for the German army seemed imminent. The return on the American investment was unlikely to be worthwhile, particularly as the Colt-Browning was the established favourite.

Though the progress of the American trials is well documented, controversy still surrounds the .45 Lugers. Work apparently began in the late summer of 1906, when 5000 cartridges were sent to Luger from Frankford Arsenal. The pistols were completed late in February 1907, two of them arriving at Springfield Armory some time prior to 28th March. One gun, believed to have been no.1, was put through the trials whilst no.2 was retained for examination. The latter still exists, though the fate of its companion is unknown.

But were there others? And, if so, how many? Deutsche Waffen- und Munitionsfabriken clearly made more than two, as at least one would have been retained in Germany as a safeguard against the loss of the guns despatched to the USA; coincidentally, .45 Luger no.4 is said to have been found in Germany in 1945 and taken to the USA as a souvenir. Another example, apparently numbered '14', was pictured in *Luger*. The late August Weiss credited his predecessor, Heinrich Hoffmann, with a statement that 'no more than six' .45-calibre guns had been made.

The .45 Luger pistol is basically a standard New Model, complete with coil spring, combination extractor/loaded-chamber indicator, and grip safety. But it is much more massive than the standard guns, the barrel is 127mm long, its magazine holds seven rounds, the grip is markedly squarer to the bore than normal, and the trigger guard is more angular. Harry Jones pictured two surviving guns in the revised edition of *Luger Variations*, commenting that the second survivor was fired 150 times in 1960 without a single stoppage. Unfortunately for Luger and DWM, the ammunition used in 1907 was not as reliable!

CHAPTER 8

Military trials and commercial exploits of the New Model Luger

Interest in the Luger as a service weapon continued after the introduction of the New Model, especially in European countries where progress had already been made.

Switzerland　The Ordonnanzpistole 1906 was adopted on 9th January 1906 to supersede the 1900 pattern. It had a 12cm 7.65mm-calibre barrel, a coil-pattern mainspring, the combined extractor/loaded-chamber indicator, a grip safety, and knurled flat-faced toggle grips. Guns made prior to the completion in 1909 of no.9050 bore the Federal Cross on a sunburst above the chamber; later guns – numbered 9051 and above – displayed the cross on a shield that, in accordance with heraldic convention, was hatched vertically for red.

Minor criticisms were received once the Lugers had been in service for some years. On 30th November 1911, therefore, five officers convened in the federal arms factory in Bern under the chairmanship of its director, Oberst René von Stürler.

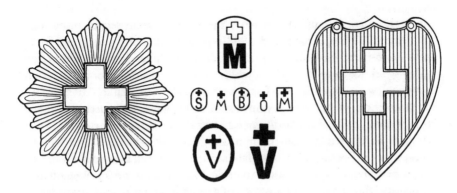

Fig. 8. The principal Swiss chamber marks were a cross-on-sunburst prior to 1909 and a cross-on-shield thereafter. The smaller marks were applied by the principal arms inspectors. *John Walter*.

119

Some parts of the army believed that the 7.65mm bullet was too small to be an effectual 'man stopper'; indeed, the artillery representative on the investigating committee, Major Brüderlin, stated his preference for the old 10.4mm revolver. He also drew attention to the adoption of the 9mm cartridge in Germany, where time and effort had been expended before deciding that a calibre of 7.65mm was too small. Many other countries – Britain and the USA, for example – were still issuing large-calibre weapons firing heavy, if slow-moving, lead or jacketed-lead bullets.

If the calibre was arguable, at least the Luger's safety features compared favourably with its contemporaries. The grip safety ensured that the pistol could not be fired until it was in the hand, and the radial lever locked the grip mechanism in the safe position. The gun could also be carried uncocked, as the striker could be set simply by pulling the toggle-grips slightly upward. The absence of an external hammer prevented thumb-cocking, but also avoided snagging on the holster or clothing; in addition, unlike some other guns, the Luger could also be dropped on a hard surface in comparative safety.

After debating the advantages of the locked breech and a powerful cartridge against the drawbacks of high price and complexity, the committee finally recommended a Browning-type close-quarters weapon (*Nahwaffe*) if it could handle a larger-diameter bullet than the 9mm rounds being used in Belgium and Sweden.

On 2nd March 1912, therefore, the pistol commission reconvened in the Bern arms factory to improve the Ordonnanzpistole 1906. Some of the original recommendations had been revised, as the locked breech had been reinstated and calibre was simply to be enlarged to at least 9mm without losing the outstanding accuracy of the 7.65mm Parabellum. This, it was hoped, would improve not only stopping-power but also the wind-riding qualities at long-range.

Several differing guns were tested – the Swiss 7.65mm service pistol; German 9mm 1904-type navy and 1908-type army Lugers; and experimental 9mm 12cm-barrelled Lugers, about twenty of which had been converted from 7.65mm service pistols in the Bern factory. Two blowback 1910-pattern Brownings were obtained from Fabrique Nationale, one each in 7.65mm Auto and 9mm Short, and a 'Spanish army pistol, Bayard' was also purchased. Eugen Heer, writing in *Die Faustfeuerwaffen bis 1850 bis zur Gegenwart*, suggested that this may have been a 9mm Campo-Giro. However, as the latter was not adopted for the Spanish army until January 1914, the gun is more likely to have been a Bergmann-Bayard ('Pistola modelo 1903, Calibro de 9'). Regardless of its identity, the Spanish weapon performed poorly and was soon discarded.

The 7.65mm Luger proved to be the most accurate, but, less predictably, performed as reliably as the simpler Brownings. At the final meeting of the trials commission, on 8th June 1912, the Ordonnanzpistole 1906 was retained for service. It had proved safer and more accurate than its rivals, and had been as reliable as could be expected.

The battleworthiness of the 7.65mm cartridge was no longer questioned as strongly as it had been in 1911, as the expense of changing to 9mm could not be justified. Design of an improved holster began immediately and modifications to the sights were made from 1913 onward, but the 7.65mm Luger remained the official service pistol until 1949.

An improvement was also made in the standard cartridge in this period, resulting in the Ordonnanz Pistolenpatrone 1903/16. The case mouth was crimped into a single cannelure midway along the body of the modified bullet ('Geschoss 1903/16'). Insignificant changes were made to the cartridge case, and the propellant charge was changed to small sheets (*Blattchen*) to improve combustion.

By 1917, the Swiss urgently needed pistols to replace the Old Model Lugers that had been discarded. Unfortunately, the last of 10,215 DWM-made New Models, no.15215, had been delivered in the summer of 1914 and the First World War was preventing further consignments.

Tooling began in the federal arms factory in Bern and the first 'Ordonnanzpistole 1906 W+F' reached the army in November 1918. Its markings included an outline Federal Cross above WAFFENFABRIK BERN in two lines on the toggle-link, chamber marks being abandoned. The Swiss-made pistols duplicated the pre-1914 German pattern, excepting that their chequered wooden grips generally had plain borders.

The popularity of the Luger in Switzerland, especially for target shooting, led to the development of the first effectual sub-calibre trainer. Patented in 1911 by Bernhard Müller (no.55,698), this single-shot barrel insert or *Einstecklauf* had the bore off-set so that the standard Luger striker could fire Flobert primer-propellant caps or rimfire cartridges. An improved version with a curved bore was patented in 1922.

Russia   According to Vladimir Fedorov, writing in *Evolyutsiya Strelkovogo Oruzhiya* in 1938, a standard 7.65mm 12cm-barrelled Old Model ('Avtomaticheskii Pistolet Borkhardta-Lyugera'), taken from commercial production, was tested at the Oranienbaum proving ground in 1904. It had been tried against the standard 7.62mm 1895-pattern Nagant service revolver, a Webley-Fosbery and a 1900-type FN-Browning blowback. The Mauser C/96, which was very popular with officers of the tsarist army, was apparently omitted simply because its operating characteristics were so well known.

The powerful 7.65mm cartridge was praised, being much more powerful than the standard Russian revolver pattern, and the Luger proved to have the best rate of fire. However, the marksmen had great difficulty in hitting the target – possibly because they were unprepared for the shift in aim

Pistolet 1900/1906

Vue de gauche, sans plaque de poignée;
culasse fermée, pistolet déchargé.

Pistolet 1900/1906

Vue de droite, sans plaque de poignée;
culasse ouverte, retenue par l'arrêtoir.

Fig. 9. These excellent engravings of the Ordonnanzpistole 06 were taken from the
official Swiss handbook.

caused by recoil or for the upward displacement of the toggle through the line of sight.

A major cataloguing problem, which Federov does nothing to resolve, is presented by New Model Lugers with crossed Mosin-Nagants above the chamber. As only the Russian army was equipped with these rifles, it has been suggested that the pistols were supplied under military contract. However, as workers in the Colt and Smith & Wesson factories in the 1870s have often testified, the army controlled the acceptance of service weapons with maniacal dedication.

The crossed-rifles mark has been reported on other handguns, including FN-Brownings. However, as none of them – including all the surviving Lugers – bear appropriate proof and inspectors' marks, military issue is very unlikely. An alternative claim that they were purchased by municipal police is also generally discredited, owing to the lack of marks such as 'Moscow City Police'. But it is possible that the pistols were sold privately to army officers, supplementing the popular Mauser C/96, or were even intended for a nobleman's private army.

The most plausible explanation is that the crossed-rifle chamber marks were applied at the request of a Russian gun-dealer, explaining not only the lack of inspectors' marks and the absence of bayonets on the rifles, but also the nickel-plating said to be found on guns remaining in Russia. Parallels could be drawn, perhaps, with the use of the American Eagle mark on Lugers sold commercially in the USA.

There were many important distributors of guns and sporting equipment – including Bitkov and Berngard in Moscow, or Chizhov in St Petersburg – but it is not yet known whether DWM had a specific Russian agent.

Suggestions that the Russian guns are actually Bulgarian have been made on the grounds that the markings on their extractors are identical. However, the two languages were written similarly until a modernised Bulgarian alphabet emerged in the 1920s. When the Lugers were supplied, therefore, marks applied to Russian and Bulgarian guns would have been alike.

A few Russian guns have recently found their way to Europe from Iran, and it is likely that they were brought to the Near East by White Russian émigrés. Their numbers are usually confined to the 560–860 block, though one numbered 313 has also been reported. The Russian guns – perhaps a thousand of them – clearly formed a separate series.

Bulgaria   The Bulgarians adopted the 7.65mm New Model Luger on 5th October 1908, immediately after gaining independence. The Old Model had been tested whilst Bulgaria was still nominally a tributary of the Sultan of Turkey.

Sales figures published by DWM in 1911–12 indicated that only 1300 7.65mm guns had been supplied since 1901. In view of the existence of Old

Fig. 10. The earliest Bulgarian Lugers displayed the pavilioned arms (left) above the chamber, though the pistols acquired in 1910 had the simplified shield (right) on the toggle-link. The small lion was a property mark. *John Walter.*

Model Lugers numbered in the 20290–20300 group with the Bulgarian arms above the chamber, the delivery of 7.65mm New Models, and the change to 9mm in 1910, it is unlikely that more than fifty Old Models had been acquired. Survivors include nos.1021, 1033 and 1261; however, all three have been rebarrelled in 9mm and were apparently renumbered at the same time.

Approximately 1250 New Model 7.65mm pistols, with grip safeties, were delivered for officers' use in 1909. They were numbered from 1 – or possibly '01' – in a separate sequence, survivors including 370 and 1237. They bore the distinctive pavillioned coat of arms above the chamber.

Portugal   The Portuguese were among the greatest Luger enthusiasts in Europe, purchasing several thousand in differing patterns.

A hundred 7.65mm Old Models were acquired for trials, the number of one survivor – 18861 – dating it to the very end of 1903 or the beginning of 1904. The test pieces also bore issue numbers (pistol 18861 displays no.62) and an encircled-triangle property mark.

Though the trials were leisurely, they ultimately brought DWM orders from both army and navy. After the murder of King Carlos I in 1908, his successor, Manuel II, sanctioned the purchase of about 5000 7.65mm long-frame New Model guns within a year of his accession. The 'Pistolas Luger-Parabellum do Exército Portuguêsa Mo.909' were delivered in 1910, distinguished by 12cm barrels and an ornate 'M2' monogram over the chambers. The extractor was marked CARREGADA, though (unlike the GNR pistol of 1935) the safety recess remained plain. The encircled-triangle property mark could be found on the left side of the receiver ahead of the trigger-plate.

A thousand short-barrelled 9mm Lugers were ordered for the Portuguese

Fig. 11. The chambers of the Lugers supplied to Portugal prior to the First World War bore these distinctive marks. *Left to right:* the army Mo. 909; the navy Mo. 910 'royal'; and the navy Mo. 910 'republican'. *John Walter.*

navy shortly after the army guns had been approved. The first 'Pistolas Luger-Parabellum da Marinha Portuguêsa Mo.910' were delivered early in 1910. But only about 800 had been despatched from Germany by 5th October, when a revolution put the king to flight. The highest reported number on a royal pistol is 769. DWM hastily changed the style of the chamber mark and delivered approximately 200 examples of the 'Republican Model', having substituted 'R.P.' (Republica Portuguêsa) for the crown in the original crown-and-anchor chamber mark. The guns all bore an 'MP' monogram navy inspector's mark.

The Netherlands Though the adoption of the Luger had been rescinded by the Dutch Parliament in December 1905, the separately constituted Netherlands Indies army (NIL, later KNIL) had also expressed an interest in acquiring a new handgun. The standard NIL M1891 revolver was supplied from the Netherlands, but, as the Hembrug factory was committed to equipping the regular army, the colonial ministry became increasingly frustrated with progress.

Ten 9mm Lugers were acquired from DWM's agent, Georges en de Watteville, and sent to the Netherlands Indies in the winter of 1906. These guns – 10cm barrelled New Models with grip safeties – had German commercial proof marks, but 'arrow/RUST' in the safety-lever recess. Their serial numbers were apparently in the 43921–43999 group.

The guns and ammunition performed particularly well in extended field trials. Finally, in April 1910, the Luger was adopted to replace the M91 NIL revolver. Four contracts were placed with DWM prior to the First World War: 1391 guns were ordered in May 1911, 750 in December 1911, 1290 in May 1913 and 750 in September 1913. Apart from the 'arrow/RUST' safety-recess marks and the stamping of GELADEN on both sides of the extractor, the NIL pistols had a crowned cursive 'W' property mark on the receiver.

Excepting six retained in the Netherlands to train officer-cadets for colonial service, all 4181 M1911 guns were despatched to the NIL headquarters on Java. A supplementary order for 400 of these Lugers was prepared in June 1914, but cancelled by the outbreak of hostilities.

Though officers' pistols remained untouched, guns issued to NCOs and mounted men acquired distinguishing marks. These originally comprised the unit mark and a weapon number, which were struck on the back of the pistol frame above the lanyard loop and on a small brass plate let into the front of the holster. A typical example read '5' above '778', signifiying the 778th gun – a single sequence containing rifles, carbines and then pistols – issued to the fifth infantry battalion.

In 1919, however, marks struck directly into the frame-metal were replaced by a special brass marking plate soldered on the front of the trigger guard. This system – applied retrospectively to many pre-1914 DWM-made Lugers – is described in greater detail in Chapter Eleven.

Great Britain   On 1st September 1911, Vickers Ltd submitted a 1908-type Luger to the Director-General of Ordnance, who passed it to the Chief Inspector of Small Arms for trial. The report of 24th October, after noting the differences from the previous guns (such as the coil spring and the combined extractor and loaded-chamber indicator), remarked that the pistol was:

...light, weighing 1lb 15ozs. with magazine, the weight of the latter being 2oz.
   The stock is inclined to suit the natural position of the hand and gives a very comfortable grip.
   The toggle joint movement of the breech mechanism, although efficient, is perhaps not so satisfactory as the horizontal breech movement, as it may offer greater facility for the entrance of sand, dirt, etc. Stripping for cleaning is very simple, and the barrel with breech mechanism is easily removed. Parts liable to wear could be replaced at no great cost.
   Range Report. Calibre: 9mm, 0.354in. Weight of bullet: 123 grains. Material of bullet envelope: steel. Weight of charge: 5.5 grains, flake propellant. Weight of round: 189 grains, rimless type. Velocity at 45ft: 1,062 ft/sec (mean value). Accuracy, 6 shots at 25yd: 1.81in wide x 2.92in high. Penetration, in deal boards, 1in apart, at 25yd: 15. Rapidity of fire: 7 rounds in 11 seconds (average). Handiness: well-balanced with a good grip angle. Sand test: no failure of any kind. Ejection good, causing no inconvenience to the firer. Certainty of action: no stoppages or misfires of any kind.

The Chief Inspector of Small Arms added a postscript to his report stating that the Luger, in common with the Webley & Scott pistol, seemed admirably suited to service requirements. However, his suggestion that comparative trials be undertaken with the Luger, the Colt-Browning and the Webley & Scott was rejected by the Small Arms Committee, and DWM was simply told that no further action would be taken.

Sales in South America

Many countries in Latin America were so pitifully poor in the 1900s that the widespread issue of expensive pistols was an unjustifiable luxury. Even though vast quantities of Mauser rifles were sold throughout the Americas – from Mexico in the north to Chile and Argentina in the south – the Luger was unable to replicate this success. Not only did its chances recede farther once the Colt-Browning had been perfected, but DWM's manufacturing facilities were stretched to capacity as soon as the German army adopted the Luger for universal service.

Brazil   The only major success in South America occurred when, after a few Old Model guns had been tested successfully in 1904-5, the army adopted the New Model Luger. Five thousand 12cm-barrelled 7.65mm examples, fitted with grip safeties, were supplied by DWM c.1907–11. A distinctive encircled-B inspection mark appeared on the left side of the receiver ahead of the trigger plate; beneath the barrel; and on the base of the magazine. The serial numbers ran upward from 1 or 01. Surviving guns – often converted to 9mm – generally show evidence of hard use.

Argentina   The army accepted the blowback 1901-type Mannlicher as the 7.65mm Pistola Mo.1905, though the Old Model Luger was undoubtedly submitted early in the twentieth century. A 7.65mm Swiss-style 'Pistola alemaña Borchard-Luger, Parabellum' was tested extensively about 1902, but the trial records were destroyed some years ago and only a single sheet of drawings survived.

Mexico   A report regarding the Luger from the British Military Attaché in Washington to the Small Arms Committee, dated 'Mexico, July 16th, 1905', stated that:

> ...the trials it has undergone in Mexico have been most satisfactory, and...the Minister of War has obtained the consent of the President to its adoption... Owing to there being no funds allotted in the Estimates it had not been possible to give at once an order to the Luger firm [DWM], but a promise to order from 6,000 to 10,000 next year [1906] had been given and he believes that a small order for 2,000 for use in special corps, President's bodyguard, &c, would be given in a few days... The pistol for Mexico is to have the latest 'German pistol'

improvements, such as the strengthening of the parts, visibility of the cartridge ready for firing, and substitution of spiral for long doubled spring, &c... The President here intends to arm all soldiers of the artillery and cavalry with this pistol, so as to do away with the carbine, for artillerymen at least'.

Additional information, dated 10th August 1905, stated that the Mexican army had been given official permission to purchase the pistols, and that issue to the artillery and the cavalry had been confirmed. However, no genuine Mexican Lugers are known; lack of funds – or nationwide unrest – prevented the purchases. The existence of the machine pistol designed by the Navarro brothers in 1914 (qv), suggests that the pistol was well known in Mexico prior to the First World War.

Bolivia   Some commercially numbered guns were supplied to the army prior to 1914, possibly in two batches as survivors include 58048, 59299, 64597 and 65475. The principal distinguishing mark is EJERCITO DE BOLIVIA, above the chamber, though at least one – perhaps of questionable authenticity – bears the Bolivian arms.

Commercial exploits

Few German archives or pre-1914 items of sales literature use the term 'Model 1906' – so popular with modern enthusiasts – except specifically in relation to the Swiss Ordonnanzpistole 1906. Most prefer 'New Model' to distinguish the perfected coil-spring design from its Old Model riband-spring predecessor.

The New Model pistols appeared on the commercial market in 1906 and rapidly supplanted the Old (1900) Model, though stocks of obsolescent parts allowed the two patterns to co-exist almost until the beginning of the First World War. Few pre-1914 manuals make much capital of the distinction, as DWM understandably concentrated on the latest design. The retailers, however, were rarely in such an unequivocal position and had to distinguish between the two – 'old' and 'new' pattern-names serving the purpose admirably.

The New Model was mechanically similar to its predecessor, excepting that the combination extractor/loaded-chamber indicator forced changes to be made in the breech-block. New Model serial numbers began where those of the 7.65mm and 9mm Old Models had stopped in the region of 25500. They reached the low 70000s by August 1914; after 1909, however, a few 9mm carbines and commercial derivatives of the Pistole 1908 were also included.

The Lugers were well received, though they were expensive and much more powerful than most commercial purchasers needed. They could never match the sales of the blowback Brownings, which had reached a million in July 1912 and stood at about 1.3 million by February 1914; DWM's entire commercial Parabellum sales, by comparison, scarcely exceeded 70,000.

Lugers were sold through the usual gun-trade and mail order outlets, but few were specially marked; it was much easier for retailers to stamp the accompanying manuals or packaging. In the USA, however, DWM dealt only with Hans Tauscher, a wholesaler based in New York City. Lugers distributed in the United States invariably bore the American Eagle over the chamber and, after 1902, also displayed GERMANY on the frame. The most popular place for this supplementary mark was underneath the serial number.

Ledgers kept by Tauscher from 1913 until 1917, when the Office of the Attorney-General confiscated his business once the USA had entered the First World War, show sales of 1697 .30 New Model American Eagle Lugers numbered between 26169 and 67871; 472 .38 New Model American Eagle Lugers numbered between 38349 and 65800; 103 .30 Old Model Luger Sporting Carbines; one .30 'Navy Commercial' Luger, number 58539; and seventy-one .38 'Navy Commercial' Lugers numbered between 25064 and 64400. It is not clear whether the term 'New Model' in these ledgers includes any 1908-type guns.

The earliest pistols sold in the United States displayed GELADEN on the extractor and GESICHERT in the safety-recess respectively, but these were soon replaced by the more appropriate LOADED and SAFE (though hybrids have been reported with polyglot Anglo-German markings).

Tauscher considered the designer's name to be more sales-worthy than 'Parabellum' and popularised the term 'Luger' in the United States prior to 1917. Stoeger perpetuated it after the First World War. Catalogues may refer to 'The Luger Automatic Repeating Pistol', 'The Luger Automatic Sporting Carbine' and even 'The Luger Automatic Pocket Carbine' – a standard pistol sold in the unusual Ideal Holster Stock.

Lugers sold in France prior to 1914 were generally handled by Manufacture Française d'Armes et Cycles ('Manufrance') of Saint-Étienne, though a few are said to bear the marks of Société Française de Munitions of Paris. A typical Manufrance gun – no.51554 – displays the distributor's name on the top surface of the barrel, applied before the gun was polished and blued.

Lugers were sold in Great Britain through several differing outlets, though never in substantial numbers. The most commonly encountered mark is W.R.CO./BIRMINGHAM, applied by Westley Richards & Company, but proof marks alone distinguish most British imports.

Among the most unusual guns made in this period were no.10158B, with an 'MM' monogram (Manuel Mondragon?) over the chamber, and some transitional carbines. A unique seven-shot pocket pistol, no.10077B, was built on an Old Model frame – cut to receive the rebound-lock – but had an unusually narrow New Model toggle system and a short grip restricting magazine capacity to seven rounds. This pistol was apparently Georg Luger's personal property. Though the presence of his 'GL' monogram on the back toggle-link is not in itself conclusive, the spare magazine and special holster were presented to Fred Datig in 1955 by Georg Luger the Younger.

Most of the co-called 'navy commercial' pistols were 9mm New Model Lugers with grip safeties, distinguished from navy issue by commercial 'crown/crown U' proofs on the receiver-side and 'crown B/crown U/crown G' on the barrels. Their numbers include 25064, 35682–38412, 43916, 51310–51357, 54099, 62151, 64302–64400 and 67943 – with gaps in the sequences – plus a handful of short-frame guns in the 56747–58634 group. Short-frame examples also lack the grip-safety mechanism.

Though survivors invariably chamber the 9mm round, at least one 7.65mm gun (no.58539, now lost) was sold by Hans Tauscher prior to 1917. Though only the pre-1914 pistols can justifiably claim to be genuine navy commercial Lugers, similar guns were made in the 1920s from cannibalised parts.

CHAPTER 9

The ultimate success: adoption of the Luger for the German Army

Completion of the protracted trials with the Luger, Mauser and Frommer pistols, which had occupied the Prussian rifle-testing commission for several years, allowed the 9mm Luger to be officially adopted on 22nd August 1908. The pistol retained the coil-type return spring and combined extractor/loaded-chamber indicator of the perfected navy pistol, but the grip safety and the upward-locking lever were replaced by a simple manual lever acting directly on the sear-bar. The laterally-moving sear was exposed on the left side of the receiver, where it could be immobilised simply by sliding a 'blocking plate' vertically out of the frame-side.

Deutsche Waffen- und Munitionsfabriken was offered a contract for 50,000 pistols, 50,000 turn-screws and 9000 cleaning rods, which were to cost the government treasury 2,313,420 Marks. Oberst Lehmann, director of the rifle factory in Spandau, signed the contract on behalf of the Prussian government on 6th November 1908; the manufacturer's representatives signed four days later; and the war ministry approved the transaction on 2nd December. A new era had begun.

DWM was asked to deliver at least 3000 pistols by 31st March 1909 – allowing issue to begin – and then deliver 2000 monthly until the order was completed in March 1911. The Spandau rifle factory accepted responsibility for the acceptance and proof of the pistols, as the DWM factory was nearby in Berlin.

Subsequent demand was to be fulfilled by the Prussian government arms factory in Erfurt, which had been granted 260,000 Marks on 16th January 1909 to commence tooling. The war ministry estimated that annual production capacity would amount to about 20,000 pistols.

Guns made by Deutsche Waffen- und Munitionsfabriken prior to 1910 were easily identifiable, as they lacked the chamber-top dates characteristic of later military issues. The proof eagle and two crowned-letter inspectors' marks lay on the left side of the receiver ahead of the trigger-plate. Assembly, inspection and

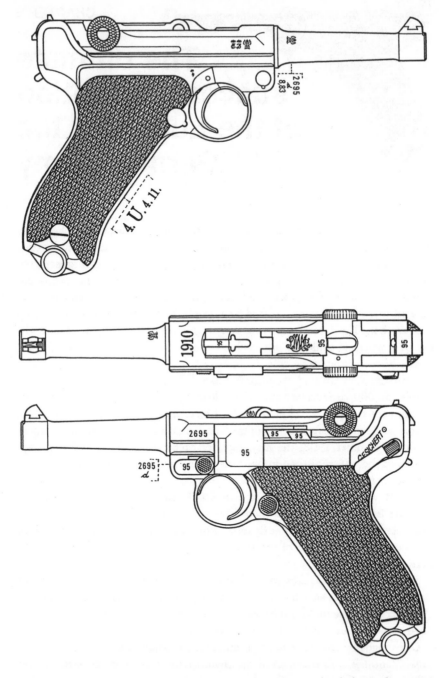

Fig. 12. The marks found on DWM-made Pistole 1908 no. 2695d, dating from 1910, were typical of those applied to German military Lugers prior to 1918. *John Walter.*

hardness-testing may have been undertaken in a single operation whilst DWM was the sole contractor, requiring only one inspector's mark, but the procedure was presumably revised once the Erfurt factory became involved. The earliest guns all lacked hold-opens and butt-heel lugs.

The perfected holster, the Pistolentasche 1908 or PT. 08, was formally approved on 4th April 1909. The flap was shaped to protect the pistol from rain, and closed by a strap-and-buckle. A pouch for the spare magazine and the cleaning rod was stitched onto the body-spine, whilst the turn-screw was carried in a compartment inside the flap.

Contracts for the holsters were placed with the leatherworking trade, but deliveries of guns rapidly outstripped consignments of holsters. Consequently, on 13th March 1910, conversion of 1891-pattern revolver holsters was approved. This entailed adding a protective flap, complete with turn-screw compartment, removing the cartridge pouch from the front of the holster body, and stitching a pouch for the magazine and cleaning rod onto the spine. The converted holsters often display nineteenth-century dates and a selection of obsolete unit markings.

Ammunition was initially delivered exclusively by the Deutsche Waffen-und Munitionsfabriken factory in Karlsruhe. The rimless straight-sided brass cases were loaded with a flat-nose nickel-jacketed bullet, containing a hardened core of lead with a small admixture of antimony. The first cartridges to be made in the Prussian munitions factory in Spandau, dating from 1909, were distinguished by 'S' in their headstamps.

Chamber-dating was introduced in 1910, when the inspectors' marks were transferred to the front right side of the receiver to allow the serial number (without the suffix letter) to take their place on the left. The quantity made in 1909 has never been confirmed, though 17,684 guns were delivered in 1910 and 28,040 in 1911.

Pistolen 1908 were issued in April/May 1909 to the independent machine-gun detachments and the machine-gun companies of the infantry regiments, then to the reserve and supplementary machine-gun units in July. The infantry, riflemen, pioneers, train and telegraph units received their pistols in October/November 1909 – accounting for all the initial deliveries, so that cavalrymen had to wait until October 1910 to receive their first pistols. By March 1911, however, issues to the cavalry were complete; and the foot artillery and the airship detachments had begun to receive their Lugers. Distribution to the field army had been completed by the end of 1911.

Proof and inspection procedures

Official manuals such as *Vorschrift zur Untersuchung und Abnahme von Pistolen 08 und deren Teilen* ('Inspection and acceptance of Pistols 08 and their parts') and *Vorschift für die Stempelung der Pistole 08 nebst einer Zeichnung* ('Regulation how to

Panel Six

PROOF AND INSPECTORS MARKS, 1911

The pistols were assembled and blued, but then dismantled to enable the parts to be gauged. Most of the pieces were assessed by eye, though critical dimensions were checked with special measuring equipment. The parts had already been numbered. The *Vorschrift* indicates their prescribed positions, '26a' on the drawings; the full number was stamped on the receiver, the frame and the barrel, with the last two digits on the breech-block, the extractor, the striker, both toggle links, the hold-open (if present), the dismantling catch, the trigger, the trigger-plate, the sear-bar, the safety-bar, the safety lever, and both grips. Final assembly was then checked by a government inspector and signified by the central of the three crowned-letter marks on the front right side of the receiver.

Once the guns had been dismantled, specific tests were undertaken. 1, the installation of the barrel was checked. 2, the milling of the front sight was approved. Inspectors approved the hardness of 3, the receiver; 4, the ejector; 5, the sear bar; 6, the breech-block; 7, the ejector; 8, the striker; 9, the firing-pin spring retainer; 10 and 11, both toggle links; 12, the spring lever; 13, the spring connector; 14, the spring guide; 15, the frame; 15a, the hold-open if present; 16, the locking bolt; 17, the trigger; and 18, the trigger lever.

Once this work had been satisfactorily completed, the principal inspector's mark 3 was struck into the receiver – the first of the three crowned letters struck into the front right side next to the proof eagle. The milling and fitting (19) of the trigger-plate was checked. The hardness of the magazine release (20) was approved. The assembly of the magazine was checked (21), the magazine base was stamped with the serial number (21a), and the base-piece was approved (21b). The hardness of the safety blade and lever was approved, 22 and 23 respectively. The fit of the grips was approved (24) and, lastly, the hardness of the grip screws was approved (25).

These parts all received crowned-letter marks. The 4.2mm version was restricted to the inside of the grips, whilst the 3.2mm pattern was struck into the barrel, receiver, breech-block, toggle links, frame, trigger plate, magazine and magazine base plate. The remainder were all 2mm types.

Re-assembled guns were fired with two super-power proof rounds to ensure they were sufficiently strong, whereafter the proof eagles or *Beschussadler* were struck into the top right side of the barrel, the front right side of the receiver and the left side of the breech-block (26b on the drawing). Two magazines – sixteen rounds – were then expended during a rapid-fire test and accuracy was assessed. Pistols that were acceptable received a third inspector's mark on the right side of the receiver (26c), nearest the proof eagle, and the land-to-land calibre was stamped into the underside of the barrel. Inspection marks were struck into the cleaning rod and turn-screw, and '+' was applied to the reserve magazine.

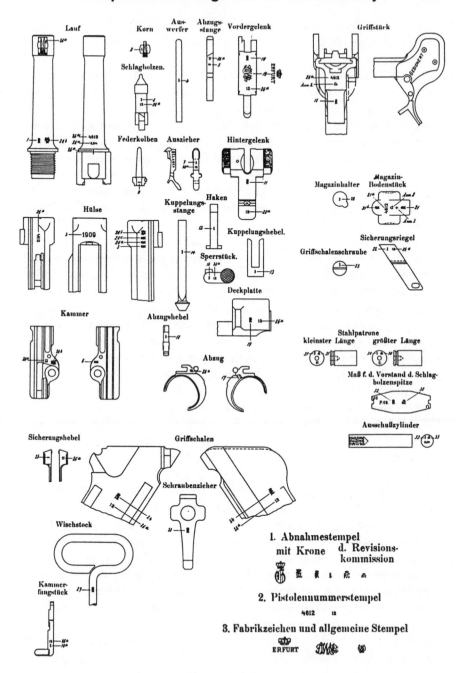

Fig. 13. These drawings show the application of the individual proof and inspectors' marks listed in the accompanying panel.

mark the Pistol 08, accompanied by a drawing') not only tell how the proof procedures were undertaken, but also identify the purpose of individual inspectors' marks.

The maker's markings, including the DWM-monogram trademark and ERFURT beneath a crown, were not precisely defined. However, there were prescribed sizes for the remaining marks. Crowned inspectors' stamps were basically tiny Fraktur letter punches. They were made in four sizes, though the 7mm-high pattern will not be found on the pistols. The remainder measured 4.2mm, 3.2mm and 2mm from the base of the letter to the apex of the crown.

Though they are difficult to read, these marks can often identify the origin and date of a German military Luger even though the chamber-mark has been erased.

Crowned-letter inspection marks have often been identified in North America as 'Contract codes' but the *Vorschriften* prove that they were applied specifically during proof and inspection. All the letters of the alphabet were used, excluding 'J', but the incidence of 'X' is surprisingly high and a few marks have been encountered with a bar beneath the letter. The bar and the 'X' apparently signify junior inspectors, but the methods of allocation are not yet known. Although attempts have been made to list the many letter-combinations found on Pistolen 1908 receivers, few have been satisfactory.

Most 1915-vintage Pistolen 1908 made by DWM display the same three letter-punches on the receiver side – 'H', 'S' and 'S'. Research undertaken by Horst Laumann, published in the *Deutsches Waffen-Journal*, shows that Oberbüchsenmacher Hoffmann was posted to Spandau in 1900 and Oberbüchsenmacher Schilling followed five years later. As Spandau was responsible for accepting the guns made in DWM's Berlin factory, links may exist between Hoffmann, Schilling and the Luger.

The appearance of the 4.2mm and 2mm crown/RC 'Revisions-Commission' marks in the 1910 regulations shows that these were not exclusive to post-1918 Allied commissions. The use of 'crown/RC' indicated an otherwise serviceable weapon that had failed inspection because of poor tolerances or minor external flaws. Rejected by the inspectors, these were submitted to the Revisions-Commission for appraisal. Guns that were then accepted for service were specially marked to absolve individuals if parts subsequently failed in service.

Serial numbers could be either 1.5mm or 2.1mm high. The documents reveal that guns were numbered in blocks of 10,000 – not 9999 – using a cyclical system in which suffix-letters distinguished successive blocks. The first 10,000 guns had plain numbers, the second series had an 'a' suffix, progressing thereafter as far through the alphabet as necessary. The letter 'j' was not used. Guns were apparently numbered on the basis of calendar years, though the governmental fiscal year ran from 1st April to 31st March.

The proof eagle was 3.2mm high and 2.9mm wide. There was a marked difference between the eagles applied by DWM and Erfurt, the latter, with an orb and sceptre, being more obviously Prussian in style. Owing to the short life of marking dies, many minor variations in detail will be found. The date, 3.2mm high by 9mm wide, appeared above the chamber after 1910. The *Vorschrift* also provides methods of distinguishing guns which had been refurbished from those that had been assembled from old parts. The former were to display dates such as '1909/13' over the chamber, the two additional 2.1mm digits showing the year of reconstruction; the latter had reversed dates in the form '1913/09', indicating a pistol assembled in 1913 from unmarked parts which were four years old. Neither form is commonly encountered on Lugers, though some receivers made at the end of one year (and dated in batches) may have been assembled in the first few weeks of the next.

A small line, 3–4mm long, struck across the sight base and blade, showed the correct installation of the barrel and front sight. A similar system denoted the alignment of the barrel and receiver. The bore diameter was struck into the underside of the barrel in 1.5mm numerals, whilst a 2mm '+' identified the second, or reserve magazine.

Proof-firing was undertaken with a special cartridge, which developed appreciably greater pressure than normal. Some rounds are simply head-stamped BESCHUSS, whilst others, often headstamped normally, may display green primer annuli or green-lacquered case heads. They should never be fired under anything other than laboratory conditions.

The adoption of the Pistole 1908 by the German army assured the success of the Luger, but, as the magnitude of the initial order occupied production facilities almost to full capacity, export and commercial sales were restricted in 1909–14. The exact quantity of pistols delivered to the army prior to the outbreak of the First World War is not yet known, though 132,375 Pistolen 1908 were received from DWM and Erfurt in 1910–13 to add to the 21,000 DWM-made guns tentatively permissible from 1909 production.

Officers were expected to purchase their handguns privately, and so pistols will be found with five-digit numbers, commercial proofs, and additional military marks. In December 1908 the war department informed all high commands and the war ministers of the German states that officers' Lugers were to cost 47.50 Marks apiece, complete with turn-screw and accessories. The price of Erfurt-made guns had dropped to 40 Marks by April 1913.

Guns acquired privately from Erfurt – unlike those from DWM – came from the regular military serial number blocks and could not be distinguished from those of NCOs. In addition, officers promoted from the ranks of the senior NCOs and warrant officers could purchase their original service pistols on receipt of their commissions.

Trials and tribulations

Attention had been drawn by 1912 to premature explosions which had occurred while packed 9mm cartridges were being handled, and the depth of the anvil in the primer was reduced so that the primer could be seated deeper in its pocket. Hindsight also showed the error of omitting the hold-open, which kept the action to the rear when the last round had been fired and ejected, and so it was soon reinstated.

The war department published details of the hold-open 'fitted to Pistolen 1908 of recent manufacture' on 6th May 1913, simultaneously noting that the Erfurt factory had been instructed to transform existing guns once they had been collected. Ironically, the hold-open had been discarded at the army's request to simplify the basic Borchardt-Luger design.

Owing to the adoption of the Lange Pistole 1908 on 3rd June 1913, a stock lug was added to the butts of standard short-barrel guns delivered after 4th August.

Variations in the height of the front sight and a lack of adequate sighting-in before the pistols left the factory contributed to poor point-blank shooting. The fifty-metre distance for which the sights were supposedly set was found by experiment to vary between eighty and 120 metres, which was clearly unacceptable. Tests had shown that a front-sight height of 15.8 ± 0.3mm would regularise the optimum sighting range, so the war ministry decreed on 12th June 1913 that modification of sights and addition of hold-opens would be undertaken simultaneously. Pistols which already had a hold-open were to be re-sighted by regimental armourers.

The Erfurt factory was supposed to convert service weapons and then, from 27th September 1913, begin work on those that had been purchased privately. Early in September, the director of the Bavarian state rifle factory suggested to his quartermaster-general that pistols should be converted locally instead of shipped to Erfurt. It was suspected that Erfurt would commence making the Lange Pistole 1908 in November, and that conversion of the Bavarian service pistols would be delayed. Inquiries sent to Erfurt and DWM elicited such unsatisfactory replies that no decision could be made for some time. Lack of knowledge of the Luger in the Amberg factory was a major problem, even though it has often been mistakenly claimed that pistols were made there.

In October 1913, after more trials had been undertaken, the rifle-testing committee revised the height of the new front sight to 15.4 ± 0.3mm. By December, Amberg had calculated the costs of re-tooling and submitted that seven months would be needed to convert the Bavarian Lugers. The state authorities rejected the plans, instead approaching both Erfurt and Deutsche Waffen- und Munitionsfabriken to obtain comparative estimates. DWM replied that pressures of work made speedy co-operation impossible; Erfurt was unwilling to begin converting the weapons until August 1914.

On 9th February 1914 the Bavarians finally placed the order with Erfurt and eventually gathered details of 20,204 Lugers, 20,068 of which required conversion. Four hundred were officers' guns, which suggests that 6735 guns had been issued to each of the three Bavarian army corps. On the basis of this average, about 170,000 guns would have equipped the entire German army – the three Bavarian corps, nineteen from Prussia, two from Saxony and one from Württemberg. This accords reasonably well not only with known deliveries – 132,375 in 1910–13 alone – but also with the most recent attempts to analyse serial numbers.

The report of the Bavarian artillery depot in Landau makes especially interesting reading, as it records the individual numbers of 2556 pistols collected for conversion, which fall within the number ranges 20–9998, 74a–9888a, 15b–8635b and 9e–1783e. No guns were listed in the 'c' or 'd'-suffix blocks.

Officers' weapons purchased from DWM commercial stocks were numbered in the 39317–41849, 42216–44790, 48448–53341 and 55802–60310 blocks. A few others – 24, 42, 75, 2099 and 4815 – had probably been issued to men commissioned from the ranks, who had taken the option of purchasing their issue pistols at a reduced rate.

The Landau lists contain two numbers (1925 and 1937) which have apparently been duplicated: they may simply be transcription mistakes, as the figures are handwritten, but could equally reflect a mixture of DWM and Erfurt guns or identically-numbered guns from different production years.

Though the Bavarians had intended to collect their guns by 31st July 1914, the political situation deteriorated so rapidly that some units refused to surrender guns unless substitutes were available. Too few revolvers remained in store, so the Bavarian Lugers were never shipped to Erfurt.

German army Lugers manufactured prior to 1914 are still occasionally found without hold-opens, and it is tempting to speculate that these may be Bavarian. This could perhaps be confirmed by attempting to correlate unit markings.

The Bulgarian Pistolen 1908

Shortly before the outbreak of the First Balkan War in 1912, when Bulgaria, Serbia, Greece and Montenegro allied against Turkey, the Bulgarian army ordered 10,000 Lugers from DWM. The pistols were standard 1908-type New Models, lacking stock lugs, though distinctive lanyard rings were mounted on the left side of the butt behind the magazine knob cut-away. The DWM monogram was struck above the chamber and a simplified coat of arms appeared on the front toggle-link. Serial numbers ran inexplicably from 1 to 5000 and 1C to 5000C.

No sooner had peace been concluded than the Bulgarians, who had already suffered severely in the First Balkan War, rashly declared war on Greece and

Serbia in June 1913. The Bulgarian armies were speedily defeated by an alliance of Greece, Serbia, Romania and Turkey; some Bulgarian Lugers may have been captured by opposing armies, but none has been identified.

The Lange Pistole 1908

The war ministry had decided as early as 1907 to equip field artillerymen with long-barrelled pistols, which would replace not only existing revolvers but also the carbines. Once re-equipment with the standard Lugers had been completed, a team led by Hauptmann Adolf Fischer began development of a suitable derivative of the basic design.

On 3rd June 1913, the Lange Pistole 1908 (LP.08) was adopted for the armies of Prussia, Saxony and Württemberg. The order received Kaiser Wilhelm II's assent on 2nd July:

> In accordance with a report made to me, I approve adoption of a self-loading pistol with shoulder stock, a sample of which has been submitted to me, under the designation 'Lange Pistole 08'. Supplementary to my order of 22nd August 1908, I hereby order that the field artillery and the airmen are to be armed with the long pistol, depending on availability of funds. Additionally, the pistol may be used to equip fortifications...

The Bavarians received a copy of the Kaiser's order on 12th July 1913. On 1st August, however, the Bavarian war ministry referred several questions to the imperial authorities in Berlin. On 28th August, a reply stated that:

> Only the non-commissioned officers and mounted men of the infantry and artillery munitions columns, who have previously carried revolvers, are to be armed with the lange Pistole 08...
>
> It is not intended to introduce the lange Pistole 08 for mounted ranks and drivers of heavy artillery...
>
> The pistol will be carried in a holster, suspended over the left shoulder on a shoulder strap and fastened to the belt...
>
> The pistol will be made by the factory in Erfurt, as well as by private contractors. It is intended – as previously – to sanction manufacture when the needs arise. The deliveries will become known when the Erfurt factory has supplied estimates of production ... due on 1st November 1913...
>
> The price has been estimated at about 58 Marks for a pistol and its shoulder stock [the P.08 cost 47.50 Marks at this time], and about 11 Marks for the pistol holster...

Duly satisfied, the Bavarians adopted the LP.08 on 12th September 1913. Though Erfurt was ordered to begin production in November, problems with the hold-open and erratic sighting of the standard pistols delayed progress.

Work was deferred until February 1914, when 209,000 long-barrel Lugers were ordered for the field artillery, the airmen and some specialist ancillary units.

The first part of the contract – for 144,000 guns – was to be completed within five years, 75,000 being made in Erfurt and 69,000 by DWM. This would re-equip the standing army, after which 65,000 would be made in Erfurt for the supplementary (Ersatz) units, the Landwehr and the Landsturm, any remaining thereafter to be held in store. The total investment approached fifteen million Marks.

The LP.08 was standard in all respects, excepting its 20cm barrel and a tangent-leaf back sight which lay immediately ahead of the receiver. A small step was milled out of the front upper edge of the receiver to accept the back under edge of the sight-block; to simplify manufacture, this step was subsequently added to all Erfurt-made P.08 receivers, though it is rarely encountered on DWM-made examples.

The sight-leaves were graduated from 100 to 800 metres. The wartime pistol manual, *Anleitung zur langen Pistole 08 mit ansteckbarem Trommelmagazin*, stated that:

> ...on account of its high firepower and easy handling, when employed as a light carbine..., [the Lange Pistole 08] can be used effectively against 'head-size' targets at a distance of 600 metres. Accuracy to 800 metres is possible if the back sight is adjusted accordingly. When careful aim is taken, all targets will be hit at 200 metres. The bullet will penetrate French steel helmets at 800 metres...

Each pistol was issued with a special board-type butt-stock, to which a leather holster was fitted. The sights of most of the guns made prior to 1917 could be adjusted with set-screws and capstan tools, facilitating long-range shooting – though it is doubtful whether a 'head size' target could be engaged effectively at 600 metres under combat conditions.

Yet the long-barrelled Luger remained surprisingly popular with the artillerymen. Though undeniably more cumbersome than the standard pistol, it was handier than the bolt-action Mauser carbine and was also semi-automatic.

CHAPTER 10

The Luger in the First World War

The Germans made rapid progress in the opening phases of the First World War, moving through Belgium to outflank the French defences. Just when victory seemed ready for the taking, Russians impetuously invaded East Prussia and forced the Germans to retaliate. Men were withdrawn from Flanders, where the westward advance of the right flank, thus weakened, faltered against stubborn resistance offered on the Marne defensive line by French and British troops. The Germans were forced to turn short of Paris, losing the key to rapid victory. Though his generals were successful in the east, the Kaiser had been denied such a major goal that the war on the Western Front degenerated into stalemate.

Though nearly 200,000 Lugers had been made by August 1914, even a total of this magnitude could not equip the army and the reserve. Germany was to mobilise more than thirteen million men by 1918, so losses of men and matériel were commensurately large.

The last navy pistols

The commencement of the First World War found the imperial navy alarmingly short of Lugers – Kiel had 580 guns in store in September 1914, but only six in October. An entry in the day-book of the navy office weapons department, dated 6th November, notes that DWM was to supply 1500 guns in November, 500 in January 1915, a thousand in February, a similar quantity in March, and 1500 in April. Though these were simply projections, work on the navy Luger had clearly redoubled. Another 8000-gun contract had probably been placed at the end of October 1914.

A little under 6000 Pistolen 1904 were delivered to Kiel between March 1915 and August 1916, when 'orders were complete'. On 29th August 1916 the navy office gave Deutsche Waffen- und Munitionsfabriken a new order (W.III.19614) asking for the rapid delivery of 8000 new guns – hopefully beginning in October, at a rate of at least 800 monthly. Deliveries to Kiel in October 1916, however, amounted to a mere 200. A hundred more appeared in November, then 400 in December and 500 in January 1917. No guns were forthcoming in February, March or April – the last report is missing from the archives – but 300 arrived in Kiel in May. Deliveries continued in small batches of between sixty and 400 guns until September, then ceased again until, between 1st January and 30th December 1918, 4231 were inventoried.

These figures have been used to suggest that three orders for third-pattern navy Lugers were placed during the First World War: one in August 1916, another in March or April 1917; and a third in November 1917. The quantities remain unknown, as the delivery pattern of Lugers to Kiel, Wilhelmshaven, and the Bruges artillery depot (for the Marinekorps) is contested. On 1st February 1918, according to Hans Reckendorf in his book *Die Handwaffen der Koeniglich Preussischen und der Kaiserlichen Marine* (1983), the Marinekorps inventory stood at 10,728 pistols. However, it is not known how many of these were Lugers, or from where they had been supplied.

The army suspended the use of unit marks in November 1916, for the duration of the war, and it is assumed that the navy followed suit. This removed a helpful indicator of the quantity and distribution of weapons in the period under review. Inventory numbers on Kiel dockyard guns ('W.K. . .') run as high as 17,000 compared with about 9000 for Wilhelmshaven ('W.W. . .'), suggesting that about two-thirds of all pistols went to Kiel. Owing to the significance of this claim in any assessment of total navy Luger production, its acceptance still raises strong passions.

The navy pistols made during the First World War were similar to their predecessors, excepting that they had short frames. The chambers were usually dated 1916 and 1917, even though surviving inventories reveal that deliveries were still being made at the end of the war.

These Lugers are much less common than their army equivalents, though the relative scarcity cannot yet be calculated. Assessments have ranged from 66,750, offered by Pat Redmond in handwritten notes circulated privately in the late 1970s, to 104,500 suggested by Charles Kenyon in *Lugers at Random* in 1969. Joachim Görtz and Hans Reckendorf have often emphasised that even the lowest of these figures considerably exceeds the total predicted by surviving archives, allowing for the existence of contracts which have yet to be found.

If it can be legitimately assumed that the navy Lugers were delivered in unbroken number-sequences, production seems to have amounted to 74,950. However, as no guns have been discovered in the second-issue 'a'-suffix block, 64,950 may be more acceptable.

Only 16,000 Lugers are known to have been ordered by the navy from DWM, disregarding the semi-experimental or pre-production guns acquired in 1904–5. One 8000-gun contract was placed in December 1904 and a duplicate in February 1916. But at least one other order must have been placed between the completion of the first contract in the Spring of 1906 and the beginning of the First World War.

Deutsche Waffen- und Munitionsfabriken claimed in 1912 to have made 20,000 pistols for the navy by the end of the previous year. Most of the other figures contained in this particular document are reasonably accurate, which suggests that the navy total should also be accepted even if it included guns that had been ordered but not necessarily delivered. As only the original 8000-gun order is known from this period, a 12,000-gun discrepancy is immediately created.

There was clearly another order, perhaps dating from the wholesale expansion of the imperial navy begun in 1909. Eight thousand Lugers would scarcely have satisfied this 'Tirpitz Plan', for which, Joachim Görtz has calculated, a minimum of 12,700 were needed. By 1914, the oldest guns had been in service for seven years and replacements would undoubtedly have been needed for those that had been discarded. The trigger system and grip safety of the Luger were prone to damage..

Twelve thousand additional guns could easily have been ordered from DWM – possibly 8000 in 1909 and 4000 in 1911 – but deliveries extended into the first weeks of the First World War. An appropriation of 60,000 Marks in the budget for 1911 and a similar sum allotted in 1912 may have paid for some of these.

Document W Ib.15307 of January 1914 does not mention the existence of any guns other than those 'to be altered' – *ie* first-pattern guns with grip safeties. In addition, the navy was so desperately short of pistols that Lugers were being withdrawn from older vessels to enable new warships to be equipped as early as 1913.

A contract for the perfected long-frame guns, lacking the grip-safety mechanism, must also have existed. The discovery of original documents in German archives, especially monthly returns made by Kiel dockyard, have contributed greatly to assessments of naval pistol requirements. Though information about the North Sea station is still lacking, a navy office decree of 18th September 1905 confirms that Kiel issued handguns not only to land-based naval units in the Baltic, but also to all serving warships – apparently regardless of station. Wilhelmshaven was responsible for equipping the land-based units in the North Sea district.

The returns also suggest that the pistols delivered from 1st January to 30th April 1918, more than 4000 of them, were all dated 1917. This is confirmed by surviving third-pattern pistols, which are invariably dated 1916–17; the few reportedly dated 1918 have almost always incorporated a standard army-type receiver with distinctive inspectors' marks.

A combination of the comparatively small production total and the loss of so many guns during the war makes the imperial navy Luger a favourite with collectors. Individual guns are still occasionally retrieved from warship wrecks, though seawater is a poor preservative. Lugers retrieved from the sunken *U-51* are typical of these relics. Built in the Krupp Germaniawerft shipyard in Kiel, the 715-tonne submarine was commissioned on 24th February 1916. Returning to base from a North Sea patrol on 14th July 1916, *U-51* was torpedoed by the British submarine *H5* only four miles north of the Aussenjade lightship. The U-boat broke in half and foundered, taking with her Kapitänleutnant Walther Rümpel, three officers and twenty-seven men. Five men escaped as the vessel sank, but two subsequently died from exposure.

The wreck was found in 1960, buried in mud, and was raised in 1968. Inside the hull were the remains of twenty crewmen, two of whom appeared to have shot themselves in the head. One Mauser carbine and four navy Lugers were retrieved, though most of their small parts had rusted away. One pistol is now in the Schifffahrts-Museum in Bremerhaven and another is owned privately; the only decipherable marking on the latter is '1916' on the front-sight base.

The Pistole 1908 in the First World War

In return for a 50,000-gun order, DWM allowed the Prussian authorities to make the Luger in the Erfurt arms factory. A duplicate set of machinery was installed there in 1909–10. The primary aim was apparently to secure the future of government employees, and also to avoid relying on a single manu-facturing source which could be paralysed by strikes or lock-outs.

Panel Seven

ISSUE OF THE LUGER IN 1914

The following details are adapted largely from *Bewaffnung des Deutschen Heeres*, the 1914 edition being produced before the LP.08 was issued in large numbers. Most of the gunners, drivers and non-commissioned officers of the field artillery carried old M79 and M83 revolvers until sufficient long-barrelled Lugers or 9mm Mauser-Pistolen C/96 became available.

Artillery The NCOs and men of the field artillery all carried Pistolen 1908. In the foot artillery, however, issue was restricted to senior NCOs, standard bearers, and medical NCOs plus the junior NCOs, trumpeters and mounted men of the haulage sections.

Cavalry Pistolen 1908 were issued to NCOs, standard-bearers, trump-eters and medical personnel of the Prussian cuirassiers and mounted riflemen; Bavarian heavy cavalry, light horse and lancers; Saxon Guard

---

cavalry, carabineers, hussars and lancers; Württemberg dragoons and lancers. Issue to Prussian dragoons, hussars and lancers was similar, with the addition of the assistant trumpeters. Pistolen 08 were also issued to cavalry under-officers undertaking the duties of staff orderlies.

Independent machine-gun units   Lugers were issued to all NCOs, trumpeters, *Kapitulanten*, drivers, NCO armourers, stretcher-bearers and medical personnel.

Infantrymen   In Bavaria, Hessen, Mecklenburg, Prussia, Saxony and Württemberg, Lugers were issued to senior NCOs ranking above *Vizefeldwebel*; to standard bearers; to regimental and battalion drummers; to range-finder operators, stretcher bearers and medical orderlies; and to all ranks of the regimental machine-gun companies. The pistols were also issued to the non-commissioned officers schools.

Pioneers   Issues were restricted to NCOs ranking above *Vizefeldwebel*; to stretcher-bearers; to medical personnel; and to the drivers and *Fahnenschmiede* of the searchlight sections.

Riflemen and sharpshooters   were issued with Pistolen 1908 if they were senior NCOs ranking above *Vizefeldwebel*; standard-bearers; range-finder operators; stretcher-bearers; medical orderlies; or attached to the machine-gun companies.

Train   Pistolen 1908 were issued to the NCOs and men of the Sanitäts-Übungs-Kompagnien, part of the Train, but not to the district commands, craftsmen's units of the clothing depots, 'semi-invalid' units, or the disciplinary unit of the Guard Corps.

Transport and lines-of-communication troops   were divided into several differing categories. Only the senior NCOs of the railway units, transport sections and 'Trials company' carried Lugers, though issue among the telegraph troops was wider – to the senior NCOs and standard bearers of the regular units, plus the riding masters, riding under-masters, sergeants and under-officers of the radio-telegraph companies. All the NCOs and men of the haulage sections of the airship troops carried Lugers, whilst the pistols were also issued to all the NCOs and other ranks of the airmen units (Fliegertruppen).

When the First World War began in August 1914, production was still meeting demand. DWM is believed to have delivered about 208,000 guns by the time war broke out, with Erfurt contributing an additional 50,000.

The finish of Erfurt-made Pistolen 1908 rarely compares favourably with DWM examples, particularly towards the end of the war, but they are similarly efficient mechanically. Erfurt guns were all dated above the chamber, commencing in 1911, and crowned-letter inspectors' letters appeared alongside the military proof mark on the right side of the receiver. The proof mark was repeated on the barrel and on the breech-block.

A mystery is presented by the absence of properly authenticated Erfurt-made Pistolen 1908 dating from 1915, though the customary handful of guns with mismatched parts has been found. The factory may not have made pistols in 1915 (which is feasible, if unlikely); or, alternatively, the guns delivered in 1915 were actually dated 1914. Analysing serial numbers seems to show a tremendous increase in output in 1914 – so did the factory simply make more basic components than could be assembled, proved and finished in the relevant year?

The supply of 1916-dated pistols to the navy in 1917, and the use of '1917' on virtually all the guns delivered in 1918, could support the theory that Erfurt used an earlier date on 1915 deliveries. But very few Lugers were acquired by the German navy during the First World War compared with the needs of the army. Joachim Görtz has suggested that, as supplies of long-barrelled guns were only just beginning to reach the field artillery when the First World War began, so the Erfurt factory was ordered to complete all 1914-dated receivers in this form. This would account not only for the '1914' invariably encountered on Erfurt-made LP.08, but also for the absence of standard guns dated 1915.

Material found in the German archives indicates that Erfurt was supposed to deliver 12,000 P.08 and 26,000 LP.08 between 1st August and 31st December 1914; 10,000 P.08 and 34,000 LP.08 from 1st January to 31st March 1915; 10,000 P.08 and 35,000 LP.08 from 1st April to 30th June 1915; and 10,000 P.08 and 35,000 LP.08 from 1st July to 30th September 1915.

The emphasis given to the so-called artillery Luger in these figures is obvious, as they suggest that 42,000 standard and 130,000 long-barrelled guns were to be made in the period under review. Yet 30,000 10cm-barrelled guns should have been completed between 1st January and 31st December 1915; even assuming that some of these were dated 1914, why are no 1915-date P.08 to be found? The question still begs a convincing answer.

Ammunition

When the First World War began, supplies of ammunition from the DWM factory in Karlsruhe and the Spandau munitions factory had proved sufficient for peacetime purposes. Once fighting had begun in earnest, the war ministry faced serious problems; production soon failed to meet escalating demand and new contractors were sought.

By the autumn of 1914, the Bavarian government factory in Ingolstadt and the Saxon plant in Dresden had both begun to make 1908-pattern cartridges, the former loading ogival bullets from the commencement of production. The first consignments from Gustav Genschow arrived in the Spring of 1915, though work in the Ingolstadt factory ceased.

The material of the bullet core changed from hard lead to a softer material from 27th August 1915 onward, and the original truncated bullet gave way in 1916 to an ogival pattern. This change was made to forestall Allied propaganda claims that the flat-headed bullet infringed the Hague Convention.

Munitionswerk Schönebeck an der Elbe and Rheinische Metallwaaren- und Munitionsfabriken of Sömmerda made their first 9mm cartridges in 1916, being followed in 1917 by Munitionsfabrik Kassel, Heinrich Huck of Nürnberg, Oberschlesisches Eisenwerke, and Lindener Zündhütchen- und Patronenfabrik of Linden bei Hannover. The nickel-plating of the bullet was replaced by tombak alloy to conserve raw material, and, from 8th March 1917, the primer cup could be made from a cheap lead/zinc alloy.

Wartime Luger production

The demands of war outstripped production capacity so rapidly that a surprising variety of handguns found their way into official service. The war ministry investigated alternative sources of Lugers – the Bavarian state manufactory in Amberg, Waffenfabrik Mauser, and even Bosch in Stuttgart – but only Anciens Établissements Pieper of Herstal-lèz-Liége was recruited, to supply hold-opens, strikers, magazine followers, safety catches, triggers, trigger-plates and other small parts directly to Erfurt.

The Bavarian rifle factory in Amberg has been mistakenly linked with production of the Pistole 1908, possibly owing to the publication of a misleading line drawing in Fred Datig's book *The Luger Pistol*. In 1913, while considering the addition of the hold-open, the Bavarians had asked the Prussians for guidance as manufacture of the Pistole 1908 was 'unknown'. Though the Amberg factory may well have repaired Lugers issued in the Bavarian army, no genuine distinctively-marked gun has ever been found.

Mystery also surrounds the Lugers said to have been made in the Spandau factory in 1918, though at least one gun – no.12 – is dated 1917. Most of them are numbered in the 12–201 group, though the authenticity of at least two of these has been questioned; guns occasionally reported with suffix letters are almost certainly spurious, their origins betrayed by Erfurt-style proof marks.

Manufacture of the Luger was so complicated that only four sets of machinery were ever made. The oldest was owned by Deutsche Waffen- und Munitionsfabriken; originally installed in the Charlottenburg factory, it was moved to new facilities in the Wittenau district of Berlin in 1916 and eventually went to the Mauser-Werke factory in Oberndorf in 1930. The second set was installed in the Prussian rifle factory in Erfurt in 1909–10; sold to Simson & Companie in 1920, it was acquired by Krieghoff in the mid 1930s to guide retooling. The only other production line was installed in the Swiss federal arms factory in Bern in 1917 after deliveries of DWM-made Lugers had been stopped by the First World War.

The history of the production machinery has been established with sufficient accuracy to question the entire Spandau story. Where was the machinery obtained, and why was none found in the plant after the First World War? The most plausible solution is that, because Spandau was the headquarters of the Revisions-Commission, a few pistols were assembled with parts retrieved from pistols which had failed proof.

Most of the so-called 'Spandau' guns are based on DWM-made receivers, which can be identified by the 'crown/T/bar', 'crown/S', 'crown/S' inspectors' marks on the right side. Some guns have the 'crown/RC' mark of the Revisions-Commission; most have additional inspectors' marks on the receivers, suggesting that they may have undergone the second and third stages of proof again.

The dating of these Spandau Lugers is still open to dispute, owing to the mixing of parts. They were probably assembled in the early part of 1918, when every available serviceable gun was required for the Spring Offensive.

The experience of war

Except for the drum magazines, described below, the only significant alteration made to the Luger during the First World War was a modification to the sear bar. Deutsche Waffen- und Munitionsfabriken had made minor changes to the rear part of the frame and the return-spring housing in 1915, but these had been present on all Erfurt-made guns and could not be detected without removing the grips.

Protected by a patent granted to Luger on 1st April 1916 (no.312,919), the modified sear allowed the mechanism to be cocked even if the safety catch was applied. A similar modification was made to navy Lugers delivered in 1916–18. Georg Luger apparently received a ten-pfennig royalty on each gun fitted with the new-pattern sear, making him a sizeable fortune ... which post-war inflation soon reduced to almost nothing.

The revisions did not affect the official designations, though guns with modified sears were often described as 'with new pattern sear-bar' (*mit Abzugsstange neuer Art*) whilst unaltered guns became 'with old-pattern sear bar' (*mit Abzugsstange alter Art*).

The Luger performed well enough in service to earn the affection of the German soldiery, as long as it was kept reasonably clean. Fortunately, the distinctive roll-over top of the standard service holster gave excellent protection from the elements. The biggest problem was the exposure of the sear bar on the left side of the receiver where, according to Hugh Pollard in *Automatic Pistols*, it was 'free to clog'. Fortunately, the Luger was relatively easy to field-strip for cleaning. A light application of oil usually restored a gun to full working order, unless the mechanism had been immobilised by a broken part or a feed jam.

The Luger was a complex piece of machinery in which the triggers, sears and trigger-plates were often adjusted individually to ensure satisfactory operation. Though the major components were interchangeable, the fit of the smaller parts was less certain. Many lives were lost during the First World War as a consequence of mismatching parts. Colin Greenwood, editor of the British magazine *Guns Review*, records the following story:

> Years ago I purchased a Luger from an elderly man who had been a captain in the British Army in the First World War. He was in the trenches in France and during an attack a German officer came within a yard of him. The German pointed a four-inch barrel Luger at him and pulled the trigger.
>
> The gun didn't fire and he had time to hit back with a shovel. He brought the gun home and for the next 48 years it stood ... in his living room.
>
> When I got it home, I discovered why it didn't fire. All the numbered parts matched except the sideplate. Someone had assembled that pistol and put back the wrong sideplate. This mistake saved that British officer's life...

However, many German soldiers felt that the automatic pistol gave them an advantage over the British and French, who were usually armed with revolvers. The value of the pistol steadily declined as the trench-war stagnated, until the most experienced men – *Frontschweine*, the Germans called them – regarded a trench-club or a sharp-edged spade as its equal.

Owing to the absence of surviving records, it is difficult to gauge how many Lugers had been made by the end of the First World War, though estimates as high as two million have been offered. DWM's fiftieth anniversary souvenir, *50. Jahre Deutsche Waffen- und Munitionsfabriken*, states that 680,000 Pistolen 1908, Lange Pistolen 08 and (presumably) Pistolen 1904 were made between 1st August 1914 and the end of the First World War. If it can be accepted that about 208,000 had been made prior to August 1914 – criticism can be made – DWM's total production in 1909–18 was about 893,000.

All that can be said for Erfurt is that, based on an analysis of serial numbers, about 735,500 guns were made between 1911 and 1918. It is now believed that they were all numbered in the same sequence, reducing the totals predicted in *Luger* (1977) where it was assumed that the standard and long-barrelled patterns had been numbered separately.

The 'emergency pistols' or *Behelfspistolen*

Though DWM and Erfurt made more than 1.6 million Lugers, there were never enough of them to equip the burgeoning German armies and the authorities were forced to issue a range of inferior weapons. Losses in the First World War were prodigious; despite the acquisition of more than two million handguns, an inventory dated 1st February 1918 revealed that the field army (including the Marinekorps) possessed only 811,109 serviceable pistols, with an additional 228,032 on home service. Most of these 1,039,141 guns were Lugers, though a substantial number of auxiliary pistols or *Behelfspistolen* would have been included.

Pistols like the curious Langenhan FL-Selbstlader, the Walther Model 4 or the Beholla had been specifically designed to interest the army; other *Behelfspistolen* were purchased from commercial agencies in Germany and occupied Belgium. A particular favourite was the 7.65mm Dreyse, made in Sömmerda by Rheinische Metallwaaren- und Maschinenfabrik, which had served many policemen in Saxony prior to 1914.

Most of these low-power guns were issued to the Train and lines-of-communication units, freeing more powerful pistols for combat duties. *Preise für Pistolen und Revolver*, produced for the war ministry in August 1917 by the department responsible for procuring weapons and military equipment, lists acceptable designs ranging from the powerful 7.63mm and 9mm Mauser C/96 down to 6.35mm 'Liége pistols' (Lütticher Pistolen) – which included Bayard, Pieper, FN-Browning and other similar blowbacks. Those that were accepted officially bore crowned-letter inspectors' marks, though these were rarely present on pistols which had been purchased privately by individual officers.

The surviving Commission Revolvers were reissued – they were sturdy, if obsolescent – and a contract was let with Waffenfabrik Mauser in 1915 for at least 150,000 C/96 pistols chambering the 9mm service-pistol cartridge. This order had not been completed by the Armistice, the highest known number being 141007.

Acting in desperation, the Bavarian army purchased about 20,000 Repetierpistolen M 12 ('Steyr-Hahn') from Österreichische Waffenfabriks-Gesellschaft in Steyr. Ten thousand were delivered in April 1916 and 6000 in March 1918, but small-scale consignments were still being received in October 1918. Unfortunately, the unit-marking scheme was suspended in 1916 and the marks applied to the Bavarian Steyr-Hahn – if any – have not been identified.

Automatic Lugers

The Germans, like many other armies, had once been keen on the pistol-carbine concept. Cavalry and mounted artillerymen were usually equipped with bolt-action magazine carbines, but these were comparatively clumsy and slow-firing. Even the earliest navy Lugers accepted a shoulder-stock/holster combination.

They had 15cm barrels and adjustable two-position back sights in the hope that experienced marksmen would be able to hit man-size targets at 200 metres or more. Experiences with these guns in rebellions in German Africa in 1905–6 had been unhelpful, but the First World War belatedly confirmed the value of light automatic weapons.

The earliest known fully-automatic conversion was patented in the USA on 13th October 1914 by Manuel and Everardo Navarro of Celaya in Guanjuarto, Mexico (no.1,113,239). A sliding spring, retained by a screw, was attached to the sear-bar. In the retracted position, this fixture had no effect on the mechanism and the weapon functioned normally. But the thumb-screw could be moved back towards the toggle-grips, forcing the spring outward as the toggle dropped to push the sear-plunger inward and fire the gun. The firing cycle could only be interrupted by releasing the grip safety, as activating the tripping spring isolated the trigger lever.

At least one Navarro-Luger pistol must have been made to establish whether the action worked well enough to patent, but relying on the sear-block on the grip safety unit to double as an interruptor would probably have strained the components.

On 31th October 1916, Heinrich Senn was granted German patent 310,499 to protect his 'trigger system for Luger self-loading pistols'. Senn, a Swiss government arms inspector, had developed a novel sear-bar plunger which could be turned through ninety degrees to control the type of fire. Unfortunately, the trigger-plate had to be removed before a turn-screw or pocket-knife blade could be used to select the type of operation desired. As the lightweight handgun was impossible to control when firing automatically, Senn also developed a bipod, a water-cooled barrel sleeve and a curved box magazine holding twenty rounds.

A solitary 'Maschinenpistole 1908' was demonstrated to the rifle-testing commission in Spandau-Ruhleben in December 1917. The otherwise standard Luger action had been modified to fire automatically from 32-round drum magazines. Performance included groups measuring 43 × 55cm at 100 metres, 100 × 105cm at 200 metres, and 168cm square at 300 metres; fifty per cent dispersion from single shots fired at 100 metres had been 10 × 15cm.

The pistol was apparently to be issued with the cooling sleeve and pivot of the Parabellum light machine-gun so that the drum magazine lay to the left. Though one surviving long-barrelled gun has a special fore-grip, the trial reports suggest that the Maschinenpistole 1908 had a rifle-type stock similar, perhaps, to those of the Luger carbines made prior to 1914.

Fully-automatic pistols emptied their magazines so quickly that the chamber rapidly heated to a point where a round could ignite without the assistance of the firing-pin. As the Luger conversions were also difficult to control, owing to lack of weight, experimentation was soon abandoned.

The drum magazine

The Lange Pistole 1908 offered a reasonable compromise to the contradictory demands of light weight and a high fire-rate. Issued to field and garrison artillerymen, airmen and other specialised units from 1914, it could be used effectively – according to the training manual – against 'head size' targets at ranges as great as 800 metres. Though this claim was incredibly optimistic, the increased range of the long-barrel gun and high rate of semi-automatic fire made it popular with the men.

Its weakness was the eight-round magazine, which was adequate enough for normal purposes but far too small to suit the storm-troops. A solution was found in the Mondragon automatic rifle, a few thousand of which had been purchased from Switzerland in 1915. Their box magazines, far too small for air service, had been replaced by spring-driven drum units. Though complicated and delicate, these drums occupied much less space beneath the breech than a conventional box of similar capacity. If drum magazines improved the utility of the Mondragon in combat, reasoned the rifle-testing commission, then a similar accessory would enhance the long-barrelled Luger.

In *Luger* in 1977, the design of the 'snail' magazine was attributed to the Hungarians Tatarek and von Benkö on the basis of a British Patent sought in 1911. Research undertaken in Germany has since revealed the patentee of the Luger magazine to have been Friedrich Blum of Budapest, who received relevant protection – DRP 302,455, 305,074 and 305,564 – in 1915–16.

Associated with Edmund Tatarek, Franz Kretz and Bela von Döry in the design of a gas-operated rifle prior to the First World War, Blum may only have provided the financial backing necessary to promote an adaption of the Tatarek-von Benkö magazine. The most obvious improvements in the Blum patents are the telescoping winding lever and angled feed-way.

The 1908-pattern drum magazine (Trommelmagazin 1908 or TM.08) increased the cartridge capacity of the Luger from eight to thirty-two, with twenty rounds in the drum body and twelve in the box-like feed-way. A spring-driven follower pushed the cartridges around the helix in the drum and up through the pistol grip into the action.

The principal drum-magazine contractor was Gebrüder Bing AG of Nürnberg, Germany's leading manufacturer of tin-plate toys; Allgemeine Elektrizitäts-Gesellschaft (AEG) made some magazines in its Ackerstrasse factory in Berlin; and Vereinigte Automaten-Fabriken Pelzer & Companie of Köln, best known for coin-in-the-slot vending machines, was also recruited.

The earliest Bing magazines had plain bottoms and telescoping winding levers, the magazine-column bracket being retained by two screws. As the cartridges were fired, the winding lever, attached to the magazine-spring, pointed to numbers stamped into the drum body ('32', '27', '22', '17', '12') to show how many unfired rounds remained.

Service experience soon showed that these bodies were not rigid enough, and changes were made. The modified or second-type Bing magazine had a single annular reinforcing rib pressed into the top surface of the body. The twin-screw magazine-column brace was then replaced by an improved nut-and-bolt fixture. Magazines will occasionally be encountered with shortened magazine-column brackets, which were altered in the field to allow uninterrupted extension of the winding lever.

The third-pattern Bing magazine had a folding winding lever, which not only gave better mechanical advantage but was less prone to bending than the sliding design; the fourth pattern incorporated all the preceding improvements in addition to a new double concentric-ring reinforcement on the bottom plate.

Production of AEG magazines was brief, but may have introduced the magazine-body reinforcing ring and nut-and-bolt magazine-column bracket that characterised the second-pattern Bing TM.08. However, Allgemeine Elektrizitäts-Gesellschaft ceased work after less than 80,000 magazines had been made; Bing's total output was at least ten times this figure.

Gebrüder Bing products are marked 'B' (Bing) over 'N' (Nürnberg); AEG's display a quadruple-hexagon trademark; and the few said to have been made in Köln by Pelzer & Companie would have borne 'VAF' (Vereinigte Automaten-Fabriken) over 'C' (Cöln) – but no authentic Pelzer magazine is known.

Issued from 1917 onward in simple canvas or elaborate leather holdalls, drum magazines were accompanied by light tinplate or sheet-steel dust covers. The official manual, *Anleitung zur langen Pistole 08 mit ansteckbarem Trommelmagazin (T.M.)*, reveals that the 'magazine box' contained five drum magazines, a loading tool and ammunition. There is no evidence that unloading tools were ever issued during the First World War, though some were made during the Weimar Republic (see Chapter Eleven).

Many drum magazines were withdrawn in 1918, to be reissued with the Bergmann-Maschinenpistolen 18 (MP.18,I). These gained a collar-type adaptor around the feed extension. Concurrently, some LP.08 were withdrawn from the artillery and assault units for the crews of gunboats and inshore minesweepers, who valued the additional firepower. A few individual guns may display navy marks, though some will date from the Weimar Republic and others from the first months of the Third Reich.

A 100-round drum magazine was supposedly designed to accompany the long-barrelled Luger, but similar claims have been advanced for a large-capacity 'TM.18' destined for the Bergmann sub-machine-gun. It is doubtful whether anything other than a few prototypes were made. Even the standard 32-round TM.08 was difficult to load, and the additional weight of the loaded 100-round TM.18 would have been a great handicap.

At least one Luger was adapted for a 30cm Maxim-pattern silencer in 1916, special cartridges being made in small numbers. They retained the standard case, DWM 480C, but the propellant charge was reduced from 0.36gm to 0.25gm and the weight of the bullet increased to 9gm. The changes reduced the muzzle velocity of the close-range cartridge or *Nahpatrone* beneath the speed of sound, but restricted effective range to a hundred metres.

Pre-1918 unit markings

Lugers dating from the imperial era will often display unit markings on the front grip strap. Until the regulations governing their applications were suspended in 1916 for the remainder of the hostilities, the jumble of letters and numbers provided vital information about the unit in which the owner of the weapon served – and often, by implication, about the campaigns in which he had fought.

Unfortunately, unit markings are difficult to decipher, particularly as the regimental armourers often failed to follow the regulations accurately. Distinctions are often very subtle. The principal document governing the pre-1918 marks was *Vorschrift Über das Stempeln der Handwaffen* (D.V.E. 185 in Prussia, D.V. 448 in Bavaria) of 1909, though many amendments – *Deckblätter* – were issued as the structure of the army was revised.

The uneven distribution of the Luger suggests that some marks are relatively common whilst others are extremely scarce. No reliable assessment of desirability has yet been made, though it would have much greater significance for collectors than the current fascination for insignificant variations in the design of the proof-eagle punches. Unfortunately, many books are so unreliable that they have done more harm than good; one US publication, for example, purporting to deal with German unit markings, contains more than 400 spelling mistakes.

Honourable exceptions are *German Small-arms Markings from Official Documents*, painstakingly compiled by Joachim Görtz and Don Bryans, and the

---

Panel Eight

TEN TYPICAL PRE-1918 UNIT MARKINGS

The following markings have been taken from Lugers in the care of the Imperial War Museum, London, except for the first listed – from the collection of Gary Adkison – and the fifth and sixth, from details supplied by James Hellyer.

B.l.M.K.D.18   A 1910-vintage DWM-made gun no.4633c. An unusual mark signifying the eighteenth gun belonging to the light munitions column ('...l.M...') attached to the Bavarian ('B...') cavalry division

('...K.D.'). Marks of this type are much more commonly encountered on revolvers.

139.R.2.11   An undated DWM-made gun no.1279b, 1909. The eleventh gun on the inventory of the second company of the 139th Infantry Regiment (Königlich Sächsisches 11. Infanterie-Regiment Nr.139).

14.U.5.16   A 1910-dated DWM-made gun no.9085c. The sixteenth gun of the fifth squadron of the 14th Lancer Regiment (1. Hannoversches Ulanen-Regiment Nr.14).

J.R.72.1.12   A 1910-dated DWM-made gun no.5179b. This signifies the twelfth pistol of the first company of the 72nd Infantry Regiment (4. Thüringisches Infanterie-Regiment Nr.72). The prefatory 'J' was unnecessary, but popular.

164.R.M.G.45   A 1913-dated Erfurt-made gun no.8125a. The second gun of the machine-gun company ('...M.G...') of the 164th Infantry Regiment (4. Hannoversches Infanterie-Regiment Nr.164).

L.L.455   A 1916-dated DWM-made gun no.2626e. This highly desirable mark is believed to have been applied by the Feldtrupp für Lenkluftschiffe, the detachment responsible for the army's dirigibles. The unit was disbanded in 1917.

108.R.7.K.M.G.12   Found on 1913-vintage DWM-made gun no.214b. This complicated unofficial mark was applied by the machine-gun troop ('...M.G...') attached to the seventh company ('...7.K...') of the 108th Infantry Regiment (Königlich Sächsisches Schützen- [Füsilier-] Regiment Nr.108).

5.G.G.M.G.5   Found on a 1913-dated DWM-made gun no.84. The fifth pistol of the machine-gun company ('...M.G...') of Garde-Grenadier-Regiment Nr.5 ('5.G.G...').

15.H.5.8   On a 1910-vintage DWM-made gun no.4581d. This simply signifies the eighth gun of the fifth squadron of the 15th Hussar Regiment (Husaren-Regiment Königin Wilhemina der Niederlande [Hannoversches] Nr.15).

G.S.M.G.61   A 1913-vintage Erfurt-made gun no.5912. Applied by the machine-gun company ('...M.G...') of the guard sharpshooters battalion ('G.S...' for 'Garde Schützen').

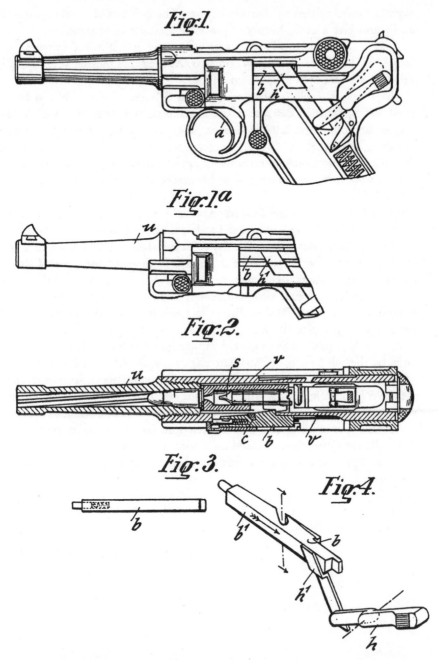

Fig. 14. Taken from German Patent 312,919 of 1916, these drawings show the modified sear, which allowed the Luger to be cocked even though the safety-catch was applied. *Deutsches Patentamt.*

bayonet books written by Anthony Carter. These deal with markings individually and give a useful history of pre-1918 German army structure.

Among the rarest pre-1918 Lugers were those issued in the colonies confiscated at the end of the First World War. As the scales of issue were so small, survivors are rare even in southern Africa.

There were sizeable 'protective forces' or Schutztruppe in German South West Africa, German East Africa and Cameroon; and lesser units such as the Polizeitruppe in German New Guinea, Togo and Samoa. The Schutztruppe markings are generally 'Sch. . .', accompanied by 'D.S.W.A.', 'D.O.A.' or 'K.', but the lesser organisations rarely applied distinctive marks. An exception was the rural gendarmerie – or Landespolizei – in German South West Africa.

The 1920 edition of the *Deutsches Kolonial-Lexicon* stated that, prior to the adoption of the Pistole 1908, the Landespolizei had used an assortment of German revolvers, Brownings, Webley & Scott pistols and the Roth-Sauer. This claim is supported by the existence of 7.65mm Roth-Sauer pistols with C-prefix numbers and Landespolizei marks, such as 'L.P.109.' on gun no.C559.

The non-standard guns were soon replaced by Lugers, surviving examples all emanating from the DWM or Erfurt factories in 1911. As the numbers of Erfurt-made examples all lack suffixes – *eg* 1091 on 'L.P.211.' and 1303 on 'L.P.3.' – they must be amongst the earliest government-made Lugers. Interestingly, they all have faint cross-hatching on the fluted safety-lever heads.

Property-mark numbers range from 55 to 237 on surviving Roth-Sauers and 3 to 396 on Pistolen 1908, which may suggest that several hundred of each were acquired.

Another rare mark is 'R.G.', encountered on Lugers issued to the imperial police (Reichs-Gendarmerie) raised for service in the Elsass-Lothringen district prior to 1914. The marks are usually found on the left side of the frame above the grip.

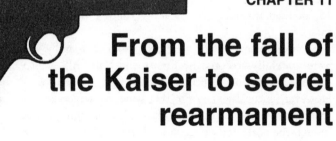

CHAPTER 11

From the fall of the Kaiser to secret rearmament

The collapse of order in Germany in 1918, typified by mutinies in the navy, forced the Kaiser to abdicate on 9th November. Power devolved in 1919 to a republican government. The state presidency was given to Friedrich Ebert, but even this failed to mollify the extreme elements in German political circles.

Left-wing Spartacists declared a short-lived independent socialist republic in Berlin, whilst less extreme 'democratic republics' were proclaimed in Bavaria, Saxony and Brunswick. The independent states were eventually subdued by the army and the Freikorps, tacitly supported by many high-ranking officers and much of the aristocracy.

The new constituent assembly met in Weimar in the spring of 1919 to create a federal Germany based on the new, less autocratic constitution. The political complexion of the Weimar Republic was much more liberal than the imperial regime had been, but was neither truly democratic nor socialist in character. Economic power was still concentrated in large industrial groups whose leaders, by and large, opposed what they saw as governmental acquiescence to Allied demands for compensation.

The Allies rapidly disarmed the Germans in the west whilst simultaneously encouraging German units to repel the Bolsheviks in the east. The history of the Freikorps raised in eastern Germany and the Baltic States is still poorly documented, but photographs exist of their soldiers carrying Lugers. Large numbers were navy pistols looted from Kiel dockyard in 1918. The *Totenkopf*, or death's head, insignia was particularly popular in the Freikorps.

Though supposedly free elections were held, stability was slow to return to public life. Not only was the presence of Allied occupation forces in western Germany bitterly resented, but the enforced detachment of Alsace, Lorraine, Upper Silesia, West Prussia and North Schleswig also substantially reduced production of coal and iron-ore.

The terms under which Germany could continue to exist had finally been agreed in Versailles on 28th June 1919. The armed forces were limited to 100,000 men, restricting their role to passively guarding borders or maintaining internal security. The air force was disbanded; armoured vehicles and chemical weapons were prohibited. The once-powerful navy was reduced to 15,000 men, manning obsolescent warships armed with nothing more powerful than 28cm guns.

Serviceable small-arms were often sold to friendly states, whilst warships were gratefully accepted by France and Italy. Allied inspectors collected the enormous total of 4,560,861 small arms, all but 6000 being destroyed. However, inconsistencies in the issue of weapons soon became evident. Handguns had originally been deemed too insignificant to control, but, even though the army and police needed them to maintain internal security, it was soon obvious that issue could not be allowed to rage unchecked.

No sooner had the signatures dried on the Treaty of Versailles than clandestine arms development began in Germany. The first steps were to acquire interests in shipyards in the Netherlands, the Bofors arms-making company in Sweden, and engineering companies in Switzerland, allowing development to be undertaken away from the prying eyes of Allied investigators. Agreement reached between Germany and the USSR in 1922 included the creation of an 'experimental agricultural station' in Kazan, where armoured vehicles could be developed in secret.

German technicians were making munitions in Russia and Hungary in the mid 1920s; overseeing the construction of submarines in the Netherlands, Finland, Spain and Turkey; developing tanks and armoured vehicles in Kazan; and training a secret air force in the skies above the Russian Steppes. However, as the development of new small-arms was accorded low priority, the Mauser rifle and the Luger pistol soldiered on.

Though the collapse of the Reichsmark delayed progress, the ailing economy was subsequently rebuilt by periodic injections of American capital until the disastrous crash of Wall Street in 1929. Even this catastrophe, which caused mass unemployment in Germany in the early 1930s, failed to halt the march of the military machine.

The first Weimar Lugers

According to the *Heeres-Verordnungsblatt* of 24th December 1919, Lugers or permissible substitutes were to be issued to all officers, senior NCOs, music masters, battalion drum-majors, armourers and armourers' assistants, senior cavalry NCOs, medical NCOs, farriers, stretcher-bearers, drivers and grooms; to corporals of the artillery, cavalry, transport and signal troops; to the gun commander and two gunners of each light machine-gun in the appropriate units; to the gun-commander and four gunners of each heavy machine-gun in the appropriate units; to a quarter of the authorised NCOs and other ranks of the infantry, riflemen (Jäger), sharpshooters (Schützen) and pioneer companies; and, for special projects, to a quarter of the authorised other ranks of the cavalry squadrons. The *Heeres-Verordnungsblatt* of 20th May 1921 gave scales of issue ranging from just twelve guns for the staff of an infantry commander to 585 for each transport-detachment depot.

The armed forces inventory sanctioned by the Allies was boosted by secretly stockpiling weapons; in 1928, for example, there were 95,032 handguns (mostly P.08), but 49,679 of them had not been declared. These were known as 'Black Weapons' (*Schwarzwaffen*), but are now generally classed amongst the many refurbishments as they generally retained some of their pre-1918 markings. Guns in the hands of the police were accounted separately, though probably only part of the real totals were disclosed.

Demilitarisation of the Erfurt small-arms factory and the eclipse of DWM left the Germans without a source of new Lugers. Even the Allies were persuaded that small-scale production was necessary to replace guns that were damaged in service or had simply worn out. Attrition had been assessed at a thousand guns annually. The Spandau factory was initially permitted to refurbish wartime guns, though the needs of the 100,000-man army were not particularly large. Ten thousand guns could be held in a strategic reserve, and the numerous state police forces could acquire Lugers of their own.

Refurbished guns of the so-called 'Double Date' variety have two dates above the chamber, one between 1910 and 1918 and the other reading '1920'. The explanation is found in the collapse of order in Germany immediately after the end of the First World War, which was accompanied by extensive looting of military stores to arm socialist revolutionaries on one side and the right-wing Freikorps on the other. As a rapid return to normality was desirable, concerted efforts were soon made to remove weapons from public circulation.

On 1st August 1920, therefore, the high command of the armed forces ordered that all small-arms and relevant accessories should be given new property marks in addition to their manufacturing dates. The goal was to identify guns which were subsequently stolen, particularly as, on 7th August 1920, parliament passed the 'Disarming of the People Law' requiring civilians to surrender firearms and accessories which had once been military. Amnesty was to run from 15th September 1920 to 28th February 1921.

The new mark was to be '1920', struck in numerals 3.1mm high. This is the only known example of a date serving as a property mark, and has no connexion with the 'Allied Control Commission' or any other agency supervising the issue of weapons in Germany. It was applied to all the Maxim machine-guns, Mauser rifles and carbines, the anti-tank rifle, the Bergmann sub-machine-gun, all Lugers, substitute handguns, bayonets, sabres and cavalry lances.

On 28th September 1920, the armed forces ministry confirmed that only army-property weapons were to be marked, privately owned officers' weapons being exempted from the programme. The service handguns were listed as the revolvers of 1879 and 1883, long- and short-barrelled 1908-model Lugers (but not the navy pattern), and the '10-shot 9mm Mauser-Pistole with shoulder stock'. Surviving *Behelfspistolen* were also to be stamped; though no details of individual patterns were given, the drawings accompanying the pronouncement showed a Beholla.

The Lugers were usually marked over the chamber above the original date, though some depots ground the previous marking away so that '1920' could be placed exactly in accordance with the official drawings. The LP.08 shoulder stock was to have been marked on the left side but, before the orders could be executed, the Allies outlawed the anti-tank rifle, the sub-machine-gun and the long-barrelled Luger in the armed forces. Refurbished handguns can be distinguished in other ways: for example, most of the parts usually display pre-1918 proof, inspectors' marks and serial numbers.

The interim '1920' was abandoned when unit markings reappeared from 9th April 1921 onward. However, a few guns delivered during the early months of 1921 – whether newly made or refurbished is questionable – displayed '1920' and '1921', the former being the property mark and the latter the actual date of manufacture.

Stockpiled wartime ammunition fulfilled the needs of the armed forces and police in the early months of the Weimar Republic, though it was obvious that production would have to recommence. In 1920, conscious of dwindling stores, the Allies allowed Deutsche Werke Aktiengesellschaft (the commercialised remnants of the Spandau small-arms and munitions factories) to prepare for production. The headstamps of the few surviving cartridges from this era indicate delivery between September 1920 and January 1921.

Article 168 of the Treaty of Versailles, accepted by the German government in May 1921, contained a list of the companies which could make arms and ammunition under Allied supervision. Many of the leading manufacturers were effectively banned from their once-lucrative activities. Only Krupp was allowed to make guns with a calibre greater than 17cm, the smaller ones being the prerogative of Rheinische Metallwaaren- und Maschinenfabrik (later Rheinmetall). The production of small-arms ammunition was restricted to Polte-Werke in Magdeburg, whilst DWM, renamed Berlin-Karlsruher Industrie-Werke AG in 1922, was prevented from making Mauser rifles or Luger pistols.

Luger production begins again

Realising that newly-made pistols would eventually be needed, the Allies permitted Simson & Companie of Suhl to purchase the Luger-making machinery from the Erfurt small-arms factory for 821,000 Reichsmarks. Simson thereafter undertook the refurbishment that had previously been the prerogative of Spandau, enabling the latter to be demilitarised, though no new guns were made in Suhl until 1925.

On 26th July 1923, the management of Berlin-Karlsruher Industrie-Werke AG, as DWM had become, offered the armed forces ministry 8000 7.65mm

1908-type Parabellums, presumably assembled from some of the pre-1918 parts. Owing to rampant inflation, BKIW would guarantee to hold the price of 1,475,000 Marks only until the end of the week. By 31st July, the price had inflated to 2,880,000 Marks for 3000 guns. These were purchased in 1923–4, the first thousand being delivered early in December 1923. Six thousand additional 10cm 9mm-calibre barrels were also acquired, presumably to convert not only the 7.65mm guns but also surviving navy and long-barrel guns to P.08 standards.

Some writers have suggested that the apparent disappearance of 5000 Lugers explains the so-called 'Vickers' delivery to the Netherlands Indies Army, but the missing guns had probably gone to Finland.

Simson & Companie delivered the first new guns made on the ex-Erfurt machinery in this period, 3000 being accepted in 1925 and a similar quantity in 1926. They displayed SIMSON & CO./SUHL on the toggle links, were dated above the chambers, and had distinctive proof and inspectors' marks.

The guns refurbished under Allied supervision, in addition to the small numbers purchased from BKIW and Simson & Companie, satisfied the immediate needs of the armed forces. Once the Allied enthusiasm for regulation waned, militarism began to grow once again. Inspired partly by an officer class which could not forgive politicians for capitulating in November 1918, and partly by those who wished to return Germany to its former glory, it was initially well hidden. One effect was to accelerate the secret stockpiling of weapons, including very many refurbished Lugers. These can be identified by their marks, as the army weapons office (Heereswaffenamt) had replaced the inspectorate of weapons and equipment in 1925.

Interest in fully-automatic pistols was kept alive in the 1920s, a suitable Luger conversion – relying on a modified sear bar and a selector in the trigger-plate – being patented by Stanislaw Gurtys of Posen in 1926 (no.492,136). No gun of this type seems to have survived, though Fred Datig, in *The Luger Pistol*, reported one displaying similar characteristics.

Machine-guns and sub-machine-guns were secretly developed in Switzerland in the late 1920s, but little was done to replace the P.08, though several commercially-available guns had been tested by the authorities from August 1927 onward. Typical of these was a 7.65mm blowback submitted in May 1930 by Franz Stock Maschinen- und Werkzeugfabrik of Berlin-Neukölln, which was considered to be insufficiently powerful even though it had 'lain well in the hand, [had] good shooting safety, and no stoppages'. Consequently, the Parabellum remained the standard service pistol until the advent of the Walther Heeres-Pistole in the late 1930s.

Lugers issued to the army during the Weimar Republic can often be identified by unit markings stamped into the front grip-strap. The earliest instructions were published in the *Heeresverordnungsblatt* on 9th April 1921, though the marks, which were temporary, consisted simply of the company and individual weapon numbers (*eg* '2.25.'). A draft of the finalised regulations appeared in November 1922, to be followed in 1923 by *Vorschrift Über die Stempelung und die Bezeichnung von Waffen und Gerät bei der Truppe* (H.Dv.464). These documents allocated abbreviations to each of the many classes of military unit.

The Police Lugers

The German state police were allowed to retain their sidearms in the immediate post-war period, when the political situation was so unstable that violence had spilled over into civilian life. However, though it is believed that the inventories were initially supervised by Allied inspectors, secret stockpiling of so many handguns make scales of issue impossible to determine.

Though Lugers predominated, 7.65mm Sauers were used in Prussia and Bavaria whilst the 7.65mm Dreyse had always been popular in Saxony. By 1930, however, the P.08 had become almost exclusively the weapon of uniformed officers. Pre-1918 military weapons refurbished by the police can usually be distinguished by supplementary proof, inspection and unit marks, even though precise details may be difficult to catalogue.

The oldest guns will often display the '1920' permission-date in addition to – or sometimes replacing – the original marking. Towards the end of the Weimar period, however, new guns were assembled by Mauser from existing DWM parts. Their toggles were often deliberately left blank and their serial numbers usually lay in the 's', 't' or 'u'-suffix blocks.

An early indication of safety problems will be found in an order prohibiting 7.65mm and 9mm Lugers being carried whilst cocked and loaded, published in the *Ministerialblatt für die Preussische innere Verwaltung* on 13th June 1923. The 7.65mm Sauer was also affected, the only specific exclusion from the restriction being the Mauser C/96. It is suspected that shots had been fired accidentally after magazines had been removed, without ensuring the chamber was empty, or when the trigger plate of a loaded gun had been removed for cleaning without uncocking the striker.

The concern over safety began a search for an effective safety system. Many inventors produced satisfactory, but often unnecessarily complicated designs in 1929–33, but few were ever made in quantity. The police do not seem to have accepted the Schiwy sear safety until the early days of the Third Reich, so details will be found in Chapter Thirteen.

Though the long-barrel Luger was rarely seen in police hands, the drum magazines were issued with the Bergmann sub-machine-guns. When Haenel developed straight magazines for the MP.28,II, surviving TM.08 were returned to store in the early 1930s. They were accompanied by accessories including a few unloading tools, converted in police armouries from pre-1918 loaders and sometimes mistakenly associated with the Luger. Semi-official status explains not only their comparative crudity but also the unexpected diversity of design.

Police markings of the Weimar era

These are commonly encountered on guns surviving from the 1919–45 era. Amongst the earliest were those applied by the Polizeiwehr Bayerns, a short-lived para-military group quickly suppressed by the Allies. Instructions published in May 1920 indicated that guns were to be marked 'Pw.B' with a suffix indicating the individul unit; 'Pw.B. 4 102', therefore, signified the 102nd gun issued to the fourth precinct.

Regulations published in Prussia in April 1922 reserved prefix letters 'S' for Schutzpolizei, 'P' for the police schools, and 'L' for the air-surveillance detachments; 'S.Ar.II 2.15.', therefore, was the fifteenth weapon issued to the second precinct of the second district of the Arnsberg area command. Berlin was divided into districts and groups, 'S.B.S. I 1.10.' being the tenth gun issued to the first precinct in the Linden ('I') district of Schutzpolizei Berlin, Gruppe Sud.

The Bavarian Landespolizei, according to documents dating from September 1930, applied distinctive marks in the form 'M.5.15' (the fifteenth gun issued to the fifth precinct of the München district) or 'N.N.A.30.' for the thirtieth gun issued to the training section of the Nürnberg-Fürth district Nachrichtentechnische Abteilung or communications squadron.

By 1932, the Prussian system had been refined to distinguish Kriminalpolizei, Schutzpolizei and Landjägerei (known prior to 26th June 1920 as the Landgendarmerie), which were responsible for investigation, urban areas and rural districts respectively. Their prefix letters were predictably 'K', 'S' and 'L', though they were often combined with additional information: 'S.Br.II.15.' was the fifteenth gun issued to the second ('II') district of the Schutzpolizei Breslau.

Care is often needed to distinguish between similar letter-groups – 'L.S.' represented the Schneidemühl district of the Landjägerei whereas 'LS' was a Landjägerei school. Other marks included 'HP.' for the Höhere Polizeischule (central police school) in Berlin; 'PTV' for the Polizeischule für Technik und Verkehr (police institute for technology and transport) in Berlin; and 'RhP.' for the Rhine river police.

The use of 'S.D.' and 'S.S.' – the marks of the Schutzpolizei in Düsseldorf and Schneidemühl respectively – are still widely misrepresented as 'Sicherheitsdienst' or 'Schutzstaffel'. Collectors worldwide seem to be very reluctant to accept the truth.

Export Lugers

The disfavour in which the Allies held DWM, or BKIW as the company had become in 1922, restricted exports. However, a link with Vickers circumvented the Versailles treaty restrictions, whilst the guns despatched to Finland attracted little notice. BKIW did not actively pursue contracts of this type until the Inter-Allied Control Commission had withdrawn from Germany in 1927.

The Netherlands   An intriguing problem is presented by the several thousand M11 pistols supplied by Vickers Ltd for the Netherlands Indies Army. It has even been claimed that these purchases date from 1915–17, overlooking not only that Britain and Germany were at war but also that there was an effective maritime blockade!

The solution to this conundrum lies in the links forged in the nineteenth century between Ludwig Loewe & Co. and the Maxim-Nordenfelt Guns & Ammunition Co. Ltd. When the First World War ended, the succesors of these partners, Vickers Ltd and Deutsche Waffen- und Munitionsfabriken, entered into a dispute over royalties due on German-made Maxim machine-guns. J.D.Scott, in *Vickers: A History* (1962) revealed that Vickers pressed claims against both DWM and Krupp, the former replying with a £75,000 claim for 'foreign territory' royalties due under an agreement reached in 1901. The case was ultimately dropped, DWM accepting an out-of-court settlement of £6000, but Vickers paid £40,000 to Krupp against a claim of £260,000 for the unauthorised use of German patents in the manufacture of fuzes.

Vickers had been DWM's agent in pre-war dealings with the British government and the two companies had a complex interwoven ownership prior to 1914. The catalyst is now known to have been Dipl.-Ing. Johannes Holl, a director of DWM, who transferred to Vickers an order placed in 1919 by the Dutch colonial ministry. The Germans were prevented from supplying the handguns by the Treaty of Versailles, whilst Vickers may have been glad of profitable work at a time when arms production in Britain had virtually ceased.

Negotiations began with the Nederlandsch-Engelsche Technische Handel Maatschappij of 's-Gravenhage, which represented Vickers in the Netherlands. A contract for 6000 handguns was signed in December 1919, followed by another – apparently for spare parts and accessories – in August 1920.

The components of the Vickers Lugers were all made by DWM, shipped to England in the white to be assembled, proved and finished in the Crayford factory. No objections were raised to pistols made in Britain, even though it must have been obvious that Vickers could not possibly have built an entire production line in such a short period. The pistols were shipped to the Netherlands in April–May 1921, apparently without the wooden grips. Most of these were made in the Geweermakersschool in Batavia, where the Vickers Lugers arrived in November 1922. The quality of Vickers' worksmanship was so poor that the Dutch apparently sent the guns across the border into Belgium, where they were checked by Fabrique Nationale d'Armes de Guerre.

These Lugers were distinguished by VICKERS/LTD. on the toggle, British proof marks, GELADEN on both sides of the extractor, and the arrow/RUST mark in the safety-lever recess. The pre-1918 origins of many components were betrayed by marks such as 'C/15' or 'C/16'. These were originally regarded as date-marks – being typical of German naval pattern – until 'C/22', 'C/24' and others were found. It seems likely that they identify sub-contractors; in common with almost all large-scale arms makers, DWM undoubtedly bought-in minor components such as screws, pins and springs.

The barrels of NIL Lugers often bear the date of replacement, which was undertaken regularly in the East Indies, but an examination of the guns owned by the Imperial War Museum in London suggests that even the original barrels may have been marked.

The colonial ministry bought 6000 guns for the East Indies, numbered 4182–10181, and a few – perhaps twenty, numbered from 1 – for service in the West Indies. As some guns were retained for presentation or promotional purposes, Vickers probably assembled about 6050 Lugers. One gun, no.10184, survives, with a suite of accessories, in a specially made case with 'V' within a naval crown on the lid-escutcheon; it also bears SAFE and LOADED instead of the Dutch marks. The highest number reported on a Vickers Luger is currently 10206.

The NIL Lugers issued to NCOs and men often bore unit markings. These had been struck into the frame above the lanyard ring prior to 1919, but were subsequently applied to small brass plates soldered on the front of the trigger-guard bow. The abbreviations gradually became so complicated that, from 1937, much larger plates – 10mm wide by 50mm long – were supposed to appear under the guard. However, none of these survive. In 1939 the marking-plates were enlarged and placed on the left side of the frame above the grip. A typical example on Vickers-made Luger no.9214 reads '10-6 R.I./16', signifying the sixteenth gun issued to the tenth company of the sixth infantry regiment; 'Mgd.Mgl./145' was the 145th gun issued to the medical corps based in Magelang hospital. A comprehensive list of these abbreviations will be found in *The Dutch Luger* by Martens & de Vries (1994).

The last of the 1911-type NIL Lugers were delivered from BKIW in August–September 1928. They were identical with previous guns, except in purely minor details, but had a new-style sear. The DWM monogram was retained on the toggle and standard crown/N proofs were used, but the crowned script 'W' inspector's mark was replaced by an encircled 'KL' monogram on the front right side of the receiver. This has often been attributed to the Royal Netherlands Air Force (Koninklijke Luchtmacht), but it is more probably 'KL within O' for Kolonien. A total of 3820 guns were purchased for the NIL, numbered 10182–14001; nineteen (14002–14020) were subsequently purchased for service in the Netherlands West Indies, where, according to a handgun inventory, eighty-eight M1911 Lugers were serving in 1941.

The navy Lugers were issued as the 'Pistool Automatisch No. 1 (Parabellum)', a designation originally applied to forty German navy Lugers acquired in the Spring of 1918. The principal difference between the NIL consignments and the No.1 pistols supplied by BKIW from 1928 onward concerned the safety arrangements, as the navy accepted a standard 1908-type gun. Owing to the elimination of the grip mechanism, the operation of the safety lever was reversed; the arrow accompanying RUST in the safety-lever recess of the No.1 points downward instead of up.

The first consignment was despatched from Berlin in May 1928 and, by the time production was moved to Oberndorf in 1930, 1484 pistols had been delivered. Numbered from 1, they had the DWM monogram on the toggle, GELADEN on both sides of the extractor, and arrow/RUST safety-lever marks. The guns delivered by Mauser prior to 1936 (numbered from 1485 to 2129) retained the DWM banner on the toggle, but their proof marks changed from 'crown/N' to 'crown/crown/U'. The subsequent Mauser-banner guns are described in Chapter Thirteen.

A few of these Lugers will be found with 'K.M.' property marks, which are believed to have been applied by the navy (Koningklijke Marine) to guns held aboard warships serving in the East Indies.

The Luger was used by several Dutch police forces in the early 1920s – guns exist marked POLITIE ROTTERDAM – and also by the home guard. In 1925, according to Mertens & de Vries, J.M.C. van Borselen & Co of Den Haag offered the Dutch government 1979 assorted Lugers amongst a variety of German weaponry. Interestingly, 1795 of them were 1904-type navy pistols, which had presumably been taken from men of the Marinekorps and the crews of interned warships returning from Flanders by way of the Netherlands.

Finland	No sooner had independence been seized from Russia in 1917 than a shortage of effectual small-arms became evident. Though substantial quantities of Mosin-Nagant rifles were taken from Helsinki arsenal, few handguns excepting obsolescent Nagant revolvers had been kept there. FN-Browning pocket automatics and Mauser C/96 pistols eked out handgun supplies until 9000 ineffective Spanish-made Ruby blowbacks – known in Finnish service as 'm/19' – were acquired from France shortly after the Armistice.

The eventual selection of the Luger as the official service weapon was influenced by familiarity with equipment issued to Finns serving in the German army during the First World War; an entire rifle battalion had been composed of Finns and Lapps. In addition, due to the deteriorating financial situation in Germany, BKIW could offer pistols at a highly attractive price.

The Luger was adopted as the Pistooli m/23 Pb. About 8000 7.65mm 1908-type pistols, with 98mm barrels, were purchased from BKIW in 1923–30. Some of them – perhaps only a few hundred – equipped the Finnish prison service, the distinctive chamber mark being applied in Berlin prior to despatch. It is basically a circle containing an enrayed star within four bars in the form of a diamond, below VANKEINHOITOLAITOS.

Many m/23 Lugers bore unit-marking discs until the system was abandoned in 1940. Other marks were simply stamped into the board-type shoulder stocks. A typical example, issued with gun no.7539, reads II.S.J.R.2.K.K.K. – the 11th gun issued to the second machine-gun company (_konekiväärikompania_) of the Savo rifle regiment, or _Savon Jäkäri-Rykmentti_. Another example has a disc marked K.K.K., J.P.4. and '8', for the machine-gun company of Jäkäri Pataljoona 4 – the fourth rifle battalion.

Markings were also applied by the Finnish navy. One surviving gun has a 25mm brass marking disc let into the right grip, reading SUV (_Sukellusvene_, 'submarine'), VESIHIISI and the issue number '91'. Twenty-five Lugers were issued to each submarine of the Vetehinen class – _Vetehinen, Vesihiisi_ and _Iku-Tursu_. Designed in Germany, these were built in 1926 by Crichton-Vulcan Oy of Turku with the assistance of AG Bremer-Vulkan of Hamburg.

Many m/23 pistols were refurbished during the 1930s, when replacement barrels – 98mm or 120mm long, 7.65mm or 9mm calibre – were made by Oy Tikkakoski Ab. In 1930–2, Arvo Saloranta developed an experimental 9mm pistol incorporating m/23 components, in addition to a blowback .22 rimfire Salobellum conversion. Unlike most comparable trainers, the Salobellum had a new receiver containing a simple reciprocating breech-block. Only about a hundred guns were converted from m/23 Lugers in 1931–2, owing to a shortage of funds; nos.2 and 98 survive.

By 1930, realising that the Parabellum did not perform particularly well in sub-zero conditions, Finnish designers had embarked on designs of their own. The first Lahti dates from this period, though the perfected version did not reach service status until the late 1930s.

With the advent of the m/35 Lahti, some m/23 pistols were passed to the protective corps (Suojeluskunta-Organisation) to replace old Russian revolvers and surviving m/19 Ruby blowbacks. However, many Lugers saw active service during the Winter War of 1939–40 and the 'Continuation War' of 1941–4. Perpetual shortages of m/23 and m/35 pistols, however, forced the Finns to purchase a few GP35 FN-Brownings for the air force and Beretta Mo.34 blowbacks for the protective corps.

Most handguns were discarded after the Continuation War with the Soviet Union, but the remaining 7.65mm m/23 Lugers were not declared obsolete until 1982 and 9mm conversions were still being retained in the 1990s to supplement the FN-Browning BDA m/80.

The original Lugers were blued, though many were eventually parkerised for service in extreme conditions. The most common property marking is 'SA' (Suomen Armeija, 'Finnish army').

Spain   The government is said to have tested the Luger in 1905, after deciding in principle to adopt the Bergmann-'Mars'. Details of the trial are not known, but the successful licensing of the cheaper Bergmann to Anciens Établissements Pieper – resolving supply difficulties – meant that it had no significance.

No distinctively Spanish-marked Parabellums are known from this era, except for some commercial examples with Spanish-language extractor/ejector markings. However, several guns were identified in *Arms Gazette* in 1980 as survivors from 'a limited amount of Luger pistols [ordered] from DWM to serve as field test pieces for issue to the . . . Civil Guard. Those Lugers sent to Spain to fill the order bear the "Civil Guard" crest on their receivers . . . [and] were issued from 1923 to 1928. Sources close to the Spanish military of today state that Spain had ordered 500 Lugers in 1923 in three separate contracts from DWM'. These pistols were supposedly 'withdrawn to Madrid Arsenal and placed into storage until 1941' before reissue to the 'Blue Division'.

Ostensibly refurbished pre-1918 German army pistols, the Guardia Civil guns display a distinctive enrayed crown over the chamber, and are numbered with '1-4 digits with or without a suffix in both 7.65mm and 9mm'. Their authenticity has been questioned, owing to the official adoption on 5th October 1922 of the 'Pistola Star de 9mm, Modelo 1922, para tropa de la Guardia Civil' (Star Model A). If the Browning-type Star was the regulation Guardia Civil pistol, why should 500 Parabellums be required only a year later? A plausible answer is that the guns were acquired in 1921–2, before the Star was approved; alternatively, they may have been intended exclusively for Gurdia Civil officers. But confirmation is still lacking.

Switzerland   By 1928, the federal arms factory in Bern had delivered 12,385 Ordonnanzpistolen 06 W+F; the price had dropped from 400 Swiss francs apiece to 225, but this still seemed excessive compared with 120 francs for an 1882-pattern revolver.

On 17th April 1928, a meeting was called between representatives of the war-technology section, the federal military department and the arms-factory staff to discuss the cost of the Luger. It was eventually realised that inherent complexity limited the potential savings in machine-time and raw materials. Simplifying machining, fitting plastic grips, and reducing the issue of magazines from three to two per gun saved a paltry ten francs. Oberst Fürrer and his supporters suggested eliminating the grip safety to save money, but were so strongly opposed by the cavalrymen that no changes were made.

According to the manufactory, the revised Luger was designated 'Pistole 06/24 W+F' – though this is still disputed by gun collectors in Switzerland. The most obvious change was the prolongation of the housing on the trigger plate and the plain-bordered wood grips; 5589 guns of this type were made between midsummer 1928 and finalisation of the 06/29 W+F pattern in May 1933.

Manufacturing 06/24-type guns allowed the pistol commission to revise the design more thoroughly. The knurling on the toggle-grips was eliminated; the locking bolt was simplified; the front grip-strap was straightened to simplify the frame forging; the machining of the receiver was altered, giving a distinctive stepped appearance; and plastic grips were adopted.

On 28th August 1928, the federal arms factory informed the war-technology section that the unit cost of the Luger could be reduced to 170 francs based on a production run of 5000 guns, or 160 francs for 10,000. This had saved nearly a third of the cost of the 1906-type pistol.

The treasury still doubted whether production in Switzerland would be viable. Acquiring 5000 guns over a six-year period would cost 800,000 francs: 250,000 francs to modify the production machinery in the Bern factory, 510,000 francs to pay sub-contractors such as SIG, and 40,000 francs for raw material. BKIW had quoted only 660,000 francs to supply 5000 1906-type guns – 132 francs apiece – but purchasing German-made guns would deprive Swiss industry of the work. It also risked disrupting supply in the event of war; memories stretched back to the First World War, which had cut Luger deliveries in this very way.

The federal parliament required very little pressure to vote to make the new handguns in Bern, particularly as the army would get an improved design instead of German-made guns which were basically obsolescent Pistolen 06 W+F.

Construction of an experimental Luger was approved on 19th January 1929, the first twenty pre-production examples (numbered V1-V21) appearing in June. The new guns passed their trials so successfully that an extra 1500, improved in minor details, were ordered at a unit cost 'not exceeding 225 francs' inclusive of the holster and accessories. Delivery was scheduled for 1930–1, an appropriation of 100,000 francs being advanced to cover the cost of the trials.

Comparative tests were then undertaken with the experimental Lugers; a Spanish Star Modelo A (chambering 9mm Bergmann-Bayard cartridges) obtained from 'Esperanza y Cia of Guernica'; the Czech vz.27 (9mm Short) from Česká Zbrojovka, Stakonice; and a Le Français (9mm Browning Long) from Manufacture Française d'Armes et Cycles of Saint-Étienne.

The rival designs were cheaper than the Luger, the Le Français costing only 61.50 francs. But none of them performed especially well. The Luger was the most accurate, its grouping at fifty metres – 8.8cm high by 6.7cm wide – being roughly half the size of that obtained from the vz.27, which had shot marginally better than the Star. The Le Français trailed a remote fourth.

Trials satisfied the Swiss that their experimental Luger was as efficient as any rival, so it was officially adopted for officers and senior NCOs on 30th

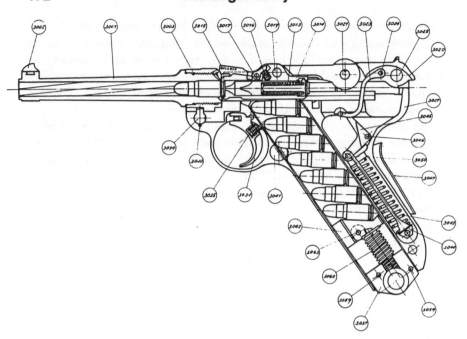

Fig. 15. The Swiss 06/29 W+F is widely regarded as the most perfect form of the Luger. *Eidgenössische Waffenfabrik Bern.*

November 1929. A revolver, the Model 82/29, had been adopted several months previously for lower-ranking NCOs and men.

The first Ordonnanzpistole 06/29 W+F, ordered in the autumn of 1930, was delivered on 29th August 1933. While the earliest guns were being assembled, however, a few hybrid 'prize' pistols – basically 06 W+F frames with 06/29 W+F receivers – were presented at the Swiss national shooting championships. Their numbers began at 33090, but fewer than ten were made.

Morocco   The mysterious Riff or 'Berber' Lugers are said to have been ordered from BKIW shortly before the pistol business was removed to Oberndorf.

The Riffs inhabited the arid tracts of north-west Africa that France and Spain had longed to incorporate in their colonial empires – expansionist plans which antagonised the tribesmen into periodic rebellion. The so-called Riff War was contested between the Spanish colonial army and forces led by Mohamed Abd-al-Karim al-Khattabi. The Spanish were decisively defeated at Anual in 1921, requiring French assistance to conclude the war in 1925. Abd-al-Karim was exiled on Réunion Island and, excepting minor skirmishes, all was quiet by 1927.

It is said that wealthy, but shadowy, backers sought to encourage a new uprising in the late 1920s. The Luger order dates from this period; August Weiss, who was then supervising BKIW's pistol production in the Berlin-Wittenau factory, recollected it as 'large for its day'. The projected rebellion collapsed before the guns could be delivered, and so they remained in store until sold to the Reichswehr in 1931–2.

The serial numbers of the guns traditionally associated with the Riff order – eg 3263u – date production to 1929, the earliest Mauser-assembled guns being in the 'v'-block. The DWM monogram on the toggle-link and crown/N proof marks were standard, so only an 'H66' acceptance mark distinguished the 'Riff Lugers' from regular commercial production.

CHAPTER 12

Commercial Lugers and accessories of the Weimar Republic

The immediate needs of the Reichswehr, restricted greatly by the Treaty of Versailles, were satisfied by the huge surplus of guns left over from the First World War. Though millions of surviving guns were destroyed under Allied supervision, surprisingly large quantities were acquired by commercial interests in the USA.

Pistols could only be sold in Germany if their calibre was 7.65mm or less, the small quantities permitted for the armed forces and the police being excepted. Barrel-length had to be less than 10cm, the purpose of this restriction being far from obvious.

Guns assembled from parts that had been on hand at the Armistice usually have the appearance of new products, though the machining of individual components often betrays their origin; some parts may even bear military inspectors' stamps. They are generally renumbered in accordance with the master-number on the frame, and may also have new serial numbers on the front left side of the receiver ahead of the trigger-plate. There will be commercial 'crown/N' proof marks and toggles which are often, but not inevitably, blank. These resulting 'mix-and-match' pistols may take unusual forms, though the most popular barrel lengths appear to have been 92, 98 and 120mm.

The stock lug and the safety marks are sometimes ground away to produce Swiss-style guns, additionally distinguished by an enrayed Federal Cross above the chamber; this was applied with a die left over from pre-1914 DWM production of Ordonnanzpistolen 1906. Grip safeties have been added to these guns, but are 'down safe' rather than the original Swiss 'up safe' pattern. Unlike genuine Swiss service pistols, GELADEN usually appears on the extractors of the German-made facsimiles.

Production resumes

The earliest newly-made 7.65mm-calibre guns by Berlin-Karlsruher Industrie-Werke, the 1922-vintage successor to DWM, had barrels of 90mm, 95mm or

98mm to comply with the Treaty of Versailles. The 'crown/N' nitro proofs were standard, and the familiar DWM monogram was retained on their toggle-links, though the quality of the finish on these guns – especially the blueing – was customarily well below pre-war standards.

Once the ardour of the Allied supervisors cooled, a wider variety of barrel-lengths was offered. Post-1922 guns will be encountered with barrels measuring 92–400mm. Fixed back sights were usually used in conjunction with the short barrels, whilst those measuring 200mm or more had the adjustable tangent-leaf patterns associated with the LP.08. So many of these sights remained in stock that Mauser was able to supply LP.08 to Siam and Persia in the mid 1930s.

The serial numbers of the genuine BKIW-made commercial Lugers begin at about 73000 and run upward to 96500. The classical safety-recess and extractor markings – GESICHERT and GELADEN – were retained on guns sold in Europe, but many of those exported to English-speaking countries displayed SAFE and LOADED.

The Luger was far from ideal by the standards of the 1920s, excepting for military use. Compared with the many compact pistols crowding the market in Germany, and especially with the vast numbers of Browning copies emanating from Spain, it was too big, too powerful and much too expensive. BKIW had attempted to market a copy of the FN-Browning Mle 10, but was sued for patent infringement. Work had stopped after only a few thousand had been made.

In the early 1920s, BKIW had been granted two registered designs protecting alterations to the Luger. Details of these have not yet been found, owing to the destruction of the appropriate records, but it is suspected that they protect the so-called 'Pocket Luger'. Four of these were produced under the personal supervision of August Weiss, two chambered for the 7.65mm Auto round and two for the 9mm Short pattern. Remarkably, one of these most unusual guns survives in the USA.

Though recoil actuation and the toggle joint were retained, the rear frame was milled flat and a Borchardt-type safety catch slid diagonally in a channel cut in the frame above the left grip. Overall length was reduced to about 160mm – about 55mm shorter than the Pistole 1908 – though the barrel measured merely 75mm and the capacity of the detachable box magazine was restricted to six rounds. The prototypes worked efficiently, but commercial production could not be justified and the project was abandoned c.1924.

A short-lived 'layer blue' was developed during the 1920s in an attempt to accelerate the finishing process from several days to a few hours. Harry Jones, in an excellent chapter on finishing in his book *Luger Variations* (1959), describes how the parts were cleaned and immersed in boiling water. The hot parts were held in the steam-jet to dry, painted with the blueing chemicals and then replaced in the water. The steam drying/chemical application process was repeated until there were five or more layers of blue – very attractive when new, but not as durable as the pre-1918 equivalent.

Guns made after about 1925 by BKIW, Simson and Mauser were simply immersed in blueing solutions, colour being determined by adjusting the chemicals, temperature, or immersion time. The resulting hues varied from a brilliantly irridescent blue to an unattractive brownish black, but were durable enough if care was taken.

Commercial interest in the Luger was comparatively small in the early years of the Weimar Republic, though a few enterprising gunsmiths – Krieghoff and Anschütz amongst them – refinished old 9mm military weapons for commercial sale. The calibre could be changed simply by substituting a 7.65mm barrel, as the cartridges shared similar case-head dimensions.

Berlin-Karlsruher Industrie-Werke sold Lugers to Heinrich Krieghoff throughout the 1920s, the earliest acquisitions being numbered in the 2191i–9853i block (with many gaps). They had the DWM toggle-mark on the links, were occasionally dated '1921' over the chamber, and had KRIEGHOFF SUHL struck rather weakly into the back of the frame above the lanyard loop.

One pistol, incorporating some wartime parts, displays KRIEGHOFF on the left side of the receiver; another, apparently an otherwise standard DWM-made commercial piece with an i-suffix number, has an unusually large H/anchor/K on the toggle link above KRIEGHOFF/SUHL. Krieghoff also refurbished war-surplus Pistolen 1908, most of which acquired small HK monograms (often encircled) on the frame, on the receiver or above the chamber.

Pistols of the Abercrombie & Fitch type, described in the North American section below, were supplied in the 1920s to Flückiger in Zürich. These bore the enrayed Federal Cross mark above the chamber and a bow-and-arrow mark enclosing 'F' and 'Z' – for Flückiger, Zürich – on the front left side of the receiver. Survivors include no.4201, apparently lacking a suffix-letter, and 4295m – an old DWM-made gun with a pre-war German barrel. A Bernerprobe was struck over the original 'crown/B, crown/U, crown/G' proof marks.

Training devices

As German economy began to recover from the collapse of the Mark, renewed interest was taken in guns and shooting. The most important developments in this era were the sub-calibre barrel inserts or *Einsteckläufe*. Renewal of interest in Germany was due to limitations on the ownership of large-calibre handguns and to restrictions placed on the size of the armed forces by the Treaty of Versailles. This also led to an increased enthusiasm for indoor ranges and shooting galleries.

A patent had been granted to Josef Ansorg as early as 1877 to protect a reduced-calibre barrel insert and an adaptor-cartridge. Though the Ansorg

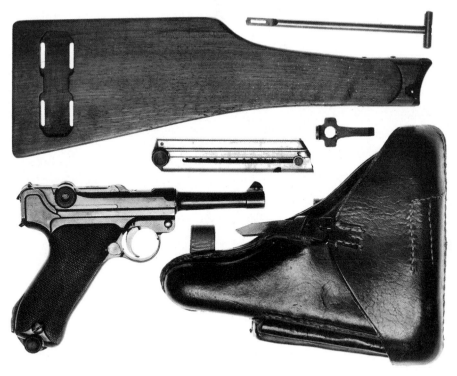

Plate 38 7.65mm m/23 Lugers, made for Finland by Berlin-Karlsruher Industrie-Werke, as DWM was then known, date from the mid 1920s. The holster was attached to the shoulder stock by straps, one of which is visible directly in front of the trigger guard of the pistol. *Sotamuseo.*

Plate 39 This distinctive chamber mark was unique to the small number of m/23 Lugers ordered by the Finnish prison service. *Rolf Gminder.*

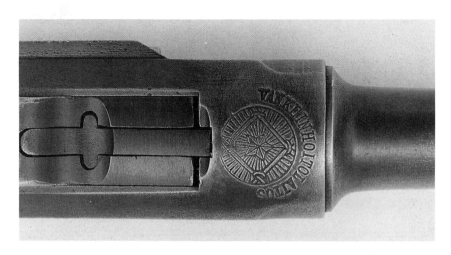

Plate 40 Cadets learn the intricacies of the Pistolen 1908 in the Friedrichsort/Ostsee navy college. The picture dates from 1930 or 1931. *Reinhard Kornmayer*.

Plate 41 Typical of the sub-calibre trainers, or Einsteckläufe, was this Swiss-made Lienhard. Chambered for the 5.6mm Nr.7 rimfire cartridge, it relied on dummy cartridge blocks to function effectively. Note the auxiliary front sight on the muzzle of the barrel-insert. *Reinhard Kornmayer*.

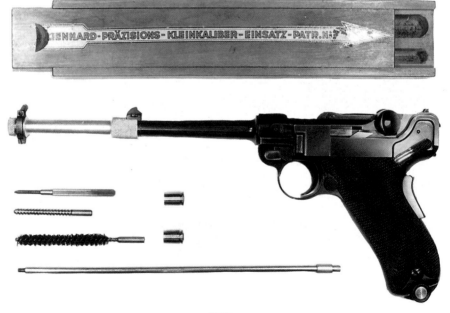

178

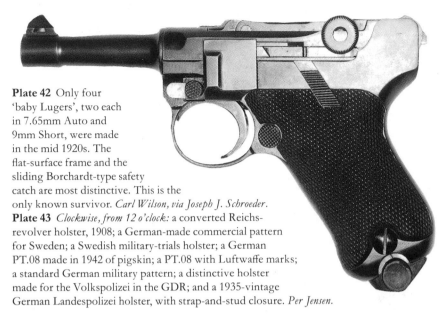

Plate 42 Only four 'baby Lugers', two each in 7.65mm Auto and 9mm Short, were made in the mid 1920s. The flat-surface frame and the sliding Borchardt-type safety catch are most distinctive. This is the only known survivor. *Carl Wilson, via Joseph J. Schroeder.*

Plate 43 *Clockwise, from 12 o'clock:* a converted Reichs-revolver holster, 1908; a German-made commercial pattern for Sweden; a Swedish military-trials holster; a German PT.08 made in 1942 of pigskin; a PT.08 with Luftwaffe marks; a standard German military pattern; a distinctive holster made for the Volkspolizei in the GDR; and a 1935-vintage German Landespolizei holster, with strap-and-stud closure. *Per Jensen.*

Plates 44, 45 This 9mm New Model or 1906-type Luger, no.13322, was made in 1928 for the Netherlands Indies Army by Berlin-Karlsruher Industrie-Werke – successor to DWM. Note the grip safety, the RUST safety mark, and the defaced brass unit-marking plate attached to the frame. *Dr Rolf Gminder; drawing by John Walter.*

Plates 46, 47 Two views of a Turkish security police (EIUM) Luger no.628, supplied by Mauser in the mid 1930s. Note the 'ates' mark on the extractor and 'emniyet' above the safety lever. A mark applied by WaA Inspector 63 is visible on the front right side of the receiver ahead of the EIUM inscription. *Dr Rolf Gminder.*

Plates 48, 49 This 'Model 1314' Luger, no.1957, was supplied by Mauser-Werke to Persia in the mid 1930s. The Farsi inscription on the right side of the receiver gives the model-date and description. *Dr Rolf Gminder.*

Plates 50, 51 This Mauser-made P.08, number 'Kü 3160', has a '42'-code toggle, a '41' chamber date, and Luftwaffe inspectors' marks (visible on the receiver). Many explanations have been given for these guns, which may have been refurbished in *c.*1943–4. Issue to coastal-protection forces seems most likely. *Dr Rolf Gminder.*

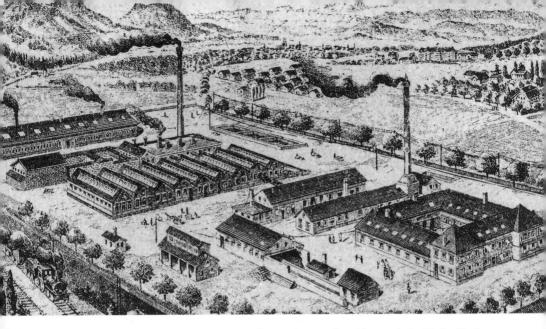

Plate 52 The Swiss government small-arms factory, the Eidgenössische Waffenfabrik, as it was in 1889. Lugers were made there from 1919 until 1947. *Bern city archives.*

Plate 55 The crew of an MG.34 anxiously scan the sky for their target. This propaganda ▷ photograph (no.R 30/4) in the 'Unser Heer' series by Film-Foto Verlag of Berlin, dates from *c*.1935. The tip of a Luger holster protrudes above the belt of the gun-commander.

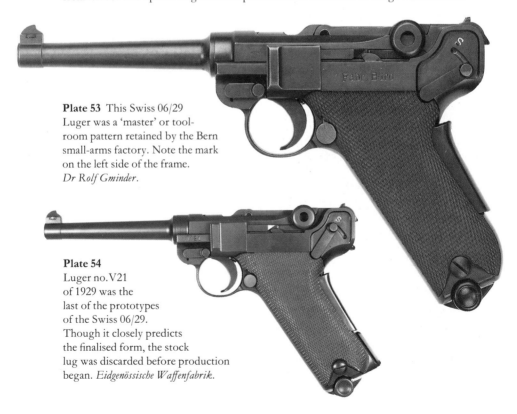

Plate 53 This Swiss 06/29 Luger was a 'master' or tool-room pattern retained by the Bern small-arms factory. Note the mark on the left side of the frame. *Dr Rolf Gminder.*

Plate 54 Luger no.V21 of 1929 was the last of the prototypes of the Swiss 06/29. Though it closely predicts the finalised form, the stock lug was discarded before production began. *Eidgenössische Waffenfabrik.*

Plate 56 The Oberndorf factory of Mauser-Werke AG in 1930, shortly before the Parabellum-making machinery was transferred from Berlin. *Mauser-Werke GmbH.*

Plate 57 Promotional literature for guns sold in the early 1930s by Gustav Genschow & Co., 'Geco' AG. *John Pearson.*

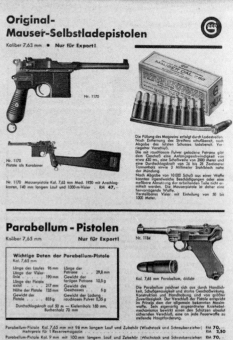

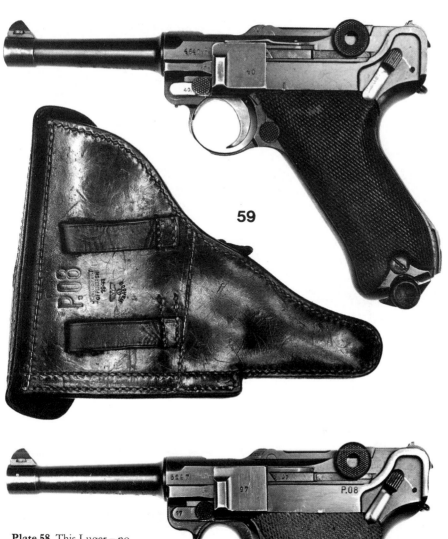

59

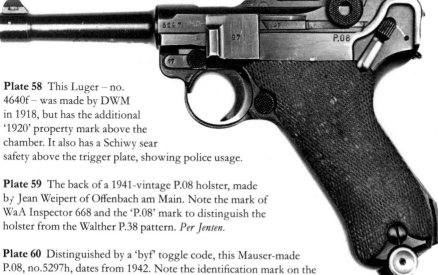

Plate 58 This Luger – no.
4640f – was made by DWM
in 1918, but has the additional
'1920' property mark above the
chamber. It also has a Schiwy sear
safety above the trigger plate, showing police usage.

Plate 59 The back of a 1941-vintage P.08 holster, made
by Jean Weipert of Offenbach am Main. Note the mark of
WaA Inspector 668 and the 'P.08' mark to distinguish the
holster from the Walther P.38 pattern. *Per Jensen.*

Plate 60 Distinguished by a 'byf' toggle code, this Mauser-made
P.08, no.5297h, dates from 1942. Note the identification mark on the
left side of the frame ahead of the safety-lever recess. *Masami Tokoi.*

△ **Plates 61–3** The barrel/receiver units of representative Lugers made during the Third Reich. Top to bottom: Mauser-Werke Persian M1314 no.1957; Krieghoff no.5220, for the Luftwaffe, 1936; and Mauser-Werke commercial P.08 6488v, 1937. *Dr Rolf Gminder*.

▽ **Plate 64** Taken in 1941 by a photographer employed by Presse-Illustration Hoffmann of Berlin, this shows the crew of an MG.34 'somewhere in Russia' in the opening phases of Operation Barbarossa. A Luger holster is visible on the gunner's belt.

Plate 65 A crewman of the battleship *Admiral Scheer*, armed with a standard 9mm P.08, ▷ hoists the German ensign aboard a merchant-ship captured during a cruise in 1940–1.

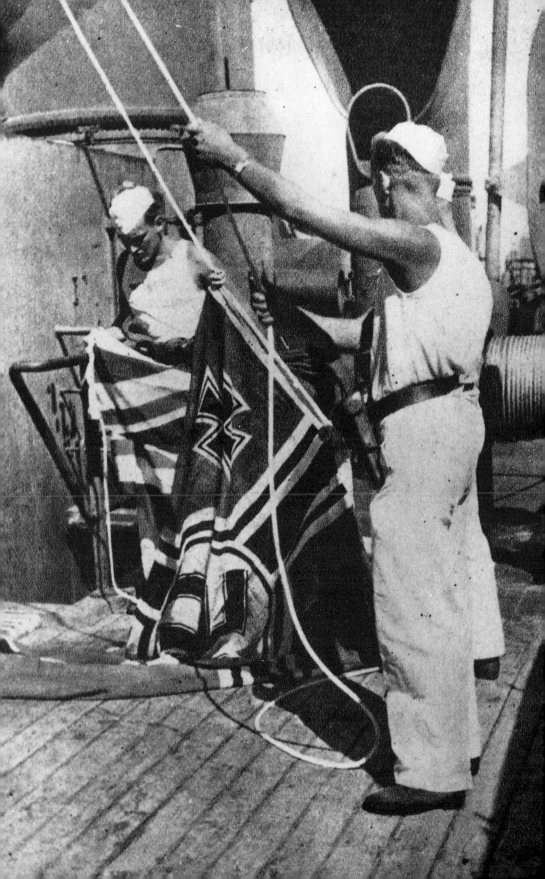

Plate 66
This 7.65mm Mauser-Parabellum 29/70, no.10.0012, clearly shows its Swiss origins in the straight-front grip and plain-gripped toggle. *Dr Rolf Gminder.*

Plate 69 This Mauser-Parabellum 06/73 is intended to duplicate the US Army trials guns of 1904, which had a cartridge-indicating device let into the left grip. The toggle-grips are partially cut away to simulate the original Old Model design. *Dr Rolf Gminder.*

Plate 67
The solitary 'Pistole 29/65 W + F' was made in the Bern small-arms factory for Samuel Cummings of Interarms, who was seeking to produce new Lugers. The contract eventually fell to Mauser-Jagdwaffen. *Dr Rolf Gminder.*

Plate 68
This experimental target-shooting version of the Swiss 06/29 Luger, P78106, was made in the Bern small-arms factory in 1947. Note the sights and the extension on the front grip strap.

Plate 70
This advertising leaflet,
published in Germany in 1986, typifies
the last years of the Mauser-Parabellum –
when a specially-decorated guns
were sold at extremely high prices.
Mauser-Jagdwaffen GmbH.

Plate 71 The navy commemorative 06/73 Mauser-Parabellum had a 15cm barrel, a facsimile of the two-position back sight, a stock lug on the heel of the butt, and a grip safety. Note the number – 'KM 001'. *Dr Rolf Gminder.*

Plate 72 One of a handful of 7.65mm-calibre 29/70 Mauser-Parabellum pocket pistols, made in the early 1970s. *Dr Rolf Gminder.*

Plate 73 This unidentified toggle-lock pistol – a .22-calibre blowback – may be a survivor the Tucker Lugers, about a thousand of which were made in the USA in the early 1960s. *Trustees of the Imperial War Museum (negative no.MH18386).*

Plates 74, 75 The Mitchell American Eagle Luger and its distinctive chamber mark. *Mitchell Arms.*

Plate 76 The Martz Safe Toggle Release installed in a wartime German P.08. Note the alteration to the safety-lever mechanism behind the magazine. *John V. Martz.*

system was never exploited commercially, Ignaz Kowar received German patent no.33,596 (1885) to protect a short sub-calibre barrel-insert firing rimfire ammunition, and the German army had soon adopted '5mm Zielmunition' for practice purposes.

The first German-made Luger trainer seems to have been registered on 20th April 1921 by Louis Hellfritzsch, best remembered for his semi-automatic pistols. Details of its construction have been lost; it may have operated semi-automatically, but no surviving example is known.

The Geco system was the first German trainer to be exploited commercially, though its introduction is difficult to date; the relevant patent, no.345,788, was granted to Gustav Genschow & Co AG ('Geco') on 23rd April 1921. The cartridge was basically a tiny bullet in a minuscule case loaded with priming compound. This generated ample power to thrust the bullet from the case with sufficient accuracy to be used for ten-metre target shooting.

The tiny cartridges, readily identifiable by their rimmed cases, could be used with equal facility in centre- and rim-fire guns. The earliest examples had conical shoulders, facilitating chambering, but later ones were cylindrical. They were usually sold as '4mm Übungsmunition Geco, Zentralfeuer und Randfeuer', describing their dual-purpose priming system perfectly.

Excepting the semi-automatic Erma pattern, the RWS/Weiss design was the most successful of the sub-calibre inserts developed prior to 1939. The Weiss cartridge was dimensionally similar to the Geco type, but was rimless, centre-fire and known universally as '4mm Übungsmunition M20'. It formed an integral part of German patent 365,264, granted on 24th April 1921 to Karl Erhard Weiss and the Nürnberg branch of Rheinisch-Westfälische Sprengstoff AG. Karl Weiss subsequently improved the basic design, receiving German patent 430,028 on 9th February 1923.

There were two principal varieties of the RWS/Weiss trainer – the original pattern of 1921, with a twist-lock at the muzzle, and the perfected 1923-vintage multi-part type retained by a lock-nut. The nut simply offset the front of the insert against the bore wall. Once the breech-block of the Luger had been retracted, to be held either by the magazine follower or the hold-open, a special spring-loaded tool was used to place the cartridge in the barrel-insert chamber. The breech was then closed to cock the striker and the gun could be fired. The recoil energy of the 4mm M20 cartridge was far too low to reload automatically, forcing the firer to retract the toggle manually and then punch the spent case from the chamber with a separate ejector rod.

Low cost, surprisingly good accuracy and the ease with which they could be adapted for differing pistols boosted the popularity of the RWS/Weiss sub-calibre inserts. They served the armed forces and the state police until the advent of the semi-automatic Kulisch/Erma system described below.

The RWS/Weiss units issued in the army had the 1923-patent 'Old Style' (*alter Art*) multi-part muzzle bush, whereas the police issue ('New Style' or *neuer Art*) were adapted to fit the existing one-piece cleaning-rod bush. RWS sub-calibre units were distributed commercially by AKAH, Waffen-Glaser and many other well-established wholesalers, and will be found with a selection of markings.

A differing system was patented by Polte-Werke of Magdeburg in February 1923 (no.450,713), protecting several methods of retaining a single-shot 4mm trainer in a pistol barrel. Though rarely encountered, Polte-made inserts were undoubtedly offered commercially. They can be recognised by a distinctive retaining plate, which locks around the front sight.

Erfurter-Maschinenfabrik B. Geipel GmbH, 'Erma-Werke', of Erfurt made single-shot trainers in the 1920s. The Model 20, chambering 4mm M20 Übungsmunition, was followed by the Model 25 adapted for the 5.6mm LfB (.22 Long Rifle) rimfire round; both relied on muzzle shrouds similar to those of the Geco and RWS/Weiss rivals.

German patent 461,610, granted on 4th April 1926 to Friedrich Gomann of Berlin, protected a sub-calibre insert held to the front sight of the Luger by a large-diameter coil spring between the barrel-body and the retaining collar.

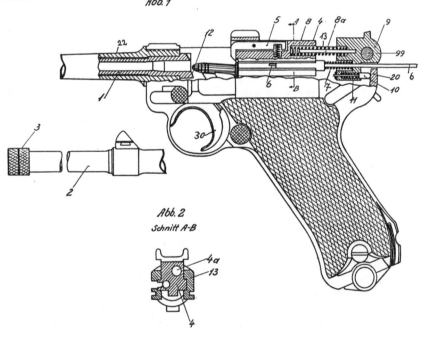

Fig. 16. The Kulisch-designed Erma Selbstlade-Einsteck-Lauf ('SEL'), from German Patent 497,683 of January 1927. *Deutsches Patentamt*.

On 12th January 1927, gunsmith Richard Kulisch was granted German patent no.497,683 to protect a 'firearm with sliding barrel', assigning rights to Erma-Werke. Unlike virtually every preceding sub-calibre insert, the Kulisch Selbstlade-Einstecklauf – or 'SEL' – operated semi-automatically. It was based on the insertion of a rifled barrel-liner/barrel-sleeve unit in the Luger barrel. The standard toggle-mechanism was replaced with a new breech-block containing two coil-pattern return springs adapted for rimfire ammunition; when cocked, the new firing pin protruded from the rear of the pistol to provide a tactile indicator.

Only a single length of barrel-liner was normally supplied, though a few were made specifically for Luger carbines. Annular sleeves sufficed to adapt the Kulisch insert to a variety of barrel lengths, conversion being undertaken simply by inserting the rifled barrel liner from the breech. The sleeve – usually made of brass after 1940 – was then placed over the protruding liner and held in place by two lock-nuts at the muzzle.

Erma-Werke provided special magazines holding five, seven or ten rounds. The barrel liner, sleeve, lock nuts, breech-block unit and magazines were usually delivered in a wooden case, which also contained a recess for the standard ejector; this had to be removed from the receiver-side before the SEL breech-block could be used.

The Kulisch trainer attracted the attention of the armed forces in 1931, as it had far greater military potential than the single-shot RWS/Weiss unit. On 8th July 1932, the 'Selbstlade-Einstecklauf (S.E.L.) für Pistole 08 mit Zielmunition 5.6mm Lang für Büchsen' was officially adopted, issue beginning in October. Two SEL were issued to accompany the first thirty 9mm Pistolen 08, and thereafter on the scale of one to twenty-five. They allowed realistic low-cost target practice to be undertaken at ranges of 25 metres.

The military SEL was issued in the 'large wooden box', which also contained a cleaning rod, a jag, a brush, and a rod guide. However, after the adoption on 15th January 1936 of the 1934-pattern 5.6mm-calibre cleaning equipment, the 'small box' was substituted. This lacked the cleaning rod and brush.

The Erma sub-calibre system was marketed commercially as the Model 30a with fixed sights or the adjustable Model 30b. It cost 32–35 Reichsmarks in 1939, compared with only about 10 Reichsmarks for the single-shot patterns, but more than 30,000 had been sold by 1939. Some went to the USA, displaying 'A.F. Stoeger/Jnc.' on the breech-block, whilst a few hundred, specially chambered for 5.6mm No.7 match cartridge, were sold in Switzerland by Walter Glaser of Zürich. The Swiss trainers were specially adapted for the Ordonnanzpistolen 1900 and 1906.

A distinctive single shot sub-calibre insert designed by Karl Enholtz of Basel was patented in Switzerland in July 1932 (no.155,806). Distinguished by a skeletal retainer locking around the front sight, it was chambered for 4mm

M20 ammunition and had a large ring-head ejector rod. A loading tube (*Laderohr*) was used to position the tiny cartridges in the breech.

Luger shoulder stocks

If the Einsteckläufe sought to provide short-range practice, developments such as the unique Benke-Thiemann folding stock were intended to improve the accuracy at long range. The basic idea was patented on 30th August 1921 by Josef Benke of Budapest, DRP 379,934, but then improved in collaboration with Georg Thiemann of Berlin. The perfected design is illustrated in German patent 452,602, granted in 1926, and was offered commercially in small numbers – not only for the Luger, but also for the Hungarian Frommer pistol.

The stock was made in Berlin by Gewehrfabrik H. Barella, which made extravagant claims for it – 'adopted in Hungary', for example. The Benke-Thiemann stock consisted of longitudinally divided sections doubling as halves of the standard pistol grip. When the stock was closed, one pivot lay ahead of the trigger guard and the other appeared behind the grip. When the stock was opened, however, the front pivot became an axis-pin for the two sections and the rear pivot anchored the stock to the grip extension. Though interesting technically, the Benke-Thiemann system was needlessly heavy, cumbersome, expensive, and too fragile to survive prolonged use; sales were meagre and very few survive.

A telescoping stock was patented in Germany in April 1924 (no.422,849) by Fritz Gomann of Berlin and Wilhelm Grunow of Charlottenburg. It could be locked to the butt-heel of the Luger by a radial level or spring catch, but was less successful than even the Benke-Thiemann pattern. No surviving example has yet been found.

The last Luger carbines

A few pistol-carbines were made in the early 1920s, though they were chambered for standard ammunition and lacked the auxiliary recoil spring found in the fore-end of most pre-1914 examples. Some of the later pistol-carbines were simply 1908-pattern receivers fitted with plain 30cm barrels, but others had chequered wooden fore-ends. Navy or LP.08 back sights were substituted for the special carbine type and grip safeties were invariably omitted. Front sights ranged from conventional P.08 patterns to ramped blades. Carbines were even made from old New Model or pre-1913 P.08 frames, new stock lugs being welded onto the butt-heel whenever necessary.

Hybrid designs were undoubtedly made during the Weimar Republic, though the authenticity of some surviving guns is questionable. These include a combination of navy and other parts – with navy 'crown, crown/M, crown/M' proofs – and a chamber marked, inexplicably, LOEWE & CO./OBERNDORF A/N. The so-called 'Dutch Commercial' guns may be military rejects, and should thus be considered as legitimate sub-variants, but the curious Cyrillic 'I' ('reversed-N') mark on the so-called 'Russian Commercial' Luger begs a better explanation than those that have been attempted.

The North American Luger

Many of the most interesting guns were produced for agents in the USA, where, until the Wall Street crash in 1929, sales prospects were infinitely better than in depressed Germany.

The Luger had been promoted enthusiastically prior to 1917 by Hans Tauscher, DWM's sole American agent since 1909. Tauscher had previously been employed by Hermann Boker & Company of New York, promoters of the Borchardt in the US Army trials of 1897, and had become friendly with Georg Luger – so friendly, indeed, that he subsequently established the engineer's name throughout English-speaking North America.

Unfortunately for Tauscher, who still retained German citizenship, his assets were seized when the USA declared war on Germany in 1917. The sequestration included rights to Luger's US Patents – 808,463, 839,978 and 851,538 were still effective – and title to the guns which were awaiting sale. Since the last bulk consignments had been received from DWM in 1913, Tauscher had sold 1801 pistols in 7.65mm and 543 in 9mm.

Post-war distribution in North America was characterised by an initial scramble, with the participation of several contractors, and then in the gradual rise of Stoeger to pre-eminence.

Widely known as the '1920 model', the earliest guns presented bewildering variety. The majority chambered the popular 7.65mm cartridge – better known in the USA as '.30 Luger' – which had always been more acceptable than the 9mm pattern. Catalogues published by the Pacific Arms Company of San Francisco illustrated the extraordinary nature of the refurbished pre-1918 guns, which could be obtained with drum magazines; with telescope sights; with barrels ranging in length from $3^5/_8$ to 24 inches; and with grip safeties.

On 11th January 1922, rights to the Luger patents and the associated pistol business were transferred by the Alien Property Commission to Hugo J. Panzer & Co Ltd of New York. The management of BKIW, as DWM had become, protested vigorously that a sole agency had already been promised to A. F. Stoeger & Company of New York; indeed, on the basis of this agreement Stoeger had acquired refurbished or parts-assembly guns from Germany as early as June 1921. The Alien Property Custodian declined to arbitrate, but the two distributors eventually agreed to recognise Stoeger as 'sole agency'. Stoeger would then sell imported guns to Panzer until the arrangement lapsed.

Few of the North American distributors excepting Stoeger were long lived, though the Pacific Arms Company was still operating in 1927. It is not clear if this agency was being supplied by Panzer or Stoeger, or had simply bought enough war-surplus guns in 1920 to survive until the Great Depression.

Abercrombie & Fitch acquired guns in Switzerland in this era, though estimates of the quantity vary from forty-nine to a highly improbable 1500 as it is unclear whether their numbers ran consecutively. It seems more likely that they were delivered in small batches, and thus that the number-range would include substantial gaps.

Most of these pistols have i-suffix numbers, but seem to include refinished pre-1918 components and commonly lack proof marks. However, they also have long frames, grip safeties, the enrayed Federal Cross chamber-mark, and DWM monograms on the toggle-links. German-style serial numbers and GELADEN extractor marks indicate that they are not simply refinished Swiss Ordonnanzpistolen 1906.

Abercrombie & Fitch Lugers were apparently sent from BKIW to Rudolf Hämmerli & Company in Lenzburg to be fitted with new 12cm barrels. Most display ABERCROMBIE & FITCH CO. NEW YORK and MADE IN SWITZERLAND in a single line along the top of the barrel, though two-line marks exist. A curious 7.65mm Pistole 1904 hybrid has been pictured by Charles Kenyon in *Lugers at Random* (1969), complete with a navy-type back sight on the toggle and a suitably adapted front sight. The gun is numbered on the side of the receiver ahead of the trigger-plate, though it lies outside the i-suffix range associated with the 1922 Abercrombie & Fitch acquisitions.

Pistol 3160i (subsequently altered to 9mm) was sold by Abercrombie & Fitch on 16th October 1922, whilst the existence of 3194i (7.65mm) has also been authenticated.

In the Spring of 1922, BKIW finally granted distribution of the Luger to A.F. Stoeger & Company. Adolf Stoeger had been born in Austria, but had held American citizenship for many years. Continual bickering between Stoeger and Hugo J. Panzer & Company, to whom the guns delivered to Hans Tauscher prior to 1917 had been given, had begun with the earliest shipment of newly-made guns from Germany. However, Panzer soon lost interest and assigned all rights in the Luger to Stoeger in March 1924.

The earliest Stoeger order for brand-new guns was apparently placed with BKIW on 7th March 1922, for 2500 7.65mm-calibre Lugers, 500 stocks and holsters, 300 spare barrels and 50,000 cartridges; 2500 boxes were to be supplied bearing Stoeger marks, whilst the 'American Eagle was to appear above the chamber as on pre-war shipments'.

On 20th May 1924, Stoeger took the unusual step of registering the DWM monogram trademark with the US Patent Office, the grant of 'Parabellum' following on 22nd July. The most important registry was 'Luger', sought on 5th October 1929, which gave Stoeger exclusive rights to a word that had already become common currency in North America.

The earliest BKIW-made pistols sent to North America probably incorporated parts which had been held in store since pre-war days. However, the distinctive American Eagle mark was rolled into the receiver above the chamber, and A.F. STOEGER INC./NEW YORK. appeared on the right side of the receiver directly below the extractor. Some guns also bore GENUINE LUGER – REGISTERED U.S. and PATENT OFFICE along the frame rail below the receiver-side mark.

The Luger was very expensive compared with the cheap handguns that abounded in North America. Sales were never large, and declined so rapidly during the Depression that Stoeger is believed to have cancelled the last order before it had been completed. Guns without the 'Genuine ... Patent Office' receiver mark were subsequently sold in Europe and to the predecessor of the Electric Company of Israel, though Stoeger's association with Mauser-Werke (to whom Luger production had been passed in 1930) endured until the beginning of the Second World War.

Enter Mauser

The First World War destroyed the export successes previously enjoyed by the German firearms industry.

Many armies experimented with new pistols between the wars, one landmark being the perfection by Fabrique Nationale d'Armes de Guerre of the Browning tipping-barrel system. Production of the GP-35 or High Power began as soon as the Belgians had shaken off the worst effects of the Depression. The US Army had accepted the Colt-Browning M1911A1 in 1926; Argentina and Norway were both making Colt-Brownings under licence. The Russians, the Poles and the French had all adapted the Browning Link for their service pistols by 1935. Elsewhere, Spain, Czechoslovakia, Japan and Mexico had adopted designs of their own. The Luger was rapidly being overtaken by sturdier and more efficient designs, relying on its reputation to gain a trickle of insignificant export orders prior to 1939.

Berlin-Karlsruher Industrie-Werke and Mauser-Werke had become part of the same holding group in the 1920s. BKIW had no interest in handguns other than the Luger, whereas Mauser was making a range of guns from tiny shirt-pocket pistols (*Westentaschenpistolen*) to modernised versions of the C/96. Sensibly, production was rationalised in 1929 – when Mauser bought the entire Luger production-line, together with the stocks of parts. Five thousand Reichsmarks were paid for rights to the Luger, the machinery was acquired for 20 Pfennige per kilogram, and 119,123 Reichsmarks were given for existing parts and unfinished forgings. A little under seven tonnes of special steel stock, which had been partially milled to shape, was purchased separately.

The machinery and relevant personnel were moved to Oberndorf under the supervision of August Weiss, who had succeeded Heinrich Hoffman as superintendent of handgun pistol production in the BKIW Berlin-Wittenau factory.

The DWM/BKIW pattern guns, seven in all, were also taken to Oberndorf. They comprised a 7.65mm commercial model; a 9mm 'Armee-Modell No.8'; a 7.65mm Swiss model, with a long barrel and a grip safety; a 9mm Netherlands navy model; a 9mm Luger with a grip safety, for the Netherlands Indies Army ('Holl. Kolonie'); a 9mm LP.08, 'no longer in production'; and a 9mm Armee-Modell of undetermined pattern, 'no longer in production'.

The last of the guns assembled in Berlin had been numbered in the 'u'-suffix block, which was subsequently completed by guns assembled in Oberndorf from Berlin-made components. Mauser then commenced on the 'v'-block. The number of the first newly-made pistol does not seem to have been recorded, though 515v was the first of a batch supplied to Stoeger in 1931. The 'v' and 'w' suffix blocks were subsequently retained for commercial and special contract use.

The extent of the commercial potential Mauser-Werke saw in the Luger is no longer easily assessed. Though the Pistole 08 was still the official handgun of the armed forces and police in Germany, the commercial markets were either very depressed or overflowing with cheaper designs. And, even in 1930, it was increasingly clear that the Pistole 08 was unlikely to remain the service weapon for long: did Mauser gamble that sufficient production was possible before a replacement appeared, or was the capital investment involved in the 1930 transfer of the production-line from Berlin so minimal that the volume of production scarcely mattered at all?

The Netherlands had ordered 302 pistols for the navy in July 1930, with the proviso that they were to be delivered in September. The temporary dislocation of production made this simple request seem impossible, but a hundred completed pistols had come from Berlin and the remaining 202 were successfully assembled from existing parts by 6th September. Inspection began in the first week of November.

Attempts were made to attract export orders throughout the early 1930s, but the high price of the Luger and the depressed state of most national economies delayed success until the Third Reich had begun.

CHAPTER 13

The rise of Hitler, and Lugers of the Third Reich

Though clandestine rearmament and weapons development had been under way for some years, the comparatively small Luger requirements were satisfied during the early 1930s by guns emanating from the Simson factory in Suhl. But any assessment of production in this era is complicated by unidentifiable inspectors' marks, the habitual omission of maker's marks, and a general lack of reliable information.

The owners of Simson & Companie, the only officially sanctioned manufacturer of Lugers for the German armed forces, were Jewish. As this did not meet with the State code, the company was simply liquidated. Simson became an NSDAP Trust (*Stiftung*) under the control of Dr Herbert Hoffman. Its assets, together with those of the Mahrholdt company, were subsequently transferred to the 'Wilhelm Gustloff-Stiftung'; Gustloff had been the leader of the National Socialist movement in Switzerland until his assassination in 1936. The new business traded as Berlin-Suhler Waffen- und Fahrzeugwerke ('BSW') until it eventually became Gustloff-Werke.

Once Mauser began production of new guns in earnest, military supply problems were largely resolved and inspectors appointed by the armed forces weapons office oversaw the acceptance of weapons. This replaced a fragmented system which had previously encompassed the army ordnance depots, the police school for technology and transport in Berlin, and inspectors seconded to the principal manufacturers.

The first of the perfected eagle/WaA marks applied by the principal weapons inspectors date from 1935. By 1941, according to Robert Whittington, writing in *German Pistols and Holsters 1934–1945*, more than 25,000 inspectors and civilian clerical staff were employed by 950 offices answering to fourteen regional bureaux.

Mauser began to deliver newly-made Lugers in the autumn of 1934, though only about 13,000 had been made by the end of the year. The acceleration in production was largely due to the enlargement of the paramilitary organisations; the impending introduction of conscription in the armed forces from 16th March 1935; the creation of an air force in all but name; and the development of effective warships to replace the antiques being crewed by the Kriegsmarine in deference to the Allies.

In 1934, however, Hitler had yet to throw off the last lingering restrictions of the Treaty of Versailles and the Germans were keen to hide the production of new guns. The introduction of coding was intended to disguise not only the quantities of weapons being made but also how many contractors had become involved.

One of the cornerstones of the coding system was the date-letter, which, on Lugers, was stamped into the receiver immediately above the chamber. The sequence is believed to have run randomly from 'A' in 1928 to 'H' in 1938, but only 'K' and 'G' are found on Mauser-made guns dating from 1934 and 1935 respectively.

Much of Mauser's production capacity was initially concentrated on refurbishing existing Lugers. These are readily identified by their proof and inspectors' marks, post-1935 examples bearing the stamps of weapons inspector no.66 ('WaA66'). A second official, using '63', was responsible for the acceptance of newly-made weapons. The work of the Oberndorf office was supervised by inspector 655 in 1937–42, and then by inspector 135 until the end of Second World War.

Pistols made in this era by Mauser-Werke AG bore 'S/42' on the toggle-links and chamber-top date-letters 'K' and 'G'. In 1935, however, Hitler rejected the remaining restrictions of the Versailles Treaty, reclaimed the Rheinland, and sanctioned the enlargement of the armed forces. The removal of secrecy made the date-coding system obsolescent, and it was promptly replaced by the production-year (stamped in full) whilst the manufacturer's code was simplified to '42' in 1939.

It is interesting that the 'S' date-code does not appear on Mauser-made pistols, though 'G' is shared by Mauser and Krieghoff. This fact has been offered in support of claims that Mauser ceased work on the military Luger in 1936, possibly after completing the first contract placed on behalf of the armed forces. Though the theory is still unproven, and probably unlikely, Mauser-Werke does seem to have undertaken much more contract work in this period.

The grand scale of the changes to the military establishment meant that demand for equipment – even handguns – rapidly outstripped production. As priority was given to the demands of the army in this era, the navy, the air force and the paramilitary organisations had all to make do with older or less effective pistols. The air force, being created from the many flying clubs and the Nationalsozialistiche Fliegerkorps (NSFK), seems to have been especially impatient.

Mauser-Werke was totally unable to meet demands for the Luger, which was notoriously difficult to mass-produce. This seems to have forced the armed forces weapons office to refuse a 10,000-gun demand from the air force.

Separate inspection facilities for the individual components of the armed forces did not exist at this time, all work being undertaken under army control. This situation explains the subsequent participation of Krieghoff.

Sempert & Krieghoff had been founded in Suhl in 1886 to make sporting guns and electrical components. About 1904, Sempert & Krieghoff purchased the gunmaking business of V.C. Schilling of Suhl; Schilling had produced large quantities of military and sporting rifles, in addition to pistols made under contract from Theodor Bergmann. However, the new owners were more keen to tender to make Mauser rifles and rapidly abandoned the irrelevant pistol business.

In 1916, Heinrich Krieghoff left his father to found his own gunmaking company, where he was joined in 1919 by his brother, Ludwig the younger. The death of the elder Ludwig Krieghoff in 1924 effectively amalgamated Sempert & Krieghoff and Heinrich Krieghoff Waffenfabrik, but each constituent continued to trade independently – Sempert & Krieghoff concentrating on sporting guns, whilst its junior partner sought military contracts.

Heinrich Krieghoff had sold substantial quantities of automatic pistols during the Weimar Republic, including No.4 Walthers and as many as 9000 DWM-made Lugers. Protection for the distinctive 'H/anchor/K' trademark, no.401,488, was sought on Christmas Eve 1928.

Krieghoff had also designed an automatic rifle, which, according to Randall Gibson in *The Krieghoff Parabellum* (1980), had been demonstrated to Hitler and senior NSDAP officials in 1934. The success of this exhibition and the proven quality of Sempert & Krieghoff sporting guns allowed Krieghoff to gain favour.

The circumstances of the grant of a pistol contract from the air sports association or Reichluftsportverband (RLV), which obscured the identity of the air force, have never been revealed. It is not known whether Krieghoff approached the association or whether the association, possibly through the influence of Hermann Göring, simply allowed Krieghoff to tender. And what was the relationship between Heinrich Krieghoff and the trustee of the Wilhelm Gustloff-Stiftung, Herbert Hoffman? Did Hoffman see a way of selling machines that were of little use? Did Krieghoff see a way of benefiting from Simson's downfall...?

Amongst the most plausible stories is one relating how Krieghoff deliberately under-bid Mauser for a 10,000 pistol contract, hoping to demonstrate that the company could be trusted with a lucrative order for machine-guns.

By 1935 Krieghoff had acquired the machinery that Simson had purchased from Erfurt in 1920. Charles Kenyon suggests, in *Lugers at Random*, that the earliest Krieghoff guns were produced on this equipment but is contradicted by Randall Gibson in *The Krieghoff Parabellum*. Conceding that some Simson-made components may have been used at the beginning of production, Gibson indicates that the machining patterns were very different. Krieghoff has always categorically denied that the old machinery was used in any way other than to guide new tooling.

Only about 15,000 sets of parts were made in a single production run in 1935–6, from which Krieghoff supplied 10,000 well-made Lugers to the air force. About 1,275–1,300 pistols (with 'P'-prefixed numbers) were sold commercially, most being salvaged from guns that had failed to meet inspection standards. Experience suggests that excessive headspace was the most common problem, which was also easily rectified.

The earliest of Krieghoff's first military pistols had 'G' (1935) and 'S' (1936) coded dates above the chamber, but progressed to '36' and then '1936'. This accounts for at least 7000 guns. Perhaps 2750–2800 were then dated 1937, the order being completed by a very tiny consignment – possibly only fifty – dated 1938. Military pistols bore the 'H/anchor/K' mark on the toggle-link.

The highest authenticated serial number on early, or 'first contract' Krieghoff Lugers is 10059, though 10918 and 10919 may have been assembled at a later date. Specially decorated models and a few commercial guns with five-digit numbers were also assembled prior to 1939. Most desirable amongst the factory-engraved presentation pieces were those that had been plated in gold or platinum, then decorated by master-engraver Hans Feuchter. Gun no.16999, dated 15th August 1939, was presented to Hermann Göring; few other recipients have ever been identified, but Heinrich Krieghoff allegedly had a triple-gun garniture in silver, gold and platinum.

It has often been claimed that Krieghoff was the sole supplier of air force Lugers, implying that none came from Mauser-Werke. Unfortunately for this superficially attractive theory, the air-force handgun inventory stood at 186,000 in September 1940; 40,251 had been delivered in 1939 and another 34,000 in 1940. As the only contract granted to Krieghoff was for merely 10,000 Lugers, Mauser had clearly been the main source of supply from 1936 onward.

The Oberndorf factory regularly made in a month as many guns as Krieghoff delivered in nine years; in September 1941, for example, Mauser dispatched 13,880 guns – 10,630 to the army, 3000 to the air force, and 250 to the navy. It has been claimed – notably by Randall Gibson in *The Krieghoff Parabellum* – that a much higher proportion of Mauser-made guns than their Krieghoff rivals failed proof, but the case is still hotly debated.

By early 1938, deliveries of the 10,000 contract guns had been completed, though some numbered above 10000 replaced the lower-numbered examples that failed proof. Most of these failures were subsequently sold commercially, but can be identified by rejection marks (small four- or five-point stars) on the front right side of the receiver instead of the military proof. However, enough components had been made to allow assembly to continue from number 13150; a few hundred souvenirs were even created in 1945 for sale to American troops.

The serial numbers of the Krieghoff-made pistols acquired by the air force during the Second World War apparently ran backward. It has been suggested that the unfinished guns were put into storage racks with the highest numbers towards the front. When they were taken from the racks to be dated, inspected, and consigned to the air force, the high numbers would be taken first. This neatly explains why the dates and numbers appear to conflict. The Krieghoff Luger remains an interesting diversion, but was of little numerical significance to the history of the pistol during the Third Reich.

Only a few insignificant changes were made to the Luger in this era, the most important being a reinforcement of the rear frame. However, Metallwaren-fabrik Bernhard Kneifel of Berlin made a few experimental die-cast zinc frames designed by employee Johannes Schwarz. Mauser-Werke purchased a few of these in the autumn of 1938 to discover whether they could withstand a prolonged battering; cast frames promised to be cheaper to make than the traditional machined forgings. The Kneifel frames were largely made of zinc, with about four per cent aluminium and a small amount of copper. Trials showed that, as tensile strength was only about two-thirds that of steel, alloy could only be used if the existing frame was radically revised.

Possibly only about ten zinc-alloy frames were made. No.5, once owned by Dr Rolf Gminder, was accompanied by a 1938 'S/42' receiver. The Kneifel frame duplicated the standard pattern except for an occasional reinforcing fillet, but the safety-lever recess contained a small red-painted dot instead of GESICHERT.

Ammunition problems

Though the changes made to the pistol were minor, substantial progress had been made in ammunition design. The development of an effective non-corrosive primer, introduced by RWS in 1926, was followed by attempts to minimise use of valuable brass. Polte-Werke experimented with steel cases in the early 1930s and, by the middle of the decade, had perfected a suitable design.

However, extruded steel cases were not only susceptible to rusting but also gave continual extraction problems until they were washed with copper and then lacquered. This gave them a distinctive reddish hue.

Lacquered steel cases proved to stick in auto-loading weapons as the chamber heated, frustrating extraction. Despite the introduction of the improved 'St+' case, the Luger was still plagued by extraction difficulties.

Changes in the material of the case were matched by the development of substitute bullets. A projectile with a sintered-iron core, developed in 1939 by Vereinigte Deutsche Metallwerke AG, was adopted in 1940 as the Pist.Patr.08 SE. Ammunition of this type initially gave serious feed problems in automatic weapons, as the bullet weighed 5.8gm instead of 8gm and its recoil impulse was too low to operate some existing weapons. By the middle of 1942, sintered-iron bullets were confined to phosphated grey-lacquered steel-case ammunition.

The 9mm Pistolenpatrone 08 mit Eisenkern (Pist.Patr.08 mE), introduced in the autumn of 1940, was loaded with a bullet with a mild steel core, a steel jacket and a lead cup in the base. The projectile weighed 6.29–6.55gm, gave a higher velocity than the standard 8gm ball round, and was always lacquered black. The steel or brass cases had black primer annuli, the steel examples having a coat of dark grey-green lacquer to facilitate extraction.

Police Lugers

Concern expressed in the 1920s by the police authorities at the growing number of accidents created renewed interest in safety systems. The most important was the Schiwy Sear Safety, patented in Germany on 19th July 1929 (no.501,267) by gunsmith Ludwig Schiwy, the owner of F.W.Vandrey & Co in Berlin. It consisted of a spring-steel bar on top of the trigger plate which sprang down into a recess in the sear bar, locking the mechanism, if the trigger plate was removed.

A differing approach was taken by two employees of BKIW, Alexander Gebauer and Georg Voss. Their system – the subject of German patent 566,002 of January 1930 – consisted of a bar riveted to the trigger-plate, reaching up and over the breech-block. A chambered cartridge raised the extractor into a slot cut in the auxiliary bar, locking the trigger-plate in place. Gebauer and Voss registered several additional designs in 1930–5, but few details survive.

The magazine safeties were intended to prevent the gun firing if the magazine had been removed. The Schiwy pattern, patented in Germany in February 1932 (no.587,781), relied on a simple bar pivoted in the back of the trigger guard below the magazine-release catch. The bar sprang into the back surface of the trigger when the magazine was removed.

The only magazine safety to be encountered in any numbers was one of several differing designs credited to Fritz Walther of Carl Walther Waffenfabrik. Protected by DRGM 1,237,949 of 1st October 1932, fifty were made for trials in 1933. A spring-steel plate was let into the left side of the frame across the magazine well. When the magazine was removed, the safety bar sprang inward until a projection on its head blocked the trigger. Guns fitted with the Walther safety can be identified by a tiny vertical slot in the lower edge of the frame behind the trigger plate, though many of the sprung plates were subsequently deactivated by removing the actuating lugs.

Safety systems were also registered in 1932 by Simson & Co and Erfurter Maschinenfabrik B.Geipel GmbH, 'Erma-Werke'. Fred Datig reproduces some of the accompanying drawings in *The Luger Pistol*, though no surviving guns have been identified. A comprehensive list of these devices has been given by Joachim Görtz and Reinhard Kornmayer in *Waffen-Revue* (1984).

Zu der Patentschrift 501 267
Kl. 72h   Gr. 1

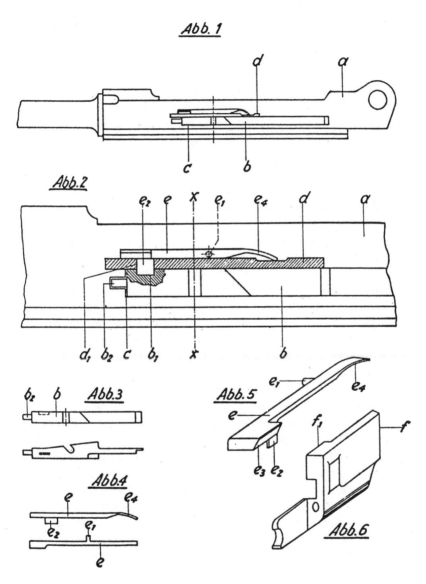

Fig. 17. The Schiwy safety.
Deutsches Patentamt.

Trials confirmed the efficacy of the Schiwy sear and Walther magazine safeties, which were adopted for the Prussian police on 30th August 1933. Even before the nationalisation of the state forces, however, the value of the fittings was being questioned; an entry published in the *Ministerialblatt des Reichs- und Preussischen Ministeriums des Innern* on 24th June 1936, for example, requested information concerning their effectiveness. It is clear that both patterns lasted into the late 1930s, but were then abandoned.

The rapid emergence of the NSDAP culminated in the installation of Hitler as Chancellor on 30th January 1933. As an act of political favour, Hermann Göring was named as minister without portfolio with tacit agreement that he would become aviation minister when the political climate allowed creation of an air force. Göring was also made minister of the interior in Prussia, allowing him to form the political police or Gestapo whilst simultaneously reorganising the state system.

The marks encountered on the handguns of the Prussian police are comparatively common on surviving guns. Many of them retained the forms popular in the 1920s, described in Chapter Eleven. Bavarian marks of this period invariably read 'P.D.M...', for Polizei-Direktion München, whereas Saxon marks are more commonly 'S.P.D...' (Schutz-Polizei Dresden). However, these are usually encountered on the Walther PP/PPK series or Sauer Behörden-Modell.

A national police force was created under the leadership of Heinrich Himmler on 16th June 1936; the state forces lost their autonomy, and the marking of police firearms was abandoned. The guns could still be recognised by the marks of the police inspectorate, which, instead of the sunbursts of the Prussians, became stylised swastika-clasping eagles accompanied by letters such as 'F' or 'L' – probably the initial of the surname of the principal inspector.

A separate state police force, the Landespolizei, had been raised in 1933 to maintain internal security. The organisation was really intended to train men for military service; when conscription was introduced in March 1935, and the unfettered enlargement of the armed forces began in October, many state police personnel (particularly the officers) immediately transferred into the army. The Landespolizei itself was disbanded in August 1935. The true status of the state police became evident when the Rheinland was reoccupied in March 1936, as the three regular infantry battalions had been reinforced by four former Landespolizei divisions raised in the demilitarised zone. Many state police weapons were also transferred to the army, explaining why Lugers bearing signs of sear and magazine-safety fittings may have additional army-style inspection markings.

Most of the Pistolen 08 delivered to the police after 1936 bore the Mauser banner on their toggles. Writing in 1977 in *World of Lugers* (volume one), Sam Costanzo recorded serial numbers as 7008v–7264v dated 1938; 7312v–8056v,

8854v–9380v, 4w–7420w and 258x–767x from 1939; 1133x–5772x from 1940; and 5819x–9995x and 31y–8282y from 1941. Few of these blocks seem to have run continuously, however, and any attempt to assess total acquisitions are fraught with danger. A few police guns are to be found with the 'SU' inspectors' marks generally associated with Simson though popularly (if mistakenly) interpreted as 'Simson-Ulbricht'. They may simply have been repaired with old parts.

Export Lugers

Several orders were attracted in the mid 1930s from a variety of sources. Unfortunately for Mauser, the quantities involved were almost always small, and the profits involved could not have been large.

The Netherlands   Dutch orders were legacies of BKIW days. Though the principal contract placed on behalf of the army in the Dutch East Indies for 9mm M1911 (grip-safety) Lugers had been completed, small quantities were made for the West Indies.

Deliveries of the 9mm Pistol No.1 were made to the Dutch navy throughout the 1930s. Guns delivered prior to January 1936, numbered from 1485 to 2129, bore the DWM monogram on the toggle-links even though they were assembled by Mauser and had distinctive Oberndorf 'crown/crown/U' proof marks.

From the autumn of 1937 onwards, when 200 were delivered, the pistols bore the Mauser banner mark on the toggles and were dated on the receiver-top. A hundred Lugers arrived in October 1938, followed by 225 in June 1939. These batches had 'v'-suffix numbers, which nevertheless continued the established navy sequence from 2330[v] onward.

Six hundred guns of a 1000-gun order scheduled for delivery in 1940 were given to the German forces after the invasion of the Netherlands; guns of this pattern were numbered 2655v–3254v, bore the 'arrow/RUST' safety-lever recess marks, and had German inspectors' marks. The remaining 400 were never completed, though surviving Dutch components – eg frames with arrow/RUST marks – were embodied in otherwise standard German P.08.

Persia   A hundred 1908-type pistols are said to have been purchased from BKIW in 1929, though no evidence other than hearsay has been offered in support. However, the first large contract was placed with Mauser in 1934 and – as Persian Lugers bear a model-date – it seems doubtful that the guns sought in the late 1920s, if indeed they were acquired at all, had any military status.

The Mauser-made pistols are easily distinguished by '1314-model short Parabellum pistol', rolled into the right side of the receiver in Farsi (Arabic) script. The date has sometimes been mistakenly identified as '1313', owing to the similarity between the Farsi numeral '4' and the Arabic '3'.

Though most Islamic countries accepted 354-day or lunar years, counted from the flight of Mohamed from Mecca to Medina in July 622, the Persians adopted a 365-day (solar) year in the 1920s. The date of the Lugers is deduced by adding 621 to the model-date 1314 – *ie* 1935.

Seventeen 10cm-barrelled P.08 numbered below 20 were sent to Persia in November or December 1935. The Shah is said to have cancelled the order, for reasons that are still unclear, but the rift was speedily healed; an entry in the diary kept by August Weiss records that a thousand pistols numbered 21–1020 left Oberndorf on 19th–20th May 1936. They were followed by a thousand more on 18th June – 1021 to 2021, excluding 1500. There may well have been a third consignment of 975–980 guns (in 1937?), totalling 3000 less the few that had either been retained by Mauser or distributed in presentations.

The 10cm-barrelled guns were accompanied by a substantial quantity of LP.08, the prototype of which, no.3001, was retained in Oberndorf. These pistols – or, at least, their barrels – were amongst the components transferred to Mauser from BKIW in 1930. Retrieved from store, they were refurbished, numbered, and fitted with sight leaves graduated in Farsi numerals.

The highest-numbered survivor is 3994, but sixty Siamese LP.08 sold by Odin International in the early 1980s, numbered between 3453 and 3551, suggest not only that the Persian guns may have been supplied in two batches but also that the total may have been only 800.

Portugal .The government ordered 12cm-barrelled 7.65mm 1906-type Lugers in 1935, destined for the national guard (Guardia Nacional Republicana or GNR). These were distinguished by the decorative monogram over their chambers, in addition to safety and extractor marks in Portuguese.

The guns were developed specifically for Austrian-made Hirtenberg ammunition, but, owing to variations in loading, were never regarded as reliable by Mauser even though the Portuguese seemed satisfied. The first consignment of 564 guns was despatched from Oberndorf in September 1935, apparently numbered from 1921v to 2484v – perhaps with gaps, as Sam Costanzo, writing in *World of Lugers* (volume one), listed 2492v and 2499v. These two stragglers could have come from the guns despatched in late September 1935, as their numbers have never been confirmed.

Whether the additional 1935 consignment was intended for the GNR has been disputed, as has the status of fifty more guns (4301v–4350v) sent to Portugal in June 1937. Notification from Portugal suggested in 1978 that only 562 guns were ever received by the national guard – the initial consignment of 564, less two guns retained as samples. If these records are to be trusted, then the supplementary guns went elsewhere.

Alternatively, since the GNR guns are said to have been received 'between 1934 and 1938', the total of 564 guns assigned to the original 1935 batch may simply have been computed on the basis of the lowest/highest serial numbers. But this would assume that the numbers ran continuously, which is sometimes dangerous.

A single 1908-pattern gun acquired by Portugal in November 1940, 4988v, chambered the 9mm round, bore '1940' on the chamber top, and had a Mauser banner on the toggle-link. The batch delivered in 1941 is assumed to have been similar. The Portuguese army was presumably assessing the merits of the 7.65mm and 9mm rounds in a bid to replace obsolescent Lugers, Savages, and Nagant-type revolvers.

The only large-scale acquisition of 9mm Lugers occurred in 1943, when several thousand 'Pistolas Parabellum do Exército, Português Mo.943' were shipped from Germany. The total is disputed, as the HWaA figure of 'four thousand' – which was clearly an approximation – does not tally with the serial numbers.

Writing in the *Deutsches Waffen-Journal* in 1969, Reinhard Kornmayer recorded numbers from 685 to 5263 (undoubtedly with 'm'-suffix numbers), suggesting that the purchase of 1943-type pistols netted 4578. However, pistol 5290m was found in southern Africa in the early 1990s, apparently in a Portuguese holster; if this can be authenticated, then the *Deutsches Waffen-Journal* claims must be reassessed.

A detailed analysis of the marks and numbers on gun 3261m, captured by the South African Army in Angola in 1975, suggests that only serial numbers were ever applied to the Mo.943. Lists purporting to be 'inventory numbers' are almost always the serial numbers without their suffixes.

Only the serial numbers distinguish the 'byf'-marked '42'-dated Portuguese Lugers from identical pistols issued in Germany. Even the regulation 'P.08' mark could be found on the left side of the frame.

The holsters made in Oporto differed perceptibly from the standard German PT.08, whilst spare magazines may have been made by the Arsenal do Exército in Lisbon. The wooden bottom plug of one of the two reserve magazines accompanying 3261m bears the Portuguese encircled-triangle mark, though the other magazine is a blued Haenel 'fxo' example.

Turkey   A few Lugers had been left behind in Turkey after 1918 by German military advisers, but no orders were sanctioned officially until the 1930s.

Most of the 9mm-calibre guns were ordered by the security police, the general directorate of security affairs (Emniyet Isleri Umum Müdürlügü, 'EIUM'). These had 10cm barrels, the full EIUM inscription rolled into the front right side of the receiver, and a 'TC' monogram – Türkiye Cümhüriyeti,

'Republic of Turkey' – on the chamber-top. Unlike the Persian guns, which are numbered in Farsi, Turkish guns have Western-style serial numbers.

The survival of guns numbered between 101 and 628 suggests that the contract may have been for a thousand. They display German 'crown/crown U' proof marks on the receiver, barrel and breech-block, but have Turkish *emniyet* (safety) and *ates* (extractor) markings. The Mauser banner appears on the toggle links, whilst the tiny marks of weapons inspector no.63 lie on the right side of the receiver, immediately ahead of the EIUM inscription, and on the frame behind the locking-bolt retaining pin.

One pistol, in addition to a 'TC' monogram above the chamber, has a star-and-crescent emblem on the front right side of the receiver accompanied by SUBAYLARA MAHSUSTUR ('for officers' use') in two lines. The weapon is otherwise similar to the EIUM pattern, with the Mauser banner on the toggle, eagle/WaA63 inspectors' marks, and standard German 'crown/crown U' proofs. No Turkish army contract has yet been authenticated.

A 'Turkish Air Force Luger' appeared in the USA in the 1980s, with an additional crescent alongside the 'TC' chamber-top monogram, and *Hava ordusuna mahsustur* ('for army air force use') on the side of the receiver. Writing in 1986 in *The Luger Book*, I questioned the spelling of the inscription and the lack of accented characters; however, the Berlitz Translation Service in London subsequently confirmed that the absence of the accents merely represented, according to the translator, 'the form of Turkish used in the 1930s'. The gun, numbered in the 9000v series with standard 'crown/crown/U' Oberndorf proof marks, is most probably genuine even though the air force still denies its existence.

However, a claim that Lugers were supplied with seventy-five Focke-Wulf Fw.190A-3 single-seat fighters sent to Turkey in 1943 still seems unacceptable. It is much more probable that the guns accompanied 24 Heinkel He.111F-1 light bombers ordered from Germany in the Spring of 1938 and delivered, with five unarmed transport derivatives, in 1938–9. As each crew mustered five men, more than a hundred Lugers could have been acquired if the scale of issue was one-per-man; even on the basis of one per bomber, there would still have been more than twenty.

Siam   In 1981, Odin International of Alexandria, Virginia, USA, advertised a large consignment of Lugers which had been authenticated by the Bangkok police department. Unlike the guns delivered to Persia in the same era, the Siamese examples have dated chambers and the Mauser banner on the toggle.

A hundred or more LP.08 apparently comprised the earliest dispatch. Dated 1936, the sixty-two sold by Odin were numbered between 3453 and 3551, a gap presumably being left in the number-sequence of the Persian 1314-model LP.08 to accommodate them. The Siamese Lugers were accompanied by standard board-type shoulder stocks bearing an impressed Mauser banner mark, though they were composed largely of old BKIW components.

Odin acquired thirty-five of the 150 9mm 10cm-barrelled Pistolen 08 purchased from Mauser in 1936, and 42 of about 200 acquired in 1937. Advertisements placed in *The Shotgun News* recorded their numbers as 4045–4240 dated 1936 and 4081–4595 dated 1937. Suffix letters, if present, were not recorded.

Yet the lists are confusing: no.4130, for example, is a 1936-vintage gun with numbers 'all matching' whilst no.4081 – also 'all matching' – is apparently dated 1937. If only a single delivery had been made in 1937–8, containing guns that had been mixed indiscriminately, the number/date inconsistencies in the Odin advertisements could be explained; but this is clearly far from satisfactory.

Most Siamese Lugers have additional issue numbers on the back of the frame above the lanyard loop, prefixed by a stylised lion-head property mark. Long-barrel guns 3539 and 3544, therefore, are also numbered '282' and '287' respectively. German 'crown/crown U' proof marks appear on the receiver, the barrel and the breech-block, whilst serial numbers follow standard German practice. The extractor and safety lever recess are unmarked.

Latvia   These Lugers were all basically Pistolen 08, but some had 9mm-calibre barrels measuring 98mm and others had 7.65mm 118mm patterns – the non-standard lengths being due to the distinctive front sight and a correspondingly shortened muzzle-crown. The total acquisition was apparently 847, 828 pistols in 9mm and the remainder in 7.65mm. One unexplained discrepancy lies in the number-sequence normally allocated to the first June 1939 consignment, 5001v–5201v, which is now known to contain six pistols sold in 1937 to the predecessor of the Electric Company of Israel. These were identified by Don Hallock and David Ginsberg in *Auto-Mag* in May 1985.

The Latvian guns were supplied from regular production and were not distinctively marked. The chambers would have been dated 1936, 1937 or 1938, the toggles had the Mauser banner mark, and the proofs would have been standard German 'crown/crown U'.

Sweden   The army purchased a few Lugers in the late 1930s, for units testing Suomi-type sub-machine-guns chambered for the 9mm Parabellum cartridge instead of the regulation 9mm M/07 (Browning Long) pattern. Some 7.65mm-calibre Lugers were acquired so that the relative merits of ammunition could be assessed.

Five 9mm guns were tested in the school of musketry, but the conclusions merely duplicated those of 1904; the Luger shot very accurately, but was too complicated and too expensive to justify widespread issue. The army eventually adopted the 9mm M/39 pistol – the Walther P.38 – but was forced to turn to the Lahti during the Second World War.

Mauser-Werke supplied the Swedish P.08-type pistols from regular 'v'-suffix commercial production, with barrels of 118mm (7.65mm) or 120mm (9mm). It is generally agreed that 285 9mm guns were acquired in September and December 1938, in batches of 275 and ten respectively, whilst thirty-four 7.65mm examples were purchased in February and August 1939.

None of these Lugers bore special markings. However, a few commercial-pattern pistols – 7551w–7889w with large gaps – were sold in Sweden in the early 1940s, distinguished by 'Kal. 7,65' on the left side of their 98mm barrels; the chambers are invariably dated 1940. Holsters will often be marked by Widforss of Stockholm, a sporting-goods distributor.

Bulgaria   Many of the original 12cm-barrelled Lugers purchased prior to 1914 survived to be altered to 9mm. This is said to have been undertaken in Oberndorf in 1940–1, once Bulgaria had joined the Axis in the Second World War, but the comparatively poor quality suggests that the work may have been undertaken locally; Mauser may simply have supplied the barrels. About 5600 P.08 were sent to Bulgaria in 1942, after procurement by the German army weapons office had ceased. These pistols undoubtedly bore standard marks – including 'byf' toggle marks and military proofs – and would have borne 'l'- and 'm'-suffix serial numbers. Owing to the domination of post-1945 Bulgaria by the USSR, details are difficult to obtain.

Switzerland   It was obvious by 1940 that the Luger had been overtaken by more modern designs. On 2nd October 1940, therefore, a five-man commission convened in the federal arms factory in Bern to consider alternatives. Trials showed that the SIG-Petter 'Neuhausen' pistol was dependable, but less accurate than either the 06/29 Luger or the 82/29 service revolver; the Spanish Astra 900 was rejected when it failed to demonstrate any superiority over its rivals.

The 06/29 Luger had returned an excellent 9cm x 6cm group at fifty metres but, as the SIG-Petters were easier to make and seemed reliable, comparative trials continued into 1941. The 7.65mm and 9mm Lugers and the SIG-Petter were then joined by the French 'Armee-Pistole aus Saint-Etienne', a Walther P.38, an FN-Browning GP Mle 35, a .38 Super Colt-Browning, and the prototype of the Pistole W + F Browning.

On 26th February 1941, a 9mm 06/29 conversion was tried against a Mauser-made P.08 and the FN-Browning GP Mle 35 with predictable results; the Swiss Luger proved to be the most accurate, but the Browning was extremely reliable.

Trials were undertaken in March 1941 with two 9mm Walther Polizei-

Pistolen and three .45 Colt-Brownings, but were then suspended until 19th May 1942. The Lugers were still shooting extremely well, particularly from a rest. Fifty-metre groups with diameters of 5.5cm (9mm) and 5.8cm (7.65mm) were much too good for the other triallists, with only the Walther P.38 bettering 15cm.

However, the testers were very impressed by the Walther double-action trigger and the simplicity and reliability of the Browning tipping-barrel system exemplified by the GP Mle 35, the Radom, and the SIG-Petter. The trials subsequently developed into a contest between the SIG-Petter and the Pistole W+F Browning, eventually resolving in favour of the former in 1949.

The experimental 9mm Lugers are said to have been P26291–P26299 'and others', though only P26291 and P26300 are mentioned in the test reports. Similar conversions of 1906 W+F and 06/24 W+F pistols are also known, but many are believed to have been undertaken commercially.

Japan Some of the Netherlands Indies army Lugers were undoubtedly seized by the Japanese during the Second World War, whilst others survived to equip the Indonesian army when the colonies gained independence in 1949. Indonesian guns – once mistakenly identified as Venezuelan – usually display small five-point stars on major components.

Pistols used by the Japanese are rarely marked; though a few ex-NIL weapons display a chrysanthemum above the chamber, their authenticity is questionable. If any of these marks date from the Second World War, it is far more likely that they were added after capture (possibly to decorate or distinguish a war trophy) than by the Japanese.

That Lugers were taken from the Japanese forces cannot be disputed – R.K. Wilson, author of the classic *Automatic Pistols* (1943), personally witnessed the surrender in Borneo in September 1945 of a gun which had been carried by a soldier of the 37th Army. Yet the claim that so many had been captured that wholesale conversion for the standard 8mm Japanese pistol cartridge had been undertaken in Java is less convincing; most of these were converted in the USA in the 1950s, when 8mm Nambu ammunition was easier and cheaper to obtain than the German 9mm type.

Commercial guns

Though the 1911-vintage 'crown/N' proof mark remained in vogue, the Mauser Lugers made prior to 1939 customarily bore 'crown/crown U' on the left side of the receiver ahead of the trigger-plate – a combination of the definitive proof for handguns (the crown) with the standard 'crown/U' view mark.

However, revision of the proof laws had commenced as early as 1937 to give greater control over the distribution of firearms. The new proof act was drafted late in 1938 and approved by the German parliament on 7th June 1939, though the new marks – including 'eagle/N' – were not used until 1st April 1940. Work continued in Oberndorf, Suhl and Zella-Mehlis, but the Frankfurt an der Oder proof house was closed. On 1st June 1940, the Austrian establishments were integrated into the system, to be followed on 23rd July 1940 by the former Czech proof house in Prague. The nitro-proof of the Prague establishment comprised a Lion of Bohemia superimposed on 'N'. One 7.65mm commercial DWM-made Luger shown in *Auto-Mag* in May 1985 displays this particular mark, together with the proof number 15547 and the date [19]43.

The popularity of sub-calibre trainers created during the Weimar Republic – principally the RWS/Weiss and Kulisch/Erma patterns – continued unabated. They were joined by the 4mm single-shot Bolte & Anschütz system, the design being registered in January 1936. The most obvious recognition feature was the improved spring-loaded retainer, which locked around the front sight.

The Swiss Lienhard was the best of the pre-war designs, excepting the semi-automatic Erma trainer. Designed by gunsmith Walter Lienhard, a renowned marksman, it allowed practice to be undertaken with the standard magazine. The 4mm or 5.6mm cartridges were simply inserted in cartridge-like auxiliary chambers or *Ladepatronen*, which were fed from the magazine by retracting the toggle manually before each shot. The auxiliary cartridges and front sights were patented in Switzerland in May 1939 (no.204,889), but improvements were filed in 1944, 1951 and 1961.

CHAPTER 14

The Second World War and the demise of the Luger

The First World War had shown that the complexity of the Luger hindered mass-production, and the advent in the 1920s of the prototype FN-Browning GP-35 did not pass unnoticed in Germany. As early as March 1927, the army weapons office had informed the infantry inspectorate that 'about 1,180 operations were required in the manufacture of the Pistole 08, 156 of which were required on the grip alone'. The simplest blowback Browning required only 55 manufacturing operations, and even the most powerful military pistols being made elsewhere in Europe rarely required more than 500.

Shortly after the Third Reich began, the army high command asked the weapons office to find a suitable replacement for the Luger. Trials began immediately but, unfortunately, few records have yet been found.

Walther, Sauer, Mauser and BSW pistols were all tested until, eventually, only the Walther Armee-Pistole remained. Objections raised to its internal hammer led in 1938 to semi-experimental exposed-hammer variants, the Militär-Pistole (IV) and the Heerespistole, before the design was deemed acceptable for service. It was adopted as the '9mm Pistole 38' on 26th April 1940, though large-scale deliveries had already commenced: about 13,000 guns had been made in 1939-40 in an 'O'-prefix series, and 4575 guns had been sent into store in April 1940 alone.

The Pistole 38 was designed by Fritz Walther and Fritz Barthelmes, the latter being responsible for the basic operating principles. The recoil-operated Walther relies on a propped-up block beneath the barrel instead of a toggle system. Trials showed it to be stronger than the Luger; a better performer in mud or snow; and easier (if not necessarily cheaper) to produce in quantity. The double-action trigger was advantageous and the cartridge feed – particularly with steel-case ammunition – was generally better than the P.08, even though the upright grip did not 'point' the gun as comfortably.

Though a great deal of effort had been applied to the production engineering of the P.38, it was still complicated; many of the individual components were concentrated in the trigger system, which was undeniably efficient, yet the

Walther contained more parts than the Luger. The simplicity sought by the army weapons office in 1927 had still not been achieved.

Production was initially entrusted to Carl Walther Waffenfabrik of Zella-Mehlis, but the army weapons office soon realised that a single manufacturer could not produce guns quickly enough to answer wartime demands. In July 1941 Mauser-Werke was ordered to begin tooling to make the P.38. Production of the Luger stopped in June 1942, but enough parts remained in store to permit large-scale assembly until December 1942. Small numbers were still being made in 1945, and the French occupation forces even managed to produce a few thousand guns in 1945–6.

Aware that the combined efforts of Walther and Mauser could not cope with unexpectedly high losses in combat, the authorities recruited Spreewerke GmbH and Böhmische Waffenfabrik at the beginning of 1942. Though Spreewerke's headquarters were sited in Berlin, the P.38 was apparently made in occupied Czechoslovakia: in 1945, several thousand sets of parts found in a factory in Hradkoú-nad-Nisou ('Werk Kratzau') were assembled for the Czech army.

Böhmische Waffenfabrik and Spreewerke each delivered their first guns in May 1942, though, oddly, the first Mauser-made weapons did not appear until December 1942. Böhmische Waffenfabrik ceased production in July 1942 after making only a hundred guns; but, by December 1942, Spreewerke had reached a monthly output of 3000.

By the end of 1942, the Pistole 38 was commonly encountered in front-line service and was prized by the Germans' opponents; the Luger was particularly desirable as a souvenir, but many soldiers sought the Walther for its double-action trigger system – a most useful feature in combat.

The Second World War

In his authoritative study *Die Pistole 08* (1982), Joachim Görtz recorded that 102,539 Pistolen 08 had been accepted in 1938 and 134,913 in 1939. Yet even these quantities were unable to meet the demands of the German armed forces, the strength of which leapt from 2.75 million men in 1939 to more than seven million in 1941.

The 1908-pattern Luger was the standard service pistol of the German army until the adoption of the P.38 in April 1940, though individual officers had always preferred the smaller Mauser, Sauer and Walther blowbacks. As the war ran its course and the Germans overran vast tracts of Europe, so many extra handguns were acquired that the issues blurred.

Responsibility for much of the German anti-aircraft defence system fell to the air force, many photographs of individual gun-batteries showing personnel with Luftwaffe insignia and Lugers. The pistols were supplied by the army weapons office through a subordinate air force procurement unit, at a monthly rate of about 3000.

The issue of Lugers to aircrew has often been debated. Among the written testimony is *Enemy in the Sky* (1976), in which Air Vice-Marshal Sandy Johnstone recorded that:

[on 24th February 1940] shortly after getting into position, we heard Red Section being vectored towards St. Abb's Head and Douglas giving the tallyho, so we left our spot and set off at full throttle to join him, and reached the area in time to watch a Heinkel 111 make a forced landing in a field nearby, with three Spitfires circling overhead. We were surprised then to see one of the Spitfires detach itself ... and then proceed to land alongside the Heinkel, but we were even more surprised when the Spitfire suddenly cartwheeled and ended up on its back. From chatter ... on the R/T it transpired it was our Squadron Commander who had come to grief so ignominiously.

However, Douglas is back at Drem again [a few miles east of Edinburgh] with a stiff neck, three Lugers and a fascinating tale...
[30th September 1940] Jack called up ... and asked me to look in at Tangmere [near Chichester in the South of England] ... as he had one of the Ju 88 pilots in the guard room who apparently wanted to meet one of his adversaries. I was more than surprised to be confronted by a fresh-faced youngster who could not have been more than eighteen years of age. He was very correct in manner ... but the gist of the message I was given was that he wanted to hand over his Luger to me as a sort of trophy of war.

Suggestions have been made that any German handgun may have been a 'Luger' to British airmen, implying that reports of this type should be treated sceptically. However, among individual guns known to have been taken from German aircrew was a standard P.08, once displayed in the arms and armour museum in Stratford upon Avon.

In October 1939, Chief Petty Officer (later Lieutenant) Robert Gibbs was serving aboard the British destroyer *Janus*. In the course of a North Sea patrol, look-outs spotted a Dornier Do.18 reconnaissance flying boat, which, hit by anti-aircraft gunfire, ditched in the sea close to the warship.

Gibbs wrote that as *Janus* approached the seaplane:

...the midship gunner opened fire at us with his machine-gun, causing no casualties but bringing a few short bursts of 0.5in quad-barrelled machine-gun fire, and about 8–10 rounds of 2pdr Pom-Pom upon the plane. This ... caused three casualties in the plane's crew of four, the pilot being killed and the navigator and midship gunner having some 0.5in holes in them. The crew surrendered, [throwing] their machine-guns overboard, by which time the ship had grappled the plane alongside the starboard after torpedo davit. The bow-gunner being first up the ship's side, I relieved him of his side-arm and pocketed it together with the other personal weapons of the crew with much pleasure ... I do not know whether the bow-gunner intended to use his weapon, as it had the first round jammed in the breech as if he had tried to get one up the spout. However, I had my Webley .45 in my left hand...

Janus then rammed and sank the Dornier, the pilot being buried at sea and the prisoners landed at Immingham. The bow-gunner told his captors that he had been transferred to the air force from the navy, a move he bitterly resented. The captured pistol proved to be no.4125u, an 'S/42' example made by Mauser in 1937.

Lugers were carried by the crews of light bombers such as the Do.17, He.111 and Ju.88 throughout the Battle of Britain, and probably on into 1941; thereafter, most of the handguns were Mauser, Sauer or Walther blowbacks. Space was at less of a premium in a bomber than in a small single-seat fighter like the Me.109.

Claims that Lugers were banned from air service in 1941 have never been supported by documentary evidence; it may simply be that more German airmen were commissioned officers, responsible for purchasing their own handguns. The mauling suffered by the Luftwaffe in the opening phases of the Battle of Britain had persuaded Hitler to order that only a single officer was to fly in each plane until losses of trained personnel had been made good. It was not uncommon in 1940 to find that the pilot of a downed bomber was a comparatively junior NCO.

Issues of Lugers in the navy were very modest, as monthly deliveries from the army weapons office rarely exceeded 250. Pistols were undoubtedly carried on warships, but the quantities concerned and responsibility for procurement have not been established. It is impossible to link pistols with individual ships on the basis of markings or serial number, except for a very few taken as war trophies or retrieved from wrecks. Wartime losses of navy small-arms would have been high, owing to the sinking of many warships: three of four battleships, for example, or 753 of 863 operational U-boats.

By the standards of the Royal Navy, the German ships often mustered very large crews; *Bismarck* carried 2092 men on her last cruise compared with 1477 aboard her victim *Hood*, older but otherwise of comparable dimensions. A typical pre-1918 dreadnought had carried about a hundred Lugers for a thousand-man crew, but the sub-machine-gun had replaced the pistol as the principal boarding weapon by 1939. It may be simply that handguns – sophisticated privately-purchased blowbacks for officers, regulation-issue Lugers for NCOs – were taken aboard ship as personal sidearms, the sub-machine-guns being issued from shipboard armouries when circumstances dictated.

The pistols issued to the navy during the Second World War included shortened and original full-length 1904-pattern navy Lugers, standard Pistolen

08, blowback Mausers and Polish Radoms. Well-known pictures show crewmen on the merchantman *Dresden* – impressed into the navy to serve the auxiliary cruiser *Atlantis* as a prison ship – guarding captured Allied crewmen with LP.08-and-stock combinations.

Though the Luger usually operated efficiently with standard ammunition, steel cases often failed to extract properly. From 1941 onward, packaging of steel-case ammunition was marked NUR FÜR MASCHINEN-PISTOLEN (for submachine-guns only) and – in January 1943 – the remaining supplies of brass-case Pistolenpatrone 08 were reserved for the Lugers. By this time, steel-case rounds were being packaged with the specific proviso that they were 'Not to be used in Pistolen 08 (intermittent jams in chamber)'.

The ferocity of the fighting, especially after the Germans invaded the Soviet Union in 1941, led to renewed interest in fully automatic pistols in the hope that they would be useful in street fighting. Typical of the designs was a Luger conversion patented in March 1943 (no.763,876) by Josef Schorn, a gunsmith of Koblenz-Lützel. Entitled 'trigger system for handguns, transforming them into machine pistols', it relied on a modified sear-bar and a pivoting fire-selector lever.

A small number of automatic LP.08 conversions were made in Stuttgart from 1942–3 until the early 1950s. One of these guns, no.0009, featured in an article in the *Deutsches Waffen-Journal* in 1981; the Maquis apparently took it from the body of a German officer killed in the French Alps in the winter of 1944. The most distinctive external features were an L-slot cut in the trigger-plate, the sliding selector on the sear-bar, and the duplication of the trigger levers.

Amongst the most interesting cartridges of the 1939–45 period was the 9mm Nahpatrone 08, based on an unsuccessful close-range cartridge developed during the First World War, which was destined for silenced weapons. Reducing the charge while simultaneously increasing the weight of the bullet to 9gm assured subsonic velocity. A few Lugers have been found with Maxim-type silencers attached to the barrel, but little of consequence is known of their history even though some of the combinations seem to date from the pre-1945 era.

Early in 1944, the Germans captured some Russian-made 7.65mm Auto cartridges, misleadingly headstamped 'Geco'. These were found to contain a small amount of poison in the bullet, subsequently identified as aconitin. The German state security bureau authorised production of comparable 9mm Kampstoff-Patrone 08 ('K.-Patr.08'), but only thirty had been produced by 13th April 1944. These poison-bullet rounds apparently contain an unusual multi-part projectile in a thin steel envelope. The after-core flew forward when the bullet hit a target, crushing a capsule of potassium cyanate to eject the poison through a channel cut in the front core. The headstamp is said to have consisted of nothing but 'K'.

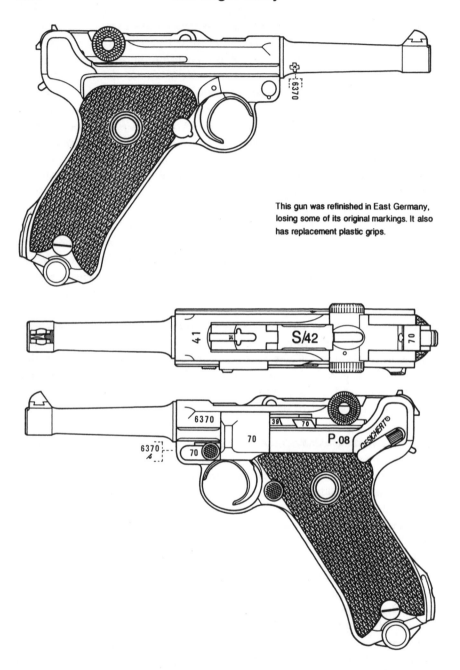

This gun was refinished in East Germany, losing some of its original markings. It also has replacement plastic grips.

Fig. 18. These drawings show the marks applied to a typical Mauser-made P.08, 'S/42' no.6370 of 1941. *John Walter*.

The decline of production

In 1940, only Mauser was making the Luger in quantity; Krieghoff was concentrating on machine-guns, though some old pistol components made in 1935–6 were assembled in 1940, and another thousand guns were delivered to the air force in 1941–3. The serial numbers of these weapons seem to run backward, as pistol no.11249 bears '1943' whilst 11957 dates from 1941. As explained previously, this is believed to have arisen from placing guns in racks with the oldest at the back. Krieghoff also assembled a few commercially saleable 'military rejects', numbered P1-P100, in this period.

Mauser continued to make Lugers for the German armed forces until the end of 1942, although a few thousand sets of components were assembled in 1943–5 for other purposes. The toggles had originally been stamped 'S/42', but this was simplified to '42' and then replaced by 'byf'. The original date-code, which appeared above the chamber, was replaced by the date in full and then by the last two digits. The army weapons office could even afford to decline the last few bulk consignments of serviceable Lugers. Official procurement stopped in November 1942, so Mauser diverted pistols to Bulgaria (5600) and Portugal ('four thousand') with the backing of the German authorities.

Finally, in 1944-5, Krieghoff produced the 9mm Pistolen 08 numbered 12943–13158; in *The Krieghoff Parabellum*, Randall Gibson argues that these guns are sufficiently different from the pre-1943 deliveries to form a distinct sub-group. They seem to be numbered from the end of the 1940 consignments, with 1000 added to the series: no guns have yet been authenticated with numbers in the 11994–12943 group.

Lugers continued to serve the armed forces, partisans, Maquisards and private armies until the end of the war. In the few weeks between the arrival of the Americans in Thuringia and the transfer of the area to the Soviet Zone, Krieghoff assembled 245–250 pistols from a collection of parts. Numbers were stamped internally, externally or not at all. Individual guns had alloy frames, Simson-made toggle-links, or non-standard barrels; some guns were blued, others were left in the white, and a few displayed the recipient's name or initials. The destruction of the Krieghoff factory by the Soviet authorities finally brought a fascinating story to an end.

Just as Krieghoff struggled to assemble Lugers for the trophy-seekers, the French were producing the P.08 and P.38 in the Mauser factory in Oberndorf. These Lugers were assembled from the components remaining in store, cannibalising anything that was needed from damaged guns. There is no evidence that any new parts were made under French supervision, though the P.38 production line was certainly reactivated. Eventually, bowing to pressure from the other Allies, the French stopped using the Oberndorf facilities on 2nd April 1946, destroyed most of the factory records, and removed much of the machinery.

By this time, however, the stature of the Luger as a souvenir had increased so greatly that, according to Ian Hogg in *German Pistols and Revolvers 1871–1945* (1971):

> ...the bridge over the river at Flensburg is practically supported by a mass of ... pistols, thrown there by the British military police who disarmed the German troops streaming back from Denmark in 1945. And it should be possible for a diver to walk from Calais to Dover on a carpet of Parabellums, so many were thrown overboard by returning British troops on hearing the stern loudspeaker warnings about what would happen ... if they were detected in the attempt to introduce illicit pistols into Britain.

Non-standard pistols

Though production of P.08 and P.38 ran into millions, even these figures failed to meet the needs of the armed forces. According to Ploetz's *Geschichte der zweiten Weltkrieges* (1960), the estimated strength of the Wehrmacht was 7.23 million in 1941 and 10.35 million in the summer of 1944. Some of the paramilitary forces could also muster millions of members.

Surviving inventories indicate that the army had 552,962 pistols in September 1940, almost all being 1908-type Lugers; the air force had 186,000 P.08; the navy had 12,914 P.08 and 23,042 7.65mm Mauser blowbacks. By December 1943, however, the total for the army had reached 1,272,696 and, by August 1944, it was 1,598,046.

The combined output of Mauser, Walther and Spreewerke alone would have been able to ensure adequate handgun supplies had it not been for escalating combat losses. Only 7569 pistols had been lost from 10th May to 31st August 1940, during the very successful campaigns in Belgium, the Netherlands, Luxembourg and France, but the invasion of the Soviet Union in June 1941 posed an entirely different problem.

Losses in the early months of Operation Barbarossa had been very low, as the Germans held the advantage. Once the Red Army began to hit back, the tide of battle turned and small-arms of all types – handguns included – were lost in great numbers; 12,381 had been lost in December 1943 and, by the summer of 1944, the situation had deteriorated farther. The inventory shrank by 52,090 pistols in July, then by 56,084 in October; more than 210,000 were lost from 1st September 1944 to 28th February 1945.

The rapid reduction in the handgun inventory soon forced the army high command to procure every available serviceable handgun. Unfortunately, the only detailed records that survive are restricted to 1939–42. Frustrating though this may be for the collector, it reflects the desperation of 1944–5 when every conceivable source of weapons was being investigated.

Panel Nine

NON-STANDARD HANDGUNS IN GERMAN
SERVICE, 1939-45

The principal German-made handguns were the P.08, the P.38 and the Mauser C/96, supported by the principal double-action blowbacks — the Mauser HSc, the Sauer 38H, the Walther PP and the Walther PPK. The assimilation of the Austrian army into the Wehrmacht in 1938 led to the standardisation of the useful, if obsolescent Steyr-Hahn ('Repetierpistole M 12'), many thousands of which were converted to chamber the standard 9mm Parabellum cartridge.

Poland and Czechoslovakia also provided effective handguns. The best of them was the sturdy Browning-link Pistole 35(p), better known as the VIS-35 or Radom. Production continued in Poland under German control, 22,474 being distributed to the army and 4000 to the navy in 1941. The Czechoslovak service pistols included the blowback vz.27 (Pistole 27[t]) and vz.38 (Pistole 39[t]), the latter being a Frantisek Myška design with a double-action trigger system. About 44,000 P.39(t) were issued to the German forces in 1939, all but 3000 to the army.

The seizure of the factory of Fabrique Nationale d'Armes de Guerre after the invasion of Belgium enabled production of the excellent FN-Brownings to continue. The locked-breech 9mm GP Mle 35 (Pistole 640[b]) was equal to any of the existing service pistols, becoming as popular with German troops as the Inglis-made variant proved to be with the Chinese, British and Canadians.

The first deliveries of these Belgian-made pistols occurred in 1940, when the army received 2520 9mm GP-35 and 2550 9mm Mle.10/22 pistols whilst the Luftwaffe received 1282 7.65mm Mle.10/22; these were issued as Pistolen 640(b), 641(b) and 626(b) respectively.

Among the lesser pistols acquired during the Second World War were the Norwegian Colt-Browning m/1914 (or Pistole 657[n]); the French MAB Mle A, MAB Mle D, Unique Mle 17, Unique Kriegsmodell, and the Mle 1935A service pistol (Pistole 625[f]); the Spanish Astra 200, Astra 300, Astra 400, Astra 600 and Star Modelo B; plus Italian Berettas seized when Italy capitulated in 1943.

By 31st December 1942, the army had been issued with P.08 and P.38; the Mauser M34 and HSc; the Walther PP and PPK; the Sauer 38H; Pistolen 27(t), 35(p), 39(t), 640(b), 641(b); and the Astra 600. The air force had P.08 and P.38; the Mauser M34 and HSc; the Walther PP and PPK; the Sauer 38H; Pistolen 37(u), 39(t) and 626(b). Comparatively few guns were carried by aircrew, but the anti-aircraft batteries (Flak-Abteilungen) were an air force responsibility. The navy had the P.08, the Mauser M34 and the Pistole 35(p).

Officers had often purchased guns of their own; in addition, in 1938, the civilian population had been ordered to surrender firearms for which there was no good use. The reissue of these guns during the Second World War, usually to non-combatants, explains the presence of inspectors' marks on such unlikely guns as the Belgian Armand Gavage automatic. Details of many of these guns will be found in the profusely illustrated books written by Jan Still.

One undesirable result of the impressment of so many differing pistols was the use of nine cartridges: 6.35mm Auto, 7.63mm Mauser, 7.65mm Auto, 7.65mm Longue, 9mm Browning Long, 9mm Parabellum, 9mm Short, 9mm Steyr and .45 ACP. There was also a special 9mm Czechoslovakian service round, dimensionally identical with 9mm Short but loaded to give greater power.

The Lugers: how many were made?

By the late 1930s, Mauser was making appreciable quantities of Pistolen 08 and annual deliveries were exceeding 100,000. According to Wolfgang Seel, in *Mauser – von der Waffenschmiede zum Weltunternehmen*, 141,514 P.08 were made in the 1939/40 financial year; 157,109 in 1940/41; 139,425 in 1941/2; 11,583 in 1942/3; 507 in 1943/4; and none in 1944/5. Mauser's financial year ran from 1st October to 30th September of the following calendar year. The total made from 1st October 1939 until the end of the war was 450,138.

Army weapons office records suggest that 126,338 P.08 were accepted in 1939; 139,220 in 1940; 151,910 in 1941; and 102,940 in 1942. Though these include unconfirmed figures for February 1939, March 1940, April 1940, September 1940, January 1942 and October 1942, and may cover differing administrative years than Mauser's own figures, the total of 520,408 seems broadly comparable. If the Army weapons office figures refer to calendar years or even the German government financial year – which began in April – then they include at least six months of deliveries prior to 1st October 1939, which would be missing from the Mauser figures given previously.

The best information currently available suggests that Mauser made 939,709 Lugers between 1st October 1935 and the end of the Second World War, in addition to 327,604 Pistolen 38. These figures include 31,633 commercial Lugers, plus 11,941 made for the forestry service, the police and export

– previously classified in the commercial category – from 1st October 1942 to May 1945.

Including an allowance for unknown numbers made in Oberndorf in the 1934/5 fiscal year, total production was about 990,000 Lugers of all types. Adding the few thousand made by Krieghoff gives a plausible grand total slightly in excess of a million made from 1st October 1934 to 8th May 1945.

CHAPTER 15

The New Luger: from Mauser-Jagdwaffen to Mitchell Arms

The last Swiss military 06/29 W+F Luger was completed in the Bern arms factory on 6th November 1946; 27,931 had been made for the armed forces alongside guns made for private sale. Estimates of commercial production range from 1316 to 1917, but are still the subject of debate. The factory subsequently modified some pistols for target shooting, but they were based on commercial examples taken from the P77942–P78258 group.

Undoubtedly the finest individual performance with a Luger was given by Heinrich Kelleter, shooting for Switzerland in the world championships held in Buenos Aires in 1949. Firing 06/29 W+F pistol no.P78108, Kelleter took the fifty-metre full-bore gold medal with a score of 559 × 600 – 96, 88, 95, 100, 88 and 92. The perfect fourth series was sensational; Fritz Häusler, in *Schweizerische Faustfeuerwaffen*, shows that all ten shots struck the top half of the 8cm-diameter bull's-eye. With thirty-six bulls in sixty shots, Kelleter beat the Finnish marksman Säärnikkö by eleven points. The Luger had a special 17cm barrel installed in the Bern factory, but retained fixed sights. It was subsequently returned, fitted with a standard 12cm barrel, and sold commercially.

Post-war Lugers

The Luger still had its uses in the Europe of the late 1940s, though even the Swiss army was seeking to replace it.

France As already noted, the French continued to operate the Oberndorf production line until 2nd April 1946, assembling P.08, P.38 and the HSc to equip the French army. Most of these French Lugers, which often have had a parkerised finish, accompanied troops dispatched to French Indo-China. There they endured long and arduous service from which many have only recently returned.

German Democratic Republic Many thousands of Lugers were refurbished for issue to the People's Police. These may contain a wide variety of parts, the numbers often being re-struck in accordance with the master number on the frame. They are generally distinguished by their plastic grips, which have a concentric-circle mark, and by the semi-matt blue finish. Made in the sequestered Haenel factory in Suhl, magazines may be marked '2/1001'.

Israel The Israeli connection with the Luger stretches back to the time of the British Mandate in Palestine. In 1937, what has since become the Electric Company of Israel purchased about thirty 1908-type guns from a Mauser agent. These were a mixture of standard Mauser-banner commercial guns and unwanted Stoeger-marked examples which had remained in Oberndorf. According to Don Hallock and David Ginsburg, writing in *Auto-Mag*, the seventeen Mauser-banner guns were numbered between 4759v and 5025v, with gaps, and the Stoegers between 409v and 472v with two higher-numbered stragglers (8732v and 8739v). These guns have attracted controversy, not least because the Banner-marked guns lie in the serial-number range often attributed to Latvia.

Substantial quantities of Lugers have been seized in Israel from members of the Palestine Liberation Organization and its offshoots. Generally ex-police Mauser Banner P.08, these may have reached the Middle East by way of the German Democratic Republic or the USSR. Refinished, appearing almost new, they are often accompanied by magazines made in the former German Democratic Republic, coded '2/1001'. Most of them also have new plastic grips with the so-called 'Vopo' concentric-circle logo. Gun 5688y, a 1942-date Mauser Banner P.08 with a police eagle/L mark, is typical of the captures.

A few Lugers were refurbished in Haifa in the 1950s and sold under the brandname 'Hanesek' ('The Gunsmith'), an appropriate Hebrew mark appearing on the left frame rail immediately ahead of the trigger-plate. This inscription has often been mistakenly attributed to 'Israeli freedom fighters'. Magazines have been manufactured in Israel by Codil Ltd.

Austria 9mm 10cm-barrelled P.08 will be encountered with the marks of the Bundesheer or Austrian federal army. These guns have often been dated to 1938–9 or 1940–2, but the standards of finish and the rounded edges of the front toggle-link suggest that they were assembled by the French after the end of the Second World War.

Some of the Lugers were sold to the Austrians in 1950–2, being transferred to the police only when new Walthers were purchased in 1958–61. They were finally sold to a German arms dealer in the mid 1970s and were dispersed on the commercial market.

The term 'Bundesheer' has only been current in Austria since independence was regained after 1945, and so the guns cannot have been marked during the Second World War. Though they often bear German 'eagle/N' proofs, supposedly dating manufacture to 1940–5, parts had been stockpiled in the Mauser plant. The quantity of pistols sold to Austria is not known, though Sam Costanzo records the observed serial numbers as 1208–2310, without suffix letters.

Rebirth of the Luger

In the early 1960s, Samuel Cummings of the American International Armament Company (Interarmco) approached Mauser-Werke and the Swiss federal factory in Bern to obtain quotes to produce new Lugers.

The Swiss factory still owned the machinery on which the 06/29 W+F Luger had been made, even though work had stopped in 1947. Design of a simplified 06/29 began in the anticipation that the equipment that remained in working order could be used to subsidise a production run. The result was the 7.65mm 'Pistole 29/65 W+F', only one of which was ever made.

The long frame and receiver were standard components, probably left over from the 1940s and the conclusion of 06/29 production. The safety lever, the plain toggle-grips, the locking bolt, the magazine release cross-bolt and the injection-moulded plastic grips (complete with little 'W+F' monograms) were also standard parts.

The 29/65 lacks the grip safety of the 06/29, and an additional rivet runs through the stem of the safety lever. The 29/65 breech-block was simplified to reduce production costs, so that its upper surface slopes almost continuously from the top of the toggle-link pivot. This and the conical barrel shoulder are most unappealing aesthetically. The characteristics of the 29/65 duplicated those of the earlier 06/29 W+F Luger, excepting that it was a few grams lighter. The only mark was a cross-on-shield on the front toggle-link, as there were neither proof marks nor serial numbers.

Cummings regarded the price quoted by the Bern factory as much too high, preferring a competitive tender made by Mauser-Werke GmbH of Oberndorf. Though the corporate structure was new, the Mauser banner trademark would still be available to assist promotional activities. Work ceased in Switzerland, much of the production machinery being sold to Mauser in 1967; the unique 29/65 W+F prototype was eventually acquired by Rolf Gminder, under whose enthusiastic direction the Mauser pistol-making business was expanded greatly in the 1970s.

The first pilot models of the new Mauser-Parabellum were made in 1968–9. They had more in common with the Bern-made 06/29 Lugers than the German P.08; the frame, receiver and barrel, in particular, showed Swiss influence. The earliest guns may even have incorporated a few Swiss-made parts.

The Mauser-Parabellum 29/70

The first guns had short grip safeties and chequered wood grips, with a plain border not unlike that of the Swiss 1906 W+F and 06/24 W+F patterns. They often displayed MAUSER PARABELLUM above 'Cal. .30 Parabellum' on the left side of the frame behind the trigger plate, though some guns had calibre designations on the top of the barrel and others were not marked at all. Proof marks were generally dated '69' (1969), but variations in detail will be encountered.

By the time series production began in November 1970, changes had been made. Chequering was added to the thumb-pieces of the magazine catch, the locking bolt and the toggle grips; and the shape of the original Swiss-pattern stepped receiver became more angularly Teutonic. The 7.65mm prototype 10.000003, dated 1971, displays these changes – but suggests that work on the 7.65mm pistols began only after small quantities of the 9mm pattern had been made.

The pistols still bore a greater resemblance to the Swiss 06/29 Luger than the German P.08, but the most obvious distinctions had blurred. They were all marketed as 'Mauser-Parabellums', but the manufacturing pattern 29/70 provides a useful distinction between the early and later ('06/73') guns.

The serial numbers of the perfected 7.65mm guns began at 10.001001, and at 11.001001 for the perfected 9mm type. Standard 7.65mm barrels measured 10cm, 12cm and 15cm, the 9mm patterns being 10cm and 15cm; alternatives could be obtained to order.

Excepting comparatively minor variations of the standard guns, few unusual 29/70-type Mauser-Parabellums seem to have been made. However, a solitary 7.65mm-calibre pocket pistol, no.10.000001, was made in 1973; it had a 75mm barrel and a Swiss-style front sight.

Pistol 11.001007 typified the earliest Mauser-Parabellums, with plain-bordered chequered walnut grips; the 'Original Mauser' banner on the toggle; and MAUSER PARABELLUM on the left side of the frame above '9mm Luger'. The calibre designation stamped into the top surface of the barrel read '9mm Para od. 38 Luger'.

Success was reflected in commercial interest, large numbers of the new pistols being purchased by Interarms. The calibre marks on these usually read '.30 Luger' and '9mm Luger', whilst SAFE and LOADED replaced GESICHERT and GELADEN on the safety-lever recess and extractor respectively. The distributor's markings – INTERARMS over ALEXANDRIA, VIRGINIA – appeared with a sunburst trademark on the front right side of the receiver.

The Mauser-Parabellums are identical mechanically with the Swiss 06/29 W+F excepting for detail refinements. Thus they bear a greater resemblance to the original New Model of 1906 than to the improved gun accepted by the German army two years later.

The grip-safety system prevented the sear moving laterally until the grip was pressed inwards against its spring. This moved the nose of the grip-lever downward into the frame and freed the sear. A radial lever in the recess milled in the left side of the frame, above the back of the grip, locked the grip safety when pushed upward. Some guns display GESICHERT or SAFE in this area, the mark being exposed only when the safety is applied.

The breech-block contained a standard New Model extractor/loaded-chamber indicator, originally patented in 1904, which was marked GELADEN or LOADED. The frames were straight-fronted, and the squared front sight block was surmounted by a blade. Proof marks appeared on the left side of the frame ahead of the trigger-plate.

A proof law accepted in 1952 had replaced the pre-war regulations, though practically no new firearms had been made in Germany since the end of the Second World War. The first post-war proof house was established in Ulm/Donau, the nitro-proof mark being little more than the Third Reich type though the accompanying eagle was greatly refined. The mark was invariably accompanied by a stylised deer's antler, adapted from the coat of arms of Württemberg. Proof houses were then opened in Eckenförde/Holstein and Hannover in 1952–3.

The proof laws were revised in 1968, the nitro-proof surviving another change; to ease the load on Ulm and Hannover, the Eckenförde establishment was moved to Kiel, and new proof houses were opened in Berlin, Köln and München. A simplified proof eagle was introduced in June 1971, but the 1968-vintage marks otherwise survived unchanged. Only the Ulm mark is encountered on the modern Mauser-Parabellums, but guns are occasionally re-proved and the München mark – a lozengy shield – graces the Erma-Lugers.

German proof marks are usually dated, an encircled '74' signifying 1974, but Mauser adopted the alternative coded version in the late 1970s. This substitutes the letters 'a' to 'j' for the numbers 0–9; 'HE', therefore, would appear on a gun made in 1974.

The Mauser-Parabellum 06/73

Once production of the 29/70 pattern was established, the first steps were taken to make the exterior of the pistols resemble the P.08. By the end of 1971, therefore, a swell-front grip had been developed and the barrel had gained a P.08-type front sight. The 29/70-style safety lever and locking bolt were initially retained. Before series production began, however, the locking-bolt thumb piece was enlarged and the knurled circular thumb piece of the safety lever was superseded by a fluted design. The opportunity was also taken to reduce the protruding housing on the trigger plate to about two-thirds of its former height.

Few of the earliest guns were numbered, though most bore Mauser's own inspection marks. Some had MAUSER PARABELLUM and the calibre mark on the left side of the frame, plus the 'Original Mauser' banner on the toggle.

The factory designation 06/73 was chosen for this new gun, the first series-made examples of which were sold in 1972. A special satin-chrome finish was

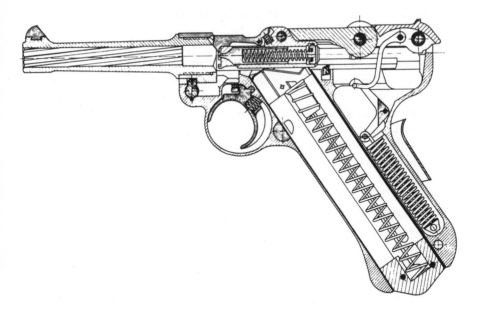

Fig. 19. A longitudinal section of the Mauser-Parabellum 06/73, showing how little change had been made to the action in seventy years. *Mauser-Werke Oberndorf GmbH.*

announced in trade journals in 1973; however, though the barrel, receiver and frame were chromed, most of the remaining parts were blued – front sight, magazine, magazine catch, safety lever, locking bolt, trigger, lockwork, grip safety, screws and pins.

Among the most interesting of the experimental guns made in the early 1970s was a solitary .45 target-pistol prototype dating from 1972. This had a large-diameter 127mm barrel and a unique parallel-edged grip. Most other features were 06/73 standard, though the grip safety mechanism was discarded to accommodate the bulky seven-round magazine. The operation of the original 'up-safe' manual lever was reversed in the mid 1970s, and a small banner mark eventually appeared on the frame-rail ahead of the trigger-plate.

Three 06/73 pocket pistols were also made in this period – no.10.000101 in 7.65mm, plus no.11.000101 and no.3 in 9mm. The 'Original Mauser' banner mark was rolled laterally into their toggle-links.

The 06/73-pattern Sportpistole prototype appeared in 1973, with a special 9mm-calibre 12cm barrel and an adjustable sight on the rear toggle link. Though differing sights were tried, there may only ever have been a single gun. The perfected Sportpistole (or Match Model), supplied to special order, initially offered a heavy 'bull' barrel and the perfected adjustable sights. From 1975 onward, however, the barrels were given flat barrel-side panels or longitudinal grooves to reduce the recoiling mass. Neither pattern retained the grip safety.

Mauser-Parabellum commemoratives

Once the initial euphoria had died away, Mauser-Jagdwaffen was confronted with a problem which had faced virtually every gunmaker who had tried to mass-produce Luger's pistol design. Production was no less exacting than it had been in the days of Deutsche Waffen- und Munitionsfabriken; in addition, the unit cost of the Mauser-Parabellum, which was not selling in tens of thousands as some of its predecessors had done, was worryingly high.

Only a few of the purchasers bought the new guns for their shooting qualities. The 29/70 and 06/73 both handled well, but had been overtaken by simpler and more robust designs even before work on them had begun. Thus the Mauser-Parabellum was clearly selling more for its historical appeal than its performance.

An answer was found in the production of limited-issue commemorative guns, aimed squarely at the collector market and priced accordingly. The first were made in 1975. The 7.65mm Bulgarian Model had dished toggle-grips, approximating to Old Model style, and a 29/70 front sight on its 12cm barrel. It had Cyrillic markings on the extractor and in the safety lever recess. An appropriate inscription lay on the left side of the frame in Old English Letter, etched in relief and faced in gold; the coat of arms found on pre-1908 Bulgarian guns was etched above the chamber, whilst a DWM monogram appeared on the toggle.

The Russian Model was essentially similar to the Bulgarian pattern, but had standard toggle grips and a 9mm-calibre 10cm barrel. The extractor was marked in Russian, though the safety-recess mark − rightly, according to linguists − remained the Bulgarian type. Crossed Mosin-Nagant rifles appeared above the chamber, with the supposed 70th-anniversary inscription on the left side of the frame in Old English Letter.

Mauser could have selected a more appropriate occasion to commemorate, owing to the controversy surrounding the consignment of guns to pre-Revolutionary Russia. The same could not be said of the third gun, which was announced in 1975 to mark the 75th anniversary of military adoption in Switzerland. This is not only unimpeachably documented but also the greatest single landmark in the history of the Luger. The 7.65mm 06/73 Swiss Model had a 12cm barrel, a cross-on-sunburst chamber mark, and a commemorative inscription in distinctively angular lettering. Unlike the Bulgarian and Russian versions, which had DWM-monogram toggles, these guns displayed the modern 'Original Mauser' banner.

The so-called 'Gamba Model' was made for Armi Renato Gamba SpA of Gardone Val Trompia, whose high-quality sporting guns were marketed in

Germany under the Mauser-Jagdwaffen umbrella. Gamba eventually negotiated a licence to produce a modified HSc pistol in Italy. The standard 9mm-
calibre 10cm barrelled 06/73 Mauser-Parabellums had a unique chamber-top
motif created from an eagle and the initials 'RG'. An identifying inscription,
including SERIE SPECIALE RENATO GAMBA was rolled into the right frame-rail.

Sales do not seem to have been high and, when the Gamba company became
involved in controversy, demand slackened still further. Consequently, several
hundred unwanted pistols were deactivated in 1976 for sale by two of Stuttgart's leading gun dealers, Jung and Gehmann. These *Dekowaffen* may be
identified by the absence of nitro proofs and omission of the special 'RG'-prefix
numbers.

Introduced in 1979 to mark the 75th anniversary of the adoption of the
Luger by the German navy, the 9mm 06/73 Navy Model had a characteristic
15cm barrel, a two-position back sight on the rear toggle link, and a stock-lug
on the heel of the butt. The left side of the frame bore an appropriate
inscription, the toggle mark was a replica of the DWM monogram, and the
serial numbers had a 'KM' prefix.

The elegant 06/73 replica carbine, which appeared in 1981 in a well-
appointed gun case, supposedly celebrated the 75th anniversary of the first
Luger of this type. However, the prototypes dated from 1900–1 and series
production of 7.65mm guns had actually begun in 1904.

Mauser-Parabellum carbines lacked the auxiliary return spring contained in
the original fore-end, but were broadly comparable in most other respects with
the guns manufactured prior to the First World War. The front sight was
mounted on a ramp, a tangent-type back sight lay on the 30cm barrel
immediately ahead of the receiver, and the walnut fore-end carried a swivel.
Chequering on the fore-end matched the detachable stock. A DWM monogram appeared on the toggle, whilst a suitable three-line inscription lay on the
left side of the frame. Serial numbers had a 'K' prefix.

The 9mm 10cm-barrelled 06/73 Cartridge Counter Model was announced in
August 1981, though the production version did not appear until the Spring of
1982. The toggle-grips were dished, the commemorative inscription appeared
in two lines on the left side of the frame, and the serial numbers were given a 'C'
prefix. A slot cut through the left grip exposed an indicator working against a
numbered scale, inspired by the Powell Cartridge Indicating Device fitted to
fifty 9mm Lugers supplied to the US Army in 1904. Consequently, the
American Eagle motif, adapted from the Great Seal of the United States,
appeared above the chamber.

An 'Army Model' was announced in October 1983 to celebrate the 75th
birthday of the Pistole 1908. The standard 9mm-calibre 10cm barrelled 06/73
Mauser-Parabellum had an Old English Letter inscription on the left side of the
frame above the grip. The dates 1908 and 1983 appeared above the chamber,

and a DWM monogram lay on the toggle. The calibre-mark on the barrel read
9MM LUGER.

The American Eagle Model was destined for sale in Germany and Switzer-
land, about eighty being released in May 1984; their barrels were marked 9MM
PARABELLUM, but the American Eagle motif appeared atop the chamber and the
DWM monogram lay on the toggle. A two-line inscription in Old English
Letter was etched in relief on the frame-side. The five-digit serial numbers had
'AE' prefixes.

The Artillery Model, orders for which were taken from January 1985
onward, was the last of the major commemorative issues. It was basically an
Army Model, described previously, with a 20cm barrel and a tangent-leaf sight
on the barrel immediately ahead of the receiver. The grip safety was eliminated,
whilst a board-pattern shoulder stock could be fitted to the lug on the butt
heel. As no appropriate anniversary could be found, the frame-side was simply
marked ERINNERUNGSMODELL/LANGE PISTOLE 08 in gold-faced relief. Serial numbers had an 'A' prefix and the DWM monogram appeared on the toggle link.

Special presentation Mauser-Parabellums have been supplied to order. The
decoration often represents the zenith of the engraver's skill, and the guns are
often much more pleasing to the eye than their Third Reich forebears. They are
still too new to have much of an impact on the collecting fraternity, but they
will be greatly sought in years to come – once the desirability of individual
patterns has been assessed and accurate information becomes available.

When *Luger* and *The Luger Book* were being written in the early 1970s and
the mid 1980s respectively, information supplied by Mauser considerably
exaggerated production quantities. Though estimates of 50,000 were being
mooted as early as 1975, production by 1985 actually totalled 5070 7.65mm-
calibre guns and 16,220 9mm examples. These excluded the artillery commemorative (250) and subsequent issues, but it seems unlikely that these added
more than a thousand to the total. The Match models are particularly desirable,
production totalling 153 and eighty-eight in 7.65mm and 9mm respectively.
And even these contained a selection of sub-variants.

The first .22 Lugers

The lure of the Luger ensured that the demand for accessories continued even
after the Second World War ended. The factory of Erfurter Maschinenfabrik
Berthold Geipel GmbH, 'Erma-Werke', had disappeared into the Russian
occupation zone under the terms of the Yalta agreement. However, several
members of the controlling family fled to western Germany, and a new Erma
business was founded in 1946 in Dachau (now a suburb of München) to make
machine-tools and roller bearings.

Eventually, Erma-Werke GmbH was approached to recreate the Kulisch-
pattern sub-calibre trainers, the success of which persuaded the management to

develop a blowback pistol. Announced in 1964, the 'Luger Programm' handgun differed greatly from the genuine locked-breech pattern, although sharing the same basic layout and similar elegant lines.

The essence of all the Erma-Lugers is a blowback toggle system, which is operated simply by propellant gas forcing the spent cartridge case rearward against the pressure of the return springs. The cam surfaces of the toggle unit probably imbue the action with a very slight delay element absent from a linear-breech mechanism, but this has never been investigated.

The return springs lie horizontally beneath the EP 22 action, whereas those of the KGP 68 and KGP 69 are angled downward. Extractors in the top of the breech-blocks double as loaded-chamber indicators.

Chambered only for the .22 Long Rifle rimfire cartridge, the EP 22 was made from 1964 until 1969. The barrel was 83mm long, the gun weighing 1010gm with its empty eight-round magazine. A special long-barrel carbine and a range of barrel-length options were available. The EP 22 was replaced by the .22 KGP 69, offered with a 10cm barrel, an eight-round magazine, and an unladen weight of 840gm. Unlike its predecessor, the KGP 69 incorporates a safety system patented in the USA in 1970 (no.3,220,310) to prevent the pistols being loaded, cocked or fired unless the magazine is in place and 'F' has been exposed by the manual safety lever. This was essential to satisfy the US Gun Control Act of 1968.

The KGP 690 – easily distinguished by its plain-bordered chequered wood grips – is an 8mm blank-firing derivative of the KGP 69, very similar externally but lacking the sophisticated safety system.

The success of the rimfire Lugers persuaded Erma to experiment with more powerful guns, though the basic blowback action was retained. The KGP 68, chambered for the 7.65mm Auto or 9mm Short cartridges, had an 89mm barrel and an overall length of 187mm; unladen weight was about 650gm. Magazines held six 7.65mm or five 9mm rounds. The KGP 68 was comparatively short-lived, owing to the introduction of the improved KGP 68A. The principal difference – apart from a new 100mm barrel – lay in the addition of the magazine safety.

Erma experimented in the early 1970s with an enlargement of the blowback system chambered for the 9mm Parabellum round, though only two examples of the KGP 70 (nos.00001 and 00002) were made. The guns were appreciably more robust than the KGP 68A, as their frames were machined from steel instead of diecast alloy, but is suspected that they were unable to handle the continual pounding from such a powerful cartridge. Work was soon abandoned.

By April 1986, Erma had made at least 40,000 EP 22 pistols, numbered from 00001. Output of KGP 68 and KGP 68A had reached 8500 and 21,600 – serial numbers running from 0001 and 100000 respectively. The total

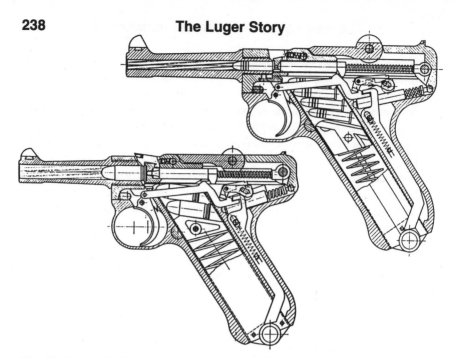

Fig. 20. Longitudinal sections of the Erma-Lugers KGP-69 (rimfire, top) and KGP-68A (centre-fire, bottom). Note the patented magazine safety bars resting on the magazine knobs. *Erma-Werke GmbH.*

quantity of KGP 69 stood at 14,130, numbered from 00001 upward, and there had been 12,200 KGP 690 blank-firers. The inexpensive blowbacks, costing less than a third of the Mauser-Parabellums, had found an important niche in the market.

The Spanish gunmaking company Echave y Arizmendi SA of Eibar copied the EP 22 as the 'Lur Panzer'. The first guns seem to have been made in 1967–8, being sold from stock until the company ceased trading in 1974. Markings provided the most obvious distinguishing characteristics, as they included LUR CAL .22 LR and an encircled EYA trademark on the receiver. The legend MADE IN SPAIN is also common, whereas the grips invariably bore a circular disc displaying either EYA or PANZER within a diamond.

Post-war accessories

The success of the single-shot trainers – some of the Swiss versions, in particular, lasted well into the post-war years – inspired new developments. Several patterns have been made by Lothar Walther of Königsbronn on the basis of Lienhard or RWS/Weiss systems, and at least one deriving from Walther's own ideas.

One of the 4mm-calibre units uses an auxiliary cartridge, whilst another has a supplementary cartridge inserter or *Ladelöffel*. One of the .22 Short patterns also uses auxiliary cartridges, but the other relies on the interposition of a separate striker plate between the standard Luger breech-block and the insert body. The use of the plate to transfer the striker-blow to the rim of the .22 cartridge allows the P.08 to be used without conversion. The Walther barrel inserts are locked in place by muzzle collars.

The pre-war Erma Selbstlade-Einstecklauf (SEL), which had been designed by Richard Kulisch in 1927, was also resurrected after the Second World War had ended. The 1946-vintage reincarnation of Erma-Werke was approached by the International Armament Company ('Interarmco') in 1954 to reproduce the sub-calibre units.

The mechanism was re-engineered by Rudolf Weiss, relying on copies of the original military drawings and two original P.08/SEL combinations supplied from the USA. Series production began in Dachau in 1956, though assembly of components made over a period of a few months was spread over six years. By 1962 about 3500 new inserts had been made; most displayed the Interarmco enrayed-sun trademark in addition to the Erma name, but others have been seen with the marks of Waffen-Glaser of Zürich.

The post-1956 units were usually despatched in stout cardboard boxes, instead of the wooden cases popular prior to 1945. The short-barrel patterns had a conical muzzle shroud, whereas those longer than 180–190mm relied on a nut and lock-nut system.

Genuine pre-war Kulisch/Erma trainers were apparently refurbished in the German Democratic Republic in the 1950s, but are rarely encountered. Additional details may eventually be forthcoming from Thuringia now that Germany has been unified.

The 1972-vintage Mauser-Jagdwaffen semi-automatic insert system was inspired by the Kulisch design, though it retained the full-size toggle grips and required transverse grooves to be milled in the receiver. Only prototypes were made before the project was abandoned.

North American Lugers

The Luger pistol has always occupied a special place in American affections, largely owing to the substantial sales of the .30-calibre version and the publicity surrounding the tests undertaken by the US Army in the early 1900s.

Harold Tucker of St Louis, Missouri, produced about a thousand .22 blowback pistols in the early 1960s, most of which were subsequently sold in Central and South America. He also made a handful of 9mm and .45 locked-breech prototypes, distinguished by their squared trigger apertures. None of these guns was successful enough to be made in quantity, though one surviving frame was pictured in *Auto-Mag* in 1984.

The widespread distribution of Erma-type blowback Lugers in North

America persuaded Stoeger Industries, Inc, of Hackensack, New Jersey, to market a range of blowback 'Stoeger Lugers'. This was facilitated by ownership of the Luger tradename dating back to the 1920s.

The Stoeger Lugers were originally built on a frame forged from an aluminium-alloy originally developed for the aircraft industry. To avoid fretting, steel bolt-ways supported the breech bolt, the sear/hammer pin, and the magazine guide. In 1980, however, a new forged-steel frame appeared, increasing weight in a search – according to the advertising material of the time – for 'extra strength and accuracy'.

The trigger mechanism was designed by Gary Wilhelm of Hamden, Connecticut, to whom US Patent 3,698,285 was granted on 15th April 1971. The sear-bar engaged the sear between its supports to give a symmetrical action and a smooth pull. Stoeger always drew attention to the inherent safety of its blowback Lugers, as the action reciprocated within the solid-back receiver. The hammer-rifled barrel was held in the frame by a hardened transverse pin. It was necessary only to remove the main frame retaining-pin and push in the 'takedown plunger' in the rear of the frame to strip the gun. The action could then be lifted clear of the receiver once the sear-bar retaining spring, on the left side of the frame above the trigger aperture, had been removed.

The Stoeger-Lugers have always been made by the Replica Arms subsidiary of Navy Arms. STLR-4 and STLL-4 models have 4.5in barrels, 'R' (right-hand) patterns having the manual safety lever on the left side of the frame whereas the 'L' (left-hand) version has the lever on the right. The sights were fixed and the grips were chequered hardwood. STLR-5 and STLL-5 patterns were similar, except for 5.5in barrels, whilst TLR-4, TLL-4, TLR-5 and TLL-5 target pistols had an adjustable back sight in a separate housing attached to the rear of the frame. Stoeger Lugers of any pattern could be purchased in a 'Luger Pistol Kit' containing the gun, a holster, a spare magazine and a magazine-loader. The 'Luger Combo' was identical, but the components were contained in a foam-lined case. Stoeger guns displayed LUGER over a minuscule REG. U.S. PAT. OFF. on the sides of the frame, within a decorative cartouche, and are also normally stamped CAL .22 L.R.

John Martz of Lincoln, California, is best known for his custom gunsmithing. Martz has made Luger carbines, 'Baby Lugers' and target-shooting Lugers in profusion, but is renowned for the MSTR or 'Martz Safe Toggle Release' patented in the USA in 1976 (no.3,956,967). One of the most useful mechanical changes embodied in the Luger in recent years, the MSTR enables the firer to trip the toggle once a fresh magazine has been inserted simply by rotating the safety lever to its downward or safe position.

A great merit of the Martz device is simplicity, as it requires only a single new part (though minor machining revisions must be made to the hold-open latch, the safety bar, the safety lever and the left grip). Insignificant changes have been made since the patent was granted, including the replacement – by a peg – of the step between the hold-open latch and the release lever, but the MSTR is as useful now as it was nearly twenty years ago.

Into the next century...?

The demise of the Mauser-Parabellum in the late 1980s was a disaster for enthusiasts who had hoped that the venerable Luger would celebrate its centenary – 1998 or 2000, depending on viewpoint – by remaining in series production. Therefore when Don Mitchell of Mitchell Arms, Inc, of Santa Ana, California, indicated a willingness to make a modernised P.08 in North America, reaction was initially disbelief. In October 1991, however, details of the Mitchell American Eagle Pistol Parabellum P-08 were released and series production began.

The Mitchell pistol approached the design of the pre-1945 P.08 so closely that some of the parts would interchange. The serial number was moved from beneath the barrel to the side of the frame, and, to comply with BATF regulations, the lug on the butt-heel was machined without the stock-attachment grooves that had characterised the German prototype.

American-made guns bore MITCHELL ARMS AMERICAN EAGLE over CAL. 9MM LUGER on the right side of the receiver, with the displayed-eagle motif above the chamber. At least one gun was engraved with arabesques, but, unfortunately, Mitchell ran into financial difficulties almost as soon as work had begun and the project was abandoned. It is suspected that no more than a few dozen guns had been made.

The demise of Mitchell threatened the survival of the Luger into the twenty-first century and threatened the celebration of its centenary. In 1997, however, Stoeger Industries – owners of the 'Luger' trademark in the USA – announced the 'Stainless Steel American Eagle Luger'. Made in Houston, Texas, by SPM, this variant retained the recoil-operated toggle mechanism (unlike the .22 rimfire 'Stoeger-Luger', which was a blowback). Most guns had matted frame recesses, butt-heel lugs that were 'suggested' instead of functional, and severe, almost squared frame contours ahead of the trigger guard. They also had seven-round magazines with displayed-eagle motifs moulded into the magazine grips. A LUGER within a floriated scroll lay on the left side of the frame above the grip, with the 'S and target' trademark ahead of STOEGER IND. AMERICAN EAGLE over CAL. 9MM LUGER on the right side of the receiver. Serial numbers began at S0001. Barrels measured 4in or 6in.

No sooner had the 9mm Stoeger-Luger been announced than the project began to flounder. It is not clear at the time of writing whether any more than a few prototypes were made in 1996–7. But we can only hope that another attempt will be made to revive what is essentially timeless design...

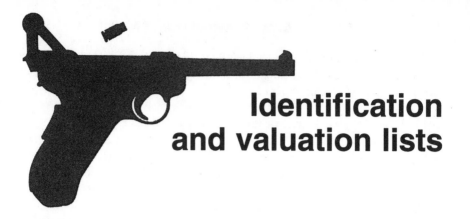

Identification and valuation lists

The enthusiasm with which the Luger has been embraced has created a vibrant collecting industry. The influence of money, unfortunately, has sometimes corrupted this business. That this should happen is largely due to the mystery that still enshrouds the pistol. Though many books have been written in the last twenty years and invaluable information has been extracted from surviving archives in Germany, some of the best-established myths persist. The 'Double-Suffix Numbered Luger' and the 'SS Luger' are simple misunderstandings of German handwriting and police markings respectively, but some people still resist the truth. Perhaps this is inevitable when the rarest guns may change hands for considerably in excess of £10,000. Indeed, there are one or two which could probably fetch ten times this sum in appropriate circumstances.

The information which follows, therefore, attempts to balance assessments of scarcity with areas in which problems will be encountered, and the factors which may add to (or detract from) the value of an individual pistol.

I have always believed passionately that demanding a premium simply on the basis of a minor inspection-mark variation cannot be justified. It would be far more useful to identify individual inspectors, undoubtedly a better indicator of desirability than a punch which may have lasted for only a thousand strikes. A gun with a unit marking should also be particularly appealing as it may be fixed in time and place; an unmarked example is all too often a dead-end historically.

The 'Rarity Index' was originally calculated on the basis of pre-1995 sales records, particularly those gleaned from auction rooms and periodicals such as *Shotgun News*. To allow for inflation, the Index should be multiplied by a factor of 1.5 to give a price in Sterling; at the time of writing, an approximate dollar equivalent can be obtained by multiplying the Sterling equivalent by 1.4 or the Index figure by 2.1.

The values have been calculated on the basis of guns with matching numbers throughout, but which, though otherwise in very good condition, show minor wear and a slight loss of finish. A gun with much of its finish gone may fetch half the predicted price, whereas a 'mint' version often costs twice as much.

Some guns pass through the salerooms so infrequently that quantities or acceptable valuations are difficult to determine; this is noted (as 'NA') where appropriate. Guns made in quantities of less than a hundred have been omitted, as have attributions made on extremely shaky evidence. For example, I have little faith in the identification of a crown/reversed-N 'Russian' proof mark, nor do I support the concentration-camp usage widely attributed to the so-called 'KL Lugers'. And so many explanations have been offered for Death's Head or 'Kü' pistols that it is impossible to decide between them.

Please contact me by way of the publisher if you would like to offer additional information; the address will be found on page four.

Abbreviations

Most of the information is listed in readily understandable form, such as the manufacturer, date (if known), calibre and barrel length – though **chm** is the chamber and **tgl** represents the toggle. In addition, **DWMC** and **DWMW** distinguish the Charlottenburg and Wittenau factories of Deutsche Waffen- und Munitionsfabriken; **L**, **S** and **Spl** are long, short and special frames respectively, 'g' indicating a grip safety. **Qty** signifies quantity; **Rl** is the rarity index; and an asterisk (*) is an average of fluctuating price.

Markings include **bca** for the full Bulgarian coat of arms; **ber** for Waffenfabrik Bern; **bls** for the Bulgarian lion-on-shield; **can** for the Portuguese crown-and-anchor; **cmn** for crossed Mosin-Nagant rifles; **csb** for the Swiss cross-on-sunburst; **csh** for the Swiss cross-on-shield; **ddt** for a double date; **dtd** for a single date; **dwm** for the well-known DWM monogram; **erf** for crown/Erfurt; **far** for Farsi (Arabic); **gnr** for the Portuguese Guardia Nacional monogram; **khf** for Krieghoff; **msj** for the Mauser-Jagdwaffen 'Original Mauser' banner; **msr** for the pre-1945 Mauser banner; **m2m** for the 'M2' monogram of Manuel II of Portugal; **per** for the Persian lion-and-sword; **rgm** for the Gamba logo (an eagle above 'RG'); **rpa** for the Portuguese republican 'R.P.' and anchor; **slm** for Simson & Co.; **tcm** for the Turkish star and crescent; **use** for the US eagle; **van** for the Finnish prison service mark ('Vankeinhoitolaitos'); **var** for 'various'; and **vck** for Vickers, Ltd. A dash ('—') signifies that the part in question was not marked.

| Maker, date | cal | brl : frame | ········· MARKINGS ········· | | | | Qty | Rl |
	mm	mm : type	chm	tgl	safety	extractor		

Old or 1900-model Lugers

Pre-production guns
DWMC, 1899–1900	7.65	120 : Lg	—	dwm	—	—	75–100	45

Bulgarian army pattern (note 1)
DWMC, c.1905	7.65	120 : Lg	bca	dwm	ОГЪНЪ	—	1000	22

German army trials pattern (notes 2, 3)
DWMC, 1903–5	9	100 : Sg	—	dwm	—	—	NA	22

German carbine pattern (note 4)
DWMC, 1902–3	7.65	300 : Lg	—	dwm	—	—	250?	*30

German commercial pattern (note 5)
DWMC, 1900–7	7.65	120 : Lg	—	dwm	—	—	6500?	7

Maker, date	cal mm	brl: frame mm : type	chm	tgl	MARKINGS safety	extractor	Qty	RI

German commercial pattern (note 6)

Maker, date	cal mm	brl: frame mm : type	chm	tgl	safety	extractor	Qty	RI
DWMC, 1903–7	9	100 : Sg	—	dwm	—	—	500	*32

Swiss M1900, army (note 5)

DMWC, 1900–5	7.65	120 : Lg	csb	dwm	—	—	5000	*9

Swiss M1900, army, supplementary type (note 7)

Bern, c.1906	7.65	120 : Lg	csb	dwm	—	—	100	12

Swiss commercial pattern (note 5)

DWMC, 1900–7	7.65	120 : Lg	csb	dwm	—	—	about 2000	10

US Army trial pattern (note 8)

DWMC, 1901	7.65	120 : Lg	use	dwm	—	—	1000	12

US commercial pattern

DWMC, 1900–7	7.65	120 : Lg	use	dwm	—	—	about 12,000	10

US commercial pattern (note 6)

DWMC, 1903–7	9	100 : Sg	use	dwm	—	—	600?	*32

Transitional or 1904-model Lugers

German M1904, navy

DWMC, 1904–6	9	150 : Lg	—	dwm	GESICHERT	GELADEN	disputed	50

New or 1906-model Lugers

Brazilian army pattern (note 1, 9)

DWMC, 1911	7.65	120 : Lg	—	dwm	—	CARREGADA	5000	7

Bulgarian army pattern (note 1)

DWMC, 1907–8	7.65	120 : Lg	bca	dwm	ОГЪНЪ	ПЪЛЕНЪ	1500	*28

Dutch M1911, East Indies army (notes 10, 11)

DWMC, 1912–14	9	100 : Sg	—	dwm	arrow/RUST	GELADEN	4181	5
Vickers, 1922–3?	9	100 : Sg	—	vck	arrow/RUST	GELADEN	6000	5
BKIW, 1928	9	100 : Sg	—	dwm	arrow/RUST	GELADEN	3820	7

German army trials pattern (note 3)

DWMC, 1906–7	9	100 : Sg	—	dwm	GESICHERT	GELADEN	500?	NA

German commercial pattern (note 12)

DWMC, 1906–14	7.65	120 : Lg	—	dwm	—	GELADEN	5000?	6
DWMC, 1906–14	9	100 : Sg	—	dwm	—	GELADEN	4000?	7

Maker, date	cal mm	brl : frame mm : type	chm	tgl	safety	extractor	Qty	RI
German commercial navy model								
DWMC, pre-1914	7.65	150 : Lg	—	dwm	GESICHERT	GELADEN	500?	*16
DWMC, pre-1914	9	150 : Lg	—	dwm	GESICHERT	GELADEN	2000?	13
German M1904, navy (note 13)								
DWMC, 1906–12?	9	150 : Lg	—	dwm	GESICHERT	GELADEN	18,500	15
DWMC, 1912–14	9	150 : Lg	—	dwm	GESICHERT	GELADEN	2550	15
Portuguese M1909, army (note 14)								
DWMC, 1908–10	7.65	120 : Lg	m2m	dwm	—	CARREGADA	5000	4–5
Portuguese M1910, navy (note 15)								
DWMC, 1909–10	9	100 : Sg	can	dwm	—	CARREGADA	800	20
DWMC, 1911	9	100 : Sg	rpa	dwm	—	CARREGADA	200	25
Portuguese M1935, national guard								
Mauser, 1935–7	7.65	120 : Sg	gnr	msr	SEGURANÇA	CARREGADA	684?	7
Russian commercial pattern								
DWMC, c.1908–11	9	100 : Sg	cmn	dwm	ОГѢНЪ	ЗАРЯДЪ	1000?	NA
Swiss M1906, army								
DWMC, 1907–9	7.65	120 : Lg	csb	dwm	—	GELADEN	4450	12
DWMC, 1909–14	7.65	120 : Lg	csh	dwm	—	GELADEN	6164	8
Bern, 1919–28	7.65	120 : Lg	—	ber	—	GELADEN	12,285	7
Swiss commercial pattern (note 16)								
DWMC, 1907–14	7.65	120 : LSg	csb	dwm	—	GELADEN	1000?	10
Mauser, 1933–6	7.65	120 : S	csb	msr	GESICHERT	GELADEN	300?	15
Swiss commercial pattern (note 17)								
DWM, originally	7.65	120 : LSg	csb	dwm	—	GELADEN	400?	9
US Army trial pattern								
DWMC, 1907	.45	127 : Splg	—	dwm	—	LOADED	5?	NA
US commercial pattern (note 18)								
DWMC, 1907–14	7.65	120 : LSg	use	dwm	SAFE	LOADED	7500?	7
DWMC, 1907–14	9	100 : Sg	use	dwm	SAFE	LOADED	3000?	8

Army or 1908-model Lugers

Maker, date	cal mm	brl : frame mm : type	chm	tgl	safety	extractor	Qty	RI
Austrian Bundesheer pattern (note 19)								
Mauser, 1941–6?	9	100 : S	dtd	byf	GESICHERT	GELADEN	500?	7
Bolivian army pattern (note 20)								
DWM, 1911–14	9	100 : S	edb	dwm	—	CARGADO	500?	12

Maker, date	cal mm	brl : frame mm : type	chm	tgl	·········· MARKINGS ·········· safety	extractor	Qty	RI
Bulgarian army pattern (note 21)								
DWM, 1910–11	9	100 : S	dwm	bls	ОГЪНЪ	ПЪЛЕНЪ	10,000	12
Dutch Pistol No. 1, navy (note 22)								
BKIW, 1928–30	9	100 : S	—	dwm	arrow/RUST	GELADEN	1484	5
Mauser, 1930–6	9	100 : S	—	dwm	arrow/RUST	GELADEN	565	6
Mauser, 1937	9	100 : S	—	msr	arrow/RUST	GELADEN	200	7
Mauser, 1938–40	9	100 : S	dtd	msr	arrow/RUST	GELADEN	925	5
Finnish M1923, army (note 23)								
BKIW, 1923–8	7.65	100 : S	—	dwm	—	—	about 7000	3
Finnish M1923, prison service								
BKIW, c.1927	7.65	100 : S	van	dwm	—	—	500?	5
German M1904, navy								
DWMC, 1914–16	9	150 : L	—	dwm	GESICHERT	GELADEN	10,000?	9
DWMW, 1916–18	9	150 : S	dtd	dwm	GESICHERT	GELADEN	25,000?	10
German M1908, air force (note 24)								
Krieghoff, 1935–6	9	100 : S	G, S	khf	GESICHERT	GELADEN	4200	9
Krieghoff, 1936	9	100 : S	36	khf	GESICHERT	GELADEN	600	12
Krieghoff, 1936–45	9	100 : S	dtd	khf	GESICHERT	GELADEN	8400	12
German M1908, army (note 25)								
Various	9	100 : S	ddt	var	GESICHERT	GELADEN	1000s	2–3
German M1908, army (notes 26-28)								
DWMC, 1909	9	100 : S	—	dwm	GESICHERT	GELADEN	15,000?	4
DWMC, 1910–13	9	100 : S	dtd	dwm	GESICHERT	GELADEN	170,000	2–3
Erfurt, 1911–13	9	100 : S	dtd	erf	GESICHERT	GELADEN	53,000	3
DWMC/W, 1914–18	9	100 : S	dtd	dwm	GESICHERT	GELADEN	500,000	2
Erfurt, 1914–18	9	100 : S	dtd	erf	GESICHERT	GELADEN	560,000	2
Simson, 1925–8	9	100 : S	dtd	sim	GESICHERT	GELADEN	10,000?	7
Simson, 1934	9	100 : S	—	S	GESICHERT	GELADEN	10,000?	7
Mauser, 1934	9	100 : S	K	S/42	GESICHERT	GELADEN	10,000	7
Mauser, 1935	9	100 : S	G	S/42	GESICHERT	GELADEN	57,500	4
Mauser, 1936–9	9	100 : S	dtd	S/42	GESICHERT	GELADEN	445,000	*3
Mauser, 1939–40	9	100 : S	dtd	42	GESICHERT	GELADEN	140,000	3
Mauser, 1940	9	100 : S	40	42	GESICHERT	GELADEN	150,000?	5
Mauser, 1941	9	100 : S	41	42	GESICHERT	GELADEN	7500	5
Mauser, 1941–2	9	100 : S	dtd	byf	GESICHERT	GELADEN	260,000	3
German M1908, army (long) (note 29)								
DWMC/W, 1914–18	9	200 : S	dtd	dwm	GESICHERT	GELADEN	215,000	6
Erfurt, 1914	9	200 : S	dtd	erf	GESICHERT	GELADEN	130,000	7
German M1908, police (note 30)								
Mauser, 1938–41	9	100 : S	dtd	msr	GESICHERT	GELADEN	30,000?	4

Maker, date	cal mm	brl : frame mm : type	chm	tgl	MARKINGS safety	extractor	Qty	RI

German commercial pattern (note 26)

Maker, date	cal mm	brl : frame mm : type	chm	tgl	safety	extractor	Qty	RI
DWMC, 1908–14	9	100 : S	—	dwm	GESICHERT	GELADEN	5500?	3–4

German commercial pattern (note 17, 31)

| Various | 7.65, 9 | 98 : S | — | var | GESICHERT | GELADEN | thousands | 2–3 |

German commercial pattern (note 31)

| BKIW, 1922–9 | 7.65 | 98 : S | — | dwm | GESICHERT | GELADEN | 14,000? | 3–4 |

German commercial pattern (notes 32, 33)

| BKIW, 1922–5 | 9 | 98 : S | — | dwm | GESICHERT | GELADEN | 250? | 9 |

German commercial pattern

| Simson, 1925–34 | 7.65 | 98 : S | — | sim | GESICHERT | GELADEN | 10,000 | 4–5 |
| Simson, 1925–34 | 9 | 100 : S | — | sim | GESICHERT | GELADEN | 12,500 | 4 |

German commercial pattern

| Mauser, 1934–9 | 7.65 | 100 : S | — | msr | GESICHERT | GELADEN | 400? | 10 |

German commercial pattern (note 33)

| Krieghoff, 1936–9 | 9 | 100 : S | — | khf | GESICHERT | GELADEN | 1280 | *9 |

German commercial pattern (notes 28, 32)

| Mauser, 1936–42 | 9 | 100 : S | — | msr | GESICHERT | GELADEN | 1000? | *7 |

German commercial pattern

| Mauser, 1938 | 9 | 100 : S | dtd | S/42 | GESICHERT | GELADEN | 300? | *5 |

German commercial pattern (notes 34, 35)

| Krieghoff, 1945 | 7.65, 9 | 100 : S | — | — | GESICHERT | GELADEN | 245? | 9 |

German commercial LP.08 (notes 2, 17, 32)

| Various | 9 | 200 : S | — | var | GESICHERT | GELADEN | NA | *7 |

German commercial navy pattern

| DWMC, 1909–13 | 9 | 150 : S | — | dwm | GESICHERT | GELADEN | 250? | 7 |

German commercial navy pattern (notes 2, 17, 32)

| DWM, originally | 7.65 | 150 : S | — | dwm | GESICHERT | GELADEN | 350? | 8 |
| DWM, originally | 9 | 150 : S,L | — | dwm | GESICHERT | GELADEN | hundreds | 7 |

Latvian army trials pattern

| Mauser, 1936–9 | 9 | 100 : S | dtd | msr | GESICHERT | GELADEN | 828 | 7 |

Persian M1314 (note 36)

| Mauser, 1936–9 | 9 | 100 : S | per | far | far | far | 3000 | 18 |

Maker, date	cal mm	brl : frame mm : type	chm	tgl	MARKINGS safety	extractor	Qty	RI
Mauser, 1936?	9	200 : S	per	far	far	far	800	12

Portuguese Mo.943
Mauser, 1943	9	100:S	dtd	byf	GESICHERT	GELADEN	4578+	2–3

Siamese police pattern (note 37)
Mauser, 1936–7	9	100 : S	dtd	msr	—	—	350 or more	6
Mauser, 1936	9	200 : S	dtd	msr	—	—	100	8

Swedish army trials pattern
Mauser, 1938	9	100 : S	dtd	msr	GESICHERT	GELADEN	285	8

Swiss commercial pattern, refurbished
DWM, originally	7.65	120 : S,L	csb	dwm	GESICHERT	GELADEN	675	7

Turkish army pattern (note 38)
Mauser, c.1936	9	100 : S	tcm	msr	emniyet	ates	hundreds?	8

Turkish security police pattern (note 39)
Mauser, 1935–7	9	100 : S	tcm	msr	emniyet	ates	1000	6

US commercial pattern (notes 18, 31, 40)
BKIW, 1922–30	7.65	98 : S	use	dwm	SAFE	LOADED	1750	4–5
BKIW, 1922–30	9	100 : S	use	dwm	SAFE	LOADED	600?	*11
Mauser, 1930–7	7.65	100 : S	use	msr	SAFE	LOADED	350?	*16
Mauser, 1930–7	9	100 : S	use	msr	SAFE	LOADED	400?	*16

1924- and 1929-model Lugers

Swiss 06/24 W+F
Bern, 1928–33	7.65	120 : SpLg —		ber	—	GELADEN	5589	8

Swiss 06/29 W+F, military pattern (note 41)
Bern, 1933–46	7.65	120 : SpLg —		csh	'S'	GELADEN	27,931	5–8

Swiss 06/29 W+F, commercial pattern
Bern, 1940–7	7.65	120 : SpLg —		csh	'S'	GELADEN	1316?	7

Mauser-Parabellum 29/70 model

Standard commercial pattern (note 42)
Mauser, 1970–3	7.65	120 : SpLg —		msj	—	GELADEN	NA	NA
Mauser, 1970–3	9	100 : SpLg —		msj	—	GELADEN	NA	NA

US commercial pattern (notes 42, 43)
Mauser, 1970–3	7.65	120 : SpLg —		msj	—	LOADED	NA	NA
Mauser, 1970–3	9	100 : SpLg —		msj	—	LOADED	NA	NA

Maker, date	cal mm	brl : frame mm : type	chm	tgl	safety	extractor	Qty	RI

Mauser-Parabellum 06/73 model

Bulgarian commemorative pattern

Maker, date	cal	brl : frame	chm	tgl	safety	extractor	Qty	RI
Mauser, 1975	7.65	120 : SpLg	coa	dwm	ОГЪНЪ	ПЪЛЕНЪ	250	8

Carbine commemorative pattern

Mauser, 1981	9	300 : SpLg	—	dwm	—	GELADEN	250	25:c

Gamba pattern

Mauser, 1975–7?	9	100 : SpLg	rgm	msj	—	GELADEN	200?	7

German Army commemorative pattern

Mauser, 1983–4	9	100 : SpL	dtd	dwm	—	GELADEN	250	10

German Artillery Model commemorative pattern

Mauser, 1985–6	9	200 : SpL	—	dwm	—	GELADEN	250	15:s

German Navy commemorative pattern

Mauser, 1979	9	150 : SpLg	—	dwm	—	GELADEN	250	15:c

Russian commemorative pattern

Mauser, 1975	9	100 : SpLg	cmn	dwm	ОГОНЪ	ЗАРЯДЪ	250	8

Sportpistole or Sportmodell (notes 43, 44)

Mauser, 1975–9?	7.65	115 : SpL	—	msj	—	GELADEN	153	NA

Standard commercial pattern (note 42)

Mauser, 1972–9?	7.65	120 : SpLg	—	msj	—	GELADEN	NA	NA
Mauser, 1972–9?	9	100 : SpLg	—	msj	—	GELADEN	NA	NA

Swiss commemorative pattern

Mauser, 1975–6	7.65	120 : SpLg	csb	msj	—	GELADEN	250	10

US Cartridge Counter commemorative pattern (note 45)

Mauser, 1982	9	100 : SpLg	use	dwm	—	LOADED?	250	10

US commercial pattern (notes 42, 43)

Mauser, 1972–9?	7.65	120 : SpLg	—	msj	—	LOADED	NA	NA
Mauser, 1972–9?	9	100 : SpLg	—	msj	—	LOADED	NA	NA

Notes

1. Often rebarrelled in 9mm, which reduces the value appreciably.

2. The toggle may be blank.

3. A crown/fraktur 'D' inspector's mark may lie on the front right side of the receiver.

4. May have presentation marks above the chamber. Has a wooden fore-end and a back sight immediately ahead of the receiver. The absence of the stock reduces value, but cased guns are very scarce.

5. There are several differing designs of grip safety and safety levers.

6. The 'fat barrel' pattern.

7. Serial numbers have an 'A' prefix.

8. Should have US Ordnance 'Flaming Bomb' inspectors' marks.

9. An encircled-'B' inspector's stamp appears on the left side of the receiver.

10. The extractor is marked on both sides.

11. Crown-over-cursive-'W' inspectors' marks appear on the side of the receiver. BKIW-made guns have an encircled 'KL' monogram on the right side of the receiver

12. Some guns had GESICHERT in the safety-lever recess.

13. Post-1912 guns were newly made with 'down-safe' levers. Older guns will be encountered with modified safety catches, which reduces their value.

14. An encircled triangle inspector's mark appears on the receiver.

15. These will also display an MP-monogram inspector's mark.

16. The safety area on DWM-made guns may display GESICHERT.

17. Refurbished pre-1918 guns, often incorporating older DWM- or Erfurt-made parts, or newly-assembled from old components.

18. The safety-receess may be blank, or even bear GESICHERT, whilst GERMANY or MADE IN GERMANY appears on the frame.

19. An 'eagle BH' property mark lies on the left side of the frame ahead of the trigger plate.

20. Some safeties are said to be marked SEGURO.

21. A small crowned-lion mark will be found on the left side of the receiver, and a lanyard ring lies on the butt-heel.

22. The last Mauser-made consignment was seized before delivery and reissued to the Wehrmacht; guns may be found with appropriate German inspectors' marks.

23. The property stamp consisted of 'SA' within a square.

24. All guns should have Luftwaffe inspectors' marks. Guns dated 1945 are extremely rare (rarity index 55).

25. The supplementary '1920' served as a property mark, and can be found on virtually any type of pre-1918 Pistole 1908.

26. No stock-lug or hold open on pre 1913 guns, but both components were then reinstated.

27. Guns dated '1914' may command a premium. No Erfurt-made guns have yet been authenticated from 1915.

28. 'P.08' appears on the left side of the frame of many post-1940 guns.

29. May have adjustable sights.

30. Often fitted with the Schiwy sear safety.

31. Various barrel lengths are known, generally from 90mm up to 400mm.

32. Some chambers may be dated.

33. Krieghoff marks may appear on the frame.

34. Toggles may have Krieghoff marks.

35. Some components have air force inspectors' stamps.

36. A two-line Farsi (Arabic) inscription appears on the right side of the receiver.

37. An inventory number and a lion-head property mark appear on the back of the frame.

38. The SUBAYLARA MAHSUSTUR mark appears on the right side of the receiver, with a star-and-crescent emblem.

39. The inscription 'Emniyet Isleri/Umum Müdürülgü' appears on the right side of the receiver.

40. Some guns display A.F. STOEGER, INC/NEW YORK on the right side of the receiver, and sometimes also GENUINE LUGER – REGISTERED U.S. PATENT OFFICE on the right frame-rail.

41. These guns often bear a sale-date - e.g., 'P.64' for 1964.

42. A few guns were made with 15cm barrels.

43. The name of Interarms of Alexandria, Virginia, will usually be found on the side of the receiver with a sunburst trademark.

44. The special heavyweight barrels may be fluted or flat-sided.

45. The left grip is slotted to expose a numbered cartridge-capacity scale.

Select Bibliography

The Luger, by attracting unrivalled attention, has been the subject of a surprisingly large number of books and a vast quantity of articles. It would be easy to provide a lengthy guide to additional reading simply by listing obscure German documents or the contents of many gun-collecting magazines, but this would be of little use to enthusiasts. Too few articles are properly documented, excepting those based on surviving archive material by researchers such as Joachim Görtz, Reinhard Kornmayer and Hans Reckendorf in Germany, or Bas Martens and Guus de Vries in the Netherlands.

The finest of the books currently available are, in my opinion, *The Dutch Luger* (which relies almost exclusively on archival material) closely followed by *Die Pistole 08*, which is also based on proper documentation.

However, each approach has its strengths and I do not wish to single out any individual book for criticism – excepting to suggest that the truth of any story other than the North American Luger is best sought in European sources.

Bender, Eugene J.: *Lugers, Holsters and Accessories of the 20th Century*. Published privately by the author, Coconut Creek, Florida, USA, 1992.

Costanzo, Sam: *World of Lugers – Proof Marks* ('Complete listing of differing variations of Proof Marks on the Luger'). Vol. 1. World of Lugers, Mayfield Heights, Ohio, USA, 1977.

Datig, Fred A.: *The German Military Pistols 1904–1930* ('Monograph II' in the series 'The Luger Pistol (Pistole Parabellum), Its History and Development from 1893–1945'). Michael Zomber Company, Culver City, California, USA, 1990.

— *The Luger Pistol (Pistole Parabellum)* ('Its history and development from 1894 to 1945'). Fadco Publishing Company, Beverly Hills, California, USA, 1955. Revised edition: Borden Publishing Company, Los Angeles, California, 1958. Since reprinted several times, without alteration.

Ezell, Edward C.: *Handguns of the World*. Stackpole Books, Harrisburg, Pennsylvania, USA, 1981. Reprinted in 1992 without alteration.

Gibson, Randall: *The Krieghoff Parabellum*. Published privately, Midland, Texas, USA, 1980.

Görtz, Joachim: *Die Pistole 08*. Verlag Stocker-Schmid, Dietikon-Zürich, Switzerland, and Motor-Buch Verlag, Stuttgart, Germany, 1985.

— (and Don Bryans) *German Small-arms Markings from Official Documents* ('as found on the Pistole 08'). Published privately by DL Research, Salem, Oregon, USA, 1995.

— (and John Walter): *The Navy Luger*. The Lyon Press Ltd, Eastbourne, England, and Handgun Press, Glenview, Illinois, USA, 1988.

Häusler, Fritz: *Schweizerische Faustfeuerwaffen – Armes de poing suisses – Swiss Handguns*. Published privately by the author, Frauenfeld, Switzerland, 1975.

Heer, Eugen: *Die Faustfeuerwaffen von 1850 bis zur Gegenwart*. Part of a series entitled 'Geschichte und Entwicklung der Militärhandfeuerwaffen in der Schweiz'. Akademische Druck- und Verlagsanstalt, Graz, Austria, 1971.

Hogg, Ian (and John Weeks): *Pistols of the World* ('The definitive illustrated guide to the world's pistols and revolvers'). Third edition, Arms & Armour Press, London, England, and DBI, Inc., Northbrook, Illinois, USA, 1992.

Hughes, Gordon: *The Luger Handbook* ('A concise guide to collecting live and deactivated 9mm Luger "Parabellum" pistols, 1904–1945'). Published privately by the author, Brighton, East Sussex, England, 1994.

Jones, Harry E.: *Luger Variations* ('Volume 1'). Privately published by the author, Torrance, California, USA; four editions, 1959–77.

Kenyon, Charles, Jr.: *Lugers at Random*. Handgun Press, Chicago, Illinois, USA, 1969. A revised-format edition was published by Handgun Press, Glenview, Illinois, in 1990.

— *Luger: The Multinational Pistol*. Richard Ellis Publications, Moline, Illinois, 1991.

Kornmayer, Reinhard: *Die Parabellum-Pistolen in der Schweiz*. Published privately by the author, Singen/Hohentwiel, Germany, 1971.

— *Kleine Geschichte der Parabellum-Pistole*. Published privately by the author, Singen/Hohentwiel, Germany, 1975.

Martens, Bas J. (and Guus de Vries): *The Dutch Luger (Parabellum). A Complete History*. Ironside International Publishers, Inc., Alexandria, Virginia, USA, 1994.

Reckendorf, Hans: *Die Militär-Faustfeuerwaffen des Königreiches Preussen und des Deutschen Reiches*. Published privately by the author, Dortmund-Schönau, Germany, 1978.

— *Die Handwafen der Koeniglich Preussischen und der Kaiserlichen Marine*. Published privately by the author, Dortmund-Schönau, Germany, 1983.

Reese, Michael, II: *1900 Luger. U.S. Test Trials*. Pioneer Press, Union City, Tennessee, revised edition, 1976.

— *Luger Tips* ('Borchardt, Commercial, DWM, Military, & Swiss Models'). Pioneer Press, Union City, Tennessee, 1976.

Reinhart, Christian: *Pistolen und Revolver in der Schweiz*. Verlag Stocker-Schmid, Dietikon-Zürich, and Motor-Buch Verlag, Stuttgart, 1988.

— (and Michael am Rhyn): *Faustfeuerwaffen II. Selbstladepistolen*. The sixth volume of the series 'Bewaffnung und Ausrüstung der Schweizer Armee seit 1817'. Verlag Stocker-Schmid, Dietikon-Zürich, Switzerland, 1976.

Rutsch, Horst: *Faustfeuerwaffen der Eidgenossen*. Motor-Buch Verlag, Stuttgart, Germany, 1978.

Still, Jan C.: *Axis Pistols* ('The Pistols of Germany and Her Allies in Two World Wars. Volume II'). Published privately by the author, Douglas, Alaska, USA, 1986.

— *Imperial Lugers and Their Accessories* ('The Pistols of Germany and Her Allies in Two World Wars. Volume IV'). Published privately by the author, Douglas, Alaska, USA, 1991.

— *The Pistols of Germany and Its Allies in Two World Wars* ('Vol. 1, Military Pistols of Imperial Germany and Her World War I Allies, and Postwar Military, Para-military and Police Reworks'). Published privately by the author, Douglas, Alaska, USA, 1982.

— *Third Reich Lugers and Their Accessories* ('The Pistols of Germany and Her Allies in Two World Wars. Volume III'). Published privately by the author, Douglas, Alaska, USA, 1988.

— *Weimar and Early Nazi Lugers and Their Accessories* ('The Pistols of Germany and Her Allies in Two World Wars. Volume V'). Published privately by the author, Douglas, Alaska, USA, 1993.

Walter, John D.: *Luger* ('An illustrated history of the handguns of Hugo Borchardt and Georg Luger, 1875 to the present day'). Arms & Armour Press, London, England, 1977. A revised edition was published by Editoriale Olimpia SpA, Firenze, Italy, in 1981.

— *Luger* ('Die illustrierte Geschichte der Faustfeuerwaffen von Hugo Borchardt und Georg Luger, 1875 bis Heute'). Motor-Buch Verlag, Stuttgart, Germany, 1982. A much-refined form of the previous book.

— *The Luger Book* ('The encyclopedia of the Borchardt and Borchardt-Luger handguns, 1885–1985'). Arms & Armour Press, London, England, 1986, and Sterling Publishing Company, New York, 1991.

Whittington, Robert D.: *German Pistols and Holsters 1934–1945. Military–Police–NSDAP*. Three volumes, published by the author in Benton, Louisiana, USA, 1970–90. The first volume was reprinted by The Gun Room Press, Highland Park, New Jersey, in 1991.

Zhuk, A.B. (John Walter, editor): *The Illustrated Encyclopedia of Handguns* ('Pistols and revolvers of the world, 1870 to the present day'). Greenhill Books, London, England, 1995.

Index

254